# NEW ENGLAND'S NATURAL WONDERS:
## an explorer's guide

JOHN S. BURK

Schiffer Publishing Ltd

4880 Lower Valley Road • Atglen, PA 19310

Designed by *Danielle D. Farmer*
Cover Design by *Bruce M. Waters*
Type set in Zurich BT/Tomboy

ISBN: 978-0-7643-3983-7
Printed in China

Schiffer Books are available at special discounts for bulk purchases for sales promotions or premiums. Special editions, including personalized covers, corporate imprints, and excerpts can be created in large quantities for special needs. For more information contact the publisher:

Published by Schiffer Publishing Ltd.
4880 Lower Valley Road
Atglen, PA 19310
Phone: 610-593-1777; Fax: 610-593-2002
E-mail: Info@schifferbooks.com

For the largest selection of fine reference books on this and related subjects, please visit our website
at *www.schifferbooks.com*
We are always looking for people to write books on new and related subjects. If you have an idea for a book, please contact us at *proposals@schifferbooks.com*

This book may be purchased from the publisher.
Please try your bookstore first.
You may write for a free catalog.

In Europe, Schiffer books are distributed by
Bushwood Books
6 Marksbury Ave.
Kew Gardens
Surrey TW9 4JF England
Phone: 44 (0) 20 8392 8585; Fax: 44 (0) 20 8392 9876
E-mail: info@bushwoodbooks.co.uk
Website: www.bushwoodbooks.co.uk

# DEDICATION

To the authors of the many
guidebooks that have
introduced people such as
myself to New England's natural
areas, flora, and fauna.

# ACKNOWLEDGMENTS

This project essentially began years ago as a series of weekend road trips, hikes, and photo safaris to all corners of New England, and gradually evolved to this guide. Along the way, I've had the good fortune to have a number of friends, colleagues, and even family members who are experts in New England's considerable natural and human history, as well as a wealth of excellent published sources.

Special thanks to Tony D'Amato, Aaron Ellison, Elizabeth Farnsworth, and David Orwig for site recommendations, passing along sources, and continuous encouragement. Thanks also to Cliff Calderwood (www.hikenewengland.com), Ed Klekowski (www.bio.umass.edu/biology/conn.river/), and Dean Goss (www.northeastwaterfalls.com) for useful Web resources. Many friends offered encouragement and/or helpful discussions along the way, including Matthias Burgi, Joe Conforti, Bob Curley, John O'Keefe, Glenn Motzkin, Nathan Rudolph, Kent Ryden, Noah Seigel, Dave Small, and Linda Woodward.

It's especially important to acknowledge the many groups responsible for protecting these special places and offering a wealth of interpretive resources. Space precludes a list of every site; among the many were Acadia National Park, Appalachian Mountain Club, Baxter State Park, Cape Cod National Seashore, Friends of Sunkhaze Meadows National Wildlife Refuge, Green Mountain National Forest, Lake Winnipesaukee Historical Society, Maine Audubon, Maine Bureau of Public Lands, Massachusetts Department of Conservation and Recreation, Meriden Land Trust, Monhegan Associates, Nature Conservancy, New Hampshire Natural Heritage Bureau, Norman Bird Sanctuary, Quechee Gorge State Park, Quoddy Head State Park, Stellwagen Bank National Marine Sanctuary, Trustees of Reservations, Vermont Department of Forests, Parks, and Recreation, and White Mountain National Forest.

For invaluable help in pulling everything together, thanks to Elaine Doughty and the Harvard Forest, and the staffs of the Athol Public Library, Clapp Library in Belchertown, Petersham Memorial Library, and Woods Memorial Library in Barre. On the photo end, thanks to Hunt's Photo in Hadley, Massachusetts, and Fuji Processing.

Thanks of course to Pete Schiffer and the staff of Schiffer Publishing, including my editor Doug Congdon-Martin, for the opportunity to pursue this project.

Finally, thanks as always to my family for continuous encouragement and support, including visits to some of these places over the years.

# CONTENTS

# INTRODUCTION

New England's landscape is indeed notable for its remarkably diverse array of natural features.

# A (VERY) BRIEF HISTORY OF A CHANGING LANDSCAPE

*Crawford Notch, a narrow valley in the White Mountains, is one of many natural areas in New England shaped by glaciers.*

*After years of exploring New England,* it seemed appropriate that the last site I visited while finishing up this guide was Mount Agamenticus, a low mountain that rises out of southern Maine's coastal plain. On this late spring evening, a good portion of New England's coast, including Capes Cod and Ann in the distance and the nearby waterfront of York, were visible to the south and east. Here the coast began its transition from a land of beaches, marshes, and bays to the rugged, rocky headlands of northern Maine. To the west, the setting sun dropped toward an entirely different landscape, where the Appalachian peaks of the White Mountains, rose on the horizon above the rolling hills of western Maine.

New England's landscape is indeed notable for its remarkably diverse array of natural features. Within its 72,000 square miles – an area comparable in size to Washington State – is the Northeast's highest mountain range, the highest mountains on the Eastern seaboard, some of the country's largest lakes, waterfalls by the hundreds, gorges, bogs, old-growth forests, salt marshes, beaches, islands, and some of the world's finest examples of dinosaur tracks, ancient volcanoes, and glacial erratics.

In addition to their scenic qualities, these areas offer a wealth of clues and insight into the region's natural history, on both short and long term scales. Features such as the Appalachian Mountains, the Connecticut River Valley dinosaur track sites, Hanging Rock Ridge in Rhode Island, and the ancient coral reef off Button Point in Lake Champlain represent hundreds of millions of years worth of geological history.

Much of the land that ultimately became New England was actually not part of the original North American continent, but was gradually pieced together over millions of years. The bulk of the region, including New Hampshire and most of Maine, Vermont, Connecticut, and central Massachusetts, was formed from volcanic islands and sediments that were attached to eastern North America during a series of processes. This was followed by a continental collision that added a land mass called "Avalonia," which included eastern Maine, much of eastern Massachusetts, Rhode Island, and eastern Connecticut.

The most recent significant event that shaped the land as we know it today was the last ice age, which ended approximately 10,000 years ago and was the latest of a dozen major glaciation periods that scientists believe to have occurred in the northern hemisphere over the past million years. This glacier originated in the uplands of northeastern Canada's Laurentide region during a period of low year-round temperatures, and gradually spread across the northern United States and western Canada. It reached its southern limit in the Northeast along New England's south coast, where it left deposits that formed the "outer lands" of Cape Cod, Martha's Vineyard, Nantucket, Block Island, and Long Island.

*Mount Hunger and the other summits of the Green Mountains were formed by continental collisions 450 million years ago.*

*This diorama, which is part of an acclaimed exhibit at Harvard Forest, depicts an early settler clearing a New England homestead. Courtesy Harvard Forest.*

As it moved across the region, the Laurentide glacier created or reshaped countless other features, including the mountains and ponds of Acadia National Park, the cirques on Mounts Washington and Katahdin, U-shaped mountain passes, sheer cliffs, gorges, waterfalls, lakes, bogs, kettle ponds, eskers (long low ridges), drumlins (low hills), and coastal areas such as Narragansett Bay and Stellwagen Bank. After the ice retreated back to the north, debris deposits and water level changes caused giant lakes to form in the Lake Champlain and Connecticut River Valleys and Narragansett Bay. Since the last ice age, lesser intervals of warming and cooling have occurred, including a period of milder temperatures approximately 3,000 to 5,000 years ago.

On a much more recent time scale, New England's landscape has undergone a remarkable cycle of change over the past 400 years. Before the arrival of European settlers, the region was the domain of Native peoples of many groups, including the Wampanoag of present-day southeast Massachusetts and Rhode Island, the Penobscot of Maine, the Abenaki of northern New England, and the Pequot of eastern Connecticut and Rhode Island. Southern New England's milder climate allowed a diverse means of sustenance, as natives were able to practice agriculture, planting crops and shifting fields in river valleys and lowlands in 8-12 year rotations that allowed the cleared land to recover. Land burning was an important practice, as it was used to clear fields and drive game into hunting areas. In the harsher climate of the northern region, tribesmen were primarily hunter-gathers who moved to water bodies seasonally. New England's native population was estimated at 70,000 in 1600, but rapidly declined to 15,000 by 1675, largely because of diseases spread by colonial settlers.

Early European visitors to the region during the 16th and 17th centuries included explorers such as Giovanni de Verrazano, John Smith, George Weymouth, Samuel de Champlain, and Henry Hudson. The written accounts of the explorers and early colonists included many valuable natural history references, including descriptions of forests, wildlife, plants, storms, and Native agricultural practices and populations. For example, in *New England's Prospect,* William Wood detailed how natives managed hunting grounds by burning open corridors into the forest.

European settlement commenced in the early 17th century, and New England's landscape was rapidly and dramatically transformed as the settlers cut the forests and cleared fields for agriculture. By the mid-19th century, more than three-quarters of southern New England is estimated to have been cleared. Though agriculture wasn't as widespread in the rugged northern regions, the forest were heavily logged for timber, and very little old-growth (virgin) forest remains today.

As the 19th century progressed, farmers abandoned the inhospitable rocky soils for the more fertile lands of the Midwest, and the process of reforestation slowly began. The advent of the Industrial Revolution during this time prompted the establishment of thousands of mills – and, unfortunately, significant industrial pollution – along the region's waterways.

The past century has seen increased general environmental awareness, the regrowth of the forests, and the establishment of many nature preserves and protected lands. A significant concern is the spread of invasive plants and forest pests, which have adversely affected native vegetation and decimated keystone tree species such as American chestnut and eastern hemlock.

Another issue is suburban development, which fragments natural areas and reduces their value for wildlife.

Thanks to these diverse natural features and climate fluctuations, New England is home to a wide variety of flora and fauna, including many species at or near their range limits. Familiar creatures of the interior woodlands include moose, white-tailed deer, black bears, bobcats, fishers, coyotes, common loons, bald eagles, and wild turkeys. In the forests of northern New England, one may view boreal forest birds such as gray jays, black-backed woodpeckers, and crossbills. The coast is home to a wide variety of wildlife, ranging from whales, sharks, and giant sea turtles to crabs, sea horses, and seabirds such as Atlantic puffins. Uncommon birds such as harlequin ducks, razorbills, and snowy owls migrate to region from the north to overwinter.

Nearly all of these species have recovered from substantial population declines caused by habitat loss and/or unregulated hunting in recent centuries. Not so fortunate were mountain lions and wolves, which have yet to officially reclaim their past territories, though many unconfirmed sightings of both have been registered in recent decades. The loss of these predators has had a lasting effect on the food chain, as evidenced by the abnormally high deer density in many areas.

The equally diverse vegetation includes a variety of forest communities and wildflowers. Southern species such as black gum, Atlantic white cedars, and rhododendrons are artifacts of the last warming period, while the alpine wildflowers that grow atop Mount Washington and a handful of other high mountains and ridges are holdover from the postglacial era, when the region's climate was similar to that of northern Canada today. The rich limestone soils of the western New England mountains support a great variety of botanic life.

This guide details roughly 120 unique natural areas that well represent this diverse landscape, from large areas such as lakes and mountain ranges to hidden old-growth forests, bogs, and waterfalls. Each chapter begins with a general overview, followed by profiles of the individual sites. Each entry includes descriptions of why the area is unique, historical anecdotes, and access information including recommended trails. Hikers should supplement this information with a relevant map and guidebook, and be prepared for the region's ever-variable weather.

It's been said that New England has too many features and areas to explore in a lifetime, but is small enough to try. There are a wealth of other worthy sites that weren't included here due to time, space, or geographic constraints, and I encourage readers to visit similar areas close to home.

A familiar sight in the north woods, breeding moose have rapidly expanded their range across southern New England states in recent years.

# ALPINE
# MOUNTAINS
## chapter
## one

*At one point in geologic time, roughly a half billion years ago, mountains that may have been higher than the Himalayas or Rockies of today rose out of New England's landscape.*

Mount Madison, seen here from Mount Adams, marks the northern edge of the alpine zone of the Presidential Range.

Well-adapted wildflowers such as diapensia (white petals) and alpine azalea grow in the harsh environments of alpine ridges.

*At one point in geologic time,* roughly a half billion years ago, mountains that may have been higher than the Himalayas or Rockies of today rose out of New England's landscape. The upheaval caused by collisions between the American, African, and Eurasian crusts caused the Green, Taconic, and Berkshire Mountains to rise out of the earth's crust approximately 450 million years ago. Some 70 million years later, another collision with Africa triggered the formation of the giant masses of granite we know today as the White Mountains. Though the relentless forces of erosion have worn away miles worth of bedrock out of these eminences, they remain as artifacts of the geologic processes that shaped the region's uplands.

New England's major mountain ranges are part of the overall Appalachian chain, which stretches from Alabama north to Quebec. It is America's oldest mountain range, as evidenced by the relatively low heights of the highest peaks, which have been worn away by erosion. The highest summits, capped by 6,684-foot Mount Mitchell in North Carolina, 6,643-foot Clingman's Dome in the Great Smoky Mountains of Tennessee, and 6,288-foot Mount Washington, New England's tallest mountain, are roughly half the height of the tallest Western peaks. All told, 67 summits in northern New England exceed 4,000 feet, including 48 in the White Mountains alone.

The highest New England peaks and ridges differ from their sister Appalachian summits in that they have treeless alpine areas with vegetation characteristic of the boreal regions of northern Canada. The hardy, well-adapted plants that grow in these harsh environments are small and low in stature, which enables them to survive strong wind and also requires less food than larger flora. They are holdovers from the end of the last ice age, when an alpine environment existed throughout the Northeast. As the climate warmed and glaciers retreated out of the region, warm-weather species gradually replaced the alpine plants in all areas except the high mountains, where the climate is comparable to the Arctic. Familiar alpine species include diapensia, which grow in large colonies, mountain cranberry, alpine bilberry, and sedges and grasses.

According to research by the Appalachian Mountain Club, in recent years the alpine plants have flowered at earlier dates than in the past, due to milder winters and earlier springs (an overall average winter temperature increase of 1.9 degrees over the past century has been documented in New Hampshire). If the long-term trend of climate warming continues, it will ultimately pose a threat to these unique communities, which are not well-adapted to competition from other species.

Those planning a hike on any of these peaks should be prepared for challenging, rugged trails and the possibility of bad weather at any time, including high winds, ice, lightning, and heavy rain or snow. Storms can form in a matter of minutes, and the weather atop a high ridge is often vastly different than at the trailhead. If the weather looks bad, leave the exposed summits and get below treeline as quickly as possible.

# MOUNT ABRAHAM

Closest Town: Warren, VT

Owner: Green Mountain National Forest, 802-747-6700

Directions: From the junction of VT 100 and the Lincoln-Warren Road in Warren, follow the Lincoln-Warren Road west for 4 miles to the height-of-land in Lincoln Gap, where there are parking areas where the white-blazed Long Trail crosses the road.

*A winter sunset lights the snow-capped summit of Mount Abraham, which rises above Lincoln Gap*

At the 4,006-foot summit of Mount Abraham, which rises above the picturesque farms and forests of Lincoln Gap in the central Green Mountains, is a tiny open alpine area comparable in size to a large room. It is one of only three such natural communities in Vermont; the others are larger zones atop the higher, more northerly peaks of Mount Mansfield and Camel's Hump. Some scientists believe that Killington Peak, the state's second-highest mountain, and Jay Peak near the Canadian border may also have supported similar communities before they were developed as ski areas.

Within this fragile, half-acre area grows a number of rare flowers that are more characteristic of the boreal regions 1,500 miles to the north, including black crowberry, a heather-like shrub that thrives in harsh environments such as rocky ledges and peat bogs, and alpine bilberry, which is distinguished by its rounded leaves. Bigelow's sedge, a threatened species that is named for an

*Stunted spruce trees border Mount Abraham's tiny alpine zone*

early mountain botanist, is among the grasses, rushes, and sedges that are present.

The spectacular 360-degree views from this narrow window include Mount Ellen and the adjacent ridge of the Monroe Skyline to the north, Killington Peak and the southern Green Mountains to the south, and Mount Ascutney, which rises alone to the east above the Connecticut River Valley. Across the valley to the northeast are Mount Lafayette

and Franconia Ridge of New Hampshire's White Mountains, while Lake Champlain and the Adirondack Mountains of New York are visible in the distance to the west.

Though not to be underestimated, the climb to Mount Abraham's summit is relatively gentle and short by the standard of New England's high mountains. From the trailhead at the height-of-land in Lincoln Gap, a segment of the Long Trail, the fabled 240-mile trail that follows the spine of the Green Mountains, offers a moderate 2.6-mile climb to the top, gaining 1,600 feet along the way. Day hikers looking to "bag" two 4,000-foot summits in one outing can continue north for 3.7 miles to the wooded, 4,086-foot summit of Mount Ellen; this out-and-back round trip is 11.6 miles. Though the portion of the Lincoln-Warren Road at the gap's height-of-land is closed in winter, hikers can park at the gates and walk up the road to the trailhead.

CAMEL'S
HUMP
MOUNTAIN

Closest Town: North Duxbury, VT

Owner: Vermont Department of Forests, Parks, and Recreation, 802-879-5682

Directions: From Interstate 89 east of Burlington, take Exit 4 and follow US 2 east. Follow River Road east along the Winooski River, then take a right on Camel's Hump Road, following signs for the state park. At the entrance, bear right to the parking area for the mountain trails.

The distinctive double-humped profile of Camel's Hump Mountain, one of the most familiar landmarks of the Green Mountains, has inspired a variety of nomenclature. It was originally known as "Tah-wak-be-dee-ee-wadso"(or "Mountain like a Seat") by the Waubanaukee Indians. The first European visitors to document the mountain were Samuel de Champlain's explorers in the early 17th century; they named it "The Crouching Lion." After Ira Allen, one of the founders of Vermont, labeled it as "Camel's Rump" on a 1798 map, dignified cartographers altered it to the "Camel's Hump" of today.

In contrast to many other peaks of the Green Mountains, Camel's Hump has a refreshingly wild, unspoiled character, free from development such as ski areas and auto roads. This is largely due to the efforts of Colonel Joseph Battell, who purchased much of the land and then donated it to the state in 1911 with the stipulation that it be maintained in a primitive state.

At the mountain's 4,083-foot summit, which is the fourth-highest peak in Vermont, is a 10-acre alpine area. Nineteenth-century botanists documented 21 uncommon plants in this open meadow, including four species that have not been recorded since then. Presently 18 state-listed endangered or threatened species, including alpine bilberry, crowberry, Labrador tea, mountain cranberry, and mountain sandwort, grow here. In order to reduce the stress and damage to the alpine plants by the thousands of hikers that visit the mountain annually, for the past 40 years rangers have been carefully marking and restricting access to the alpine zone.

The panoramic views include the Lake Champlain Valley and Adirondack Mountains to the west, the White Mountains to the southeast, the Worcester Range to the northeast, and Mount Mansfield and the adjacent ridges of the Green Mountains to the north and south. On clear days, it is possible to see the highest mountains in three states – Vermont's Mount Mansfield, New Hampshire's Mount Washington, and Mount Marcy in New York.

The summit and forests above 2,500 feet are part of a designated wilderness zone, while the area below is managed for multiple uses, including wildlife habitat, recreation, and timber harvesting. The forests, which include northern hardwoods at lower elevations and subalpine spruce-fir groves near the summit, have recovered from extensive logging that continued until the early 20th century, and a large fire in 1903. A current threat to these trees is acid rain; the mountain has been the center of pioneering studies by the University of Vermont.

The 24,000-acre Camel's Hump State Park encompasses the mountain and a surrounding forest buffer. The shortest approach to the summit is from the west via the Burrows Trail, which begins at a trailhead east of Huntington Center and makes a 2.1-mile climb to its junction with the Long Trail near the summit. The Burrows Trail can also be combined with the Forest City and Long Trails as a 6.4-mile circuit that adds some nice ridge views from the Long Trail (which makes a north-south traverse over the mountain). From the east, the Monroe Trail, the reservation's most popular route, makes a 3.1-mile climb from the ranger's cabin.

# MOUNT MANSFIELD

The rising moon peeks above the open summit ridge of Mount Mansfield, the highest peak of the Green Mountains.

Closest Town: Stowe, VT

Owner: Vermont Department of Forests, Parks, and Recreation, 802-879-5682

Directions: For the auto road and Long Trail, from Interstate 89, take Exit 10 and follow VT 100 north to the village of Stowe. From Stowe, continue on VT 108 north for 5.5 miles to the auto road entrance on the left ($25 toll) and 8.1 miles to the Long Trail parking area.

An autumn snowstorm clears the "Chin," the true summit of Mount Mansfield.

The spectacular summit ridge of Mount Mansfield is often described as resembling the profile of a human face looking skyward when viewed from below. From north to south, the prominent peaks of this visage are the "Adam's Apple," "Chin" (the true summit and highest point in Vermont at 4,393 feet), "Nose," and "Forehead." Though Mount Mansfield is lower than other New England mountains with alpine areas, its unbuffered exposure to wind and storms and northerly location keep forests from developing at elevations above 4,000 feet. As a result, the ridge is home to Vermont's largest alpine zone, a 250-acre area that is much larger than those atop Camels Hump and Mount Abraham.

The characteristic alpine flowers of New England, including diapensia, mountain cranberry, mountain sandwort, alpine bilberry, and black crowberry, all grow here. Their low profile and tiny, waxy leaves allow them to survive the winds and dry, thin soils at these heights. The fragility of these communities is evidenced by the fact that it can take as long as 1000 years for a mere inch of soil to form. The ridge is also home to several rare high-elevation peat bogs that fill subtle depressions in the bedrock. At the margins of the alpine zone are clumps of thick, stunted spruce and fir trees that are known as *krummholz,* which is a German word for "crooked wood."

The 37,242-acre Mount Mansfield State Forest protects the majority of the mountain, while the alpine zone is managed by the University of Vermont. The east slopes are home to a popular ski area in a basin that was likely formed by an alpine glacier. The shortest hiking route to the summit is via the Long Trail in Smuggler's Notch. From a roadside parking area, the trail climbs at a moderately steep grade for 1.7 miles to the Taft Lodge, then emerges above the trees and reaches the summit at 2.3 miles. A longer but more scenic option is the spectacular 3.4-mile (one way) Sunset Ridge trail, which begins at Underhill State Park and follows the open ridge to the summit.

For those looking for a much easier route to the top, the privately managed auto toll road begins on Route 108 north of Stowe and climbs to a parking area at the Nose at the site of an old inn. From here, it's a fairly easy, though somewhat rocky 1.5-mile walk along the ridge to the summit.

# MOUNT MOOSILAUKE

*A large alpine meadow, hiking trails, and the remains of an old hotel are attractions of the popular summit of Mount Moosilauke in the western White Mountains.*

Closest Town: North Woodstock, NH

Owner: White Mountain National Forest, 603-536-6100

Directions: For the Beaver Brook Trail, from North Woodstock, follow NH 112 west for 6 miles to the trailhead and parking area on the left (west) side of the road, near Beaver Pond in Kinsman Notch. For the Glencliff Trail, from the junction of NH 25 and High Street in Glencliff, follow High Street for slightly more than a mile to the trailhead and parking area.

Though Mount Moosilauke is nearly 1,500 feet lower than Mount Washington, it undeniably has the air and majesty of a big mountain. It rises alone out of the western edge of the White Mountains, high above the Connecticut River Valley. Atop its 4,802-foot summit, which is the tenth-highest peak in the White Mountains, is a large alpine meadow, formed by the continuous forces of unbuffered wind, ice, and snow.

The most abundant plant of this expansive zone is highland rush, a grass that gives the meadows a splash of color when it turns reddish-brown in late summer. Wildflowers include mountain sandwort, which is well-adapted to colonizing disturbed areas, three-toothed cinquefoil, and mountain cranberry. Interestingly, a handful of species that are common

on other New England alpine peaks are absent on Moosilauke. One possible reason for this is that the summit may have become forested during a warming period thousands of years ago, then reverted to its present condition when the climate cooled.

In the darker forests on the mountain's lower northeast slopes are the cascades of Beaver Brook, which drops more than 600 feet over the steep ledges before draining into Beaver Pond at the base of the mountain in Kinsman Notch. Along its course are four distinct waterfalls and other cascades.

The first known of many visitors to Mount Moosilauke was local hunter Chase Witcher, who followed the tracks of a moose over the mountain in 1785. The first scientific ascent was by Alden Partridge in 1817, who detailed the forests, the tangled clumps of spruce at treeline, and the summit's "entirely bald mass of bare granite." 1860 saw the opening of a popular summit hotel known as the Prospect House, which tourists reached by riding horse carriages up rocky bridle paths. A stone foundation is the only evidence of the building, which was destroyed by a storm in 1942. In 1869, the country's first mountain weather station, a forerunner to the Mount Washington Observatory, was temporarily established at the summit.

The mountain's trail network offers approaches to the summit from all directions. One of the most interesting routes is the Beaver Brook Trail, which begins at Kinsman Notch and makes a moderately steep ascend along the cascades and waterfalls for 1.2 miles, with steps and iron rungs in places. After passing the upper falls, it becomes somewhat easier; at 1.5 miles it reaches a shelter and then continues along a series of ridges to the summit at 3.9 miles. Though not overly difficult, the lower portion is steep and rocky, and extra care should be given when conditions are wet or icy. Waterfall enthusiasts have the option of following the trail to the upper cascades, then backtracking for a 2.4-mile outing.

From the west, the Glenclif Trail offers a hike of similar length and overall difficulty, though it is somewhat safer in that it bypasses the steep areas along the cascades. Both the Beaver and Glenclif Trails are segments of Appalachian Trail. Several other popular routes begin at the Moosilauke Ravine Lodge, including the Gorge Brook (at 3.7 miles, the most direct route), Snapper Ski, and Carriage Road Trails.

On the steep northeast slopes of Mount Moosilauke, Beaver Brook drops 600 feet in a long chain of cascades.

MOUNT
LAFAYETTE
&
FRANCONIA
RIDGE

*The spectacular Franconia Ridge is home to alpine plants and one of the most scenic trails in the eastern United States.*

*The summit of Mount Lafayette offers views across Franconia Notch to Cannon Mountain.*

**Closest Town:** Lincoln, NH

**Owner:** New Hampshire Division of Parks and Recreation, White Mountain National Forest, 603-536-6100

**Directions:** Take Interstate 93 to Lincoln, and continue to follow the highway north into Franconia Notch, where it becomes the Franconia Notch Parkway. Continue past Exit 34A and The Basin, then exit the highway at a sign marked "Trailhead Parking," where there is parking and access to the Falling Waters and Old Bridle Path trails.

With a long, exposed ridge that includes two 5,000-foot peaks, the Franconia Ridge is one of the most spectacular mountain areas in the eastern United States. Indeed, many veteran Appalachian Trail hikers consider it the most scenic segment of the entire, 2,200-mile route. Capped by the summits of 5,260-foot Mount Lafayette, 5,089-foot Mount Lincoln, and 4,880-foot Little Haystack, it is the second-highest mountain range in New England, after only the Presidential Range. The ridge forms the steep east wall of Franconia Notch, one of several dramatic mountain passes in the White Mountains *(see Mountain Passes chapter).*

Spread along Mount Lafayette's summit and a narrow band along the crest of the ridge is a 230-acre alpine area that is one of the largest such communities in New England. A short distance north of Mount Lincoln's summit is one of several shrub communities, where Labrador tea is predominant. An uncommon alpine flower that grows in scattered areas is mountain avens, which is easily identified by its bright yellow flowers. Outside of the White Mountains, it is only found at one other place in the world, an island off of Nova Scotia. The most visible species is diapensia, which grows in large patches along the ridge. The areas around the peaks are largely bereft of vegetation now, as the ridge is a very popular hiking area that sees more than 10,000 pairs of boots annually.

The views from the long section of trail above treeline are exceptional, and one can spend hours trying to distinguish the surrounding peaks and ridges. Westward lies 4,077-foot Cannon Mountain, rising high above the opposite side of Franconia Notch, and the distant ridges of the Green and Adirondack Mountains. To the northeast, Mount Washington and the Presidential Range rise above the Pemiwegassett Wilderness.

The main approaches to the ridge are the Falling Waters Trail and Old Bridle Path, which begin at the same trailhead in Franconia Notch and are often combined as a challenging, though not overly strenuous circuit that is considered is one of the classic hikes of the White Mountains. This 8.8-mile route, which gains a total of 3,900 feet along the way, follows the ridge across the three main peaks, and also offers close-up views of the waterfalls and cascades along Dry Brook (fully detailed in Waterfalls chapter). The Falling Waters Trail is generally preferred as an ascent route, as the steep section along the cascades can be difficult during wet or icy weather. While an out-and-back hike on the Old Bridle Path bypasses the cascades and the ridge walk, it offers the option of a slightly shorter outing and a more direct route to Mount Lafayette's summit. Hikers should be prepared for bad weather and fog, which can form in a matter of minutes, along the ridge.

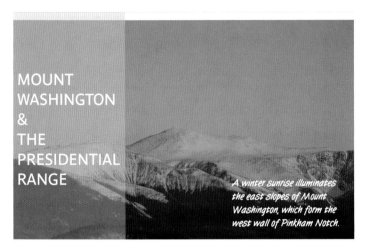

# MOUNT WASHINGTON & THE PRESIDENTIAL RANGE

*A winter sunrise illuminates the east slopes of Mount Washington, which form the west wall of Pinkham Notch.*

Closest Town: North Conway, NH

Contact: White Mountain National Forest, 603-536-6100, Appalachian Mountain Club Pinkham Notch Visitor Center, 603-466-2721

Directions: To reach the Pinkham Notch Visitor Center from the south, from the center of North Conway, follow NH 16 north for 18 miles to the entrance on the left. From the north, from the junction of NH 16 and US 2 in Gorham, follow NH 16 south for 10 miles.

On April 11 and 12, 1934, a powerful early spring storm enveloped Mount Washington and the Presidential Range, bombarding the mountains with hurricane-force winds. Around noon on the 12th, the meteorologists in the weather observatory atop Mount Washington noticed the windows of the stout building bulging as the gusts continued to mount in intensity. By early afternoon, sustained winds exceeded 200 miles per hour, capped at 1:21 PM by a 231 mph gust recorded by observer Salvatore Pagliuca. For many years, this reading stood as the highest wind speed ever recorded on the planet, until a 253 mph gust was recorded by an automated Australian station during a 1996 cyclone.

Remarkably harsh weather is a matter of course atop the Northeast's highest mountain range, a 12-mile long ridge capped by New England's five highest summits. From south to north, the significant peaks, which are all named for presidents, are Mounts Eisenhower (4,761 feet), Monroe (5,385 feet), Washington (6,288 feet), John Quincy Adams (5,410 feet), John Adams (5,798 feet), and Madison (5,363 feet). An average of more than 100 inches of precipitation is recorded annually, and snow often lingers into the summer months.

The unusual weather, which has claimed the lives of a number of unprepared hikers, results from a combination of geographic factors. The range is situated at the general convergence of the Atlantic, Gulf, and Pacific storm tracks, and its high ridge forces the prevailing winds of the Mount Washington Valley into the cool high elevations, often resulting in sudden storms, intense winds and dense fog. In 1870, the United States Signal Service established the first weather station atop Mount Washington; it operated until 1892 and was followed in 1932 by the current observatory.

Given these extreme conditions, it's not surprising that the Presidential Range is home to the largest alpine area east of the Rockies, an eight square-mile treeless zone that stretches from Mount Eisenhower to Mount Madison. In spite of its harsh environment and short growing season, the ridge hosts 110 species of vascular plants, including 75 alpine specialists. Many of Mount Washington's natural features, including Huntington and Tuckerman's Ravines, are named for past botanists.

Mount Washington is the southern range limit for moss campion, an attractive pink or violet-hued wildflower that is common in the western mountains but rare in eastern North America. An even smaller pink flower is alpine azalea, a dwarf shrub that grows in dense mats early in the growing season. Carpets of diapensia, New England's most familiar alpine flower, grow in places such as the Alpine Garden and Cow Pasture. Mountain avens, which is endemic to the White Mountains, is most common near snow bank sites and in boggy areas. As the summer progresses, alpine goldenrod and bluebells (also known as harebells) add bright splashes of color to the barren zone.

The spectacular cirques on Mount Washington's upper east slopes are another

*Early spring skiers and snowboarders enjoy a nearly pristine Tuckerman's Ravine, a cirque formed by alpine glaciers.*

legacy of the ice age. These ravines were formed by alpine glaciers, which were small glaciers that predated the massive continental ice sheets. The largest of these is the Great Gulf, which has a 1,600-foot headwall that separates Mount Washington from the northern peaks of the range. Tuckerman's Ravine, which has an 800-foot wall, is famous for its spring skiing, which draws thousands of visitors to the "snow bowl" annually.

Many moderate to challenging hiking trails ascend the various peaks of the range. Three of Mount Washington's most popular routes begin at the Pinkham Notch Visitor Center on Route 16, including the 4.2-mile (one way) Tuckerman's Ravine trail, the Lion's Head, which is the same distance but somewhat rougher and steeper, and the Boott Spur, which offers excellent views from the opposite side of the ravine. The nation's oldest hiking trail is the Crawford Path, which makes a longer but less strenuous 8.2-mile approach to Washington's summit over the southern portion of the range from the trailhead near Saco Lake at Crawford Notch. An especially interesting route up Mount Adams, the second-highest summit, is the Air Line Trail, which begins at the "Appalachia" parking area on Route 2 in Randolph. After emerging above the trees, it follows the narrow, exposed crest of Durand Ridge before reaching the summit at 4.3 miles, after gaining 4,500 feet from the trailhead.

A much easier approach to the summit is via the privately owned auto toll road ($25 toll), which begins in Pinkham Notch north of the visitor center and winds steeply for eight miles to the summit, allowing drivers to experience a full range of natural communities within a matter of minutes. The cog railroad, which opened in 1869, makes a steep three-mile climb to the summit from Marshfield Station in Crawford Notch. Several early locomotives, including "Old Peppersass," the first engine to climb to the summit, are on display at the visitor center.

BIGELOW
&
SADDLEBACK
MOUNTAIN
RANGES

*The 4,145-foot West Peak is the crest of Bigelow Mountain's long, scenic ridge, and the highest point in Maine outside of Mount Katahdin.*

**Closest Town:** Stratton, ME

**Owner:** Maine Bureau of Parks and Lands, 207-778-8231

**Directions:** For the Bigelow Mountain trails, from the center of Stratton follow ME 16/27 east for 4.5 miles, then turn north on the dirt Stratton Brook Road. Continue 1.6 miles to the parking area, which includes an information sign with a trail map.

When Major Timothy Bigelow made the first known ascent of the mountain that would ultimately be named after him, he had a practical reason for seeking the long views. Bigelow was a division commander under Benedict Arnold during the American Revolution, and he used the vistas to scout the surrounding countryside of western Maine during their expedition to invade Quebec in 1775. Today, the views from the ridges of Bigelow and sister Saddleback Mountains continue to attract hikers to their rugged heights. These two mountain ranges, which are divided by the narrow Carrabasset River Valley, are home to nine of Maine's 14 mountains that exceed 4,000 feet.

Bigelow Mountain's long, rolling ridge rises high above the south shores of Flagstaff Lake, an artificial reservoir that is home to nesting bald eagles. The highest peaks of the ridge are the twin summits of West and

*Moose and beavers frequent Stratton Brook Pond, which lies in the valley between Bigelow and Saddleback Mountains.*

Avery Peaks (4,145 and 4,088 feet respectively), which are separated by Bigelow Col. To the west are North and South Horn, which rise above Horns Pond, a scenic mountain tarn. The ridge is mostly forested but open at elevations above 3,800 feet with roughly 170 acres of alpine terrain. The largest open areas are around West and Avery Peaks, where plants such as goldenrod, alpine bilberry, sweetgrass, and mountain sandwort thrive.

Some 200 years after Bigelow's ascent, the citizens of Maine, in response to a proposal to develop the range as a large ski area billed as "the Aspen of the East," voted to establish the 36,000-acre Bigelow Mountain Preserve. The most direct route to West and Avery Peaks is via the Fire Warden's Trail, which branches off the Horns Pond Trail above Stratton Brook Pond and reaches Bigelow Col in 4.6 miles, with a steep section below the summit. Here one can walk west for 0.3 miles to West Peak, or east for 0.4 miles to Avery Peak. There is also the option of a 12.4-mile circuit that combines the Horns Pond, Fire Warden, and Appalachian Trails; the Horns Pond Trail offers a much gentler climb to the ridge. A one-way traverse of the ridge is 16.7 miles from trailheads at both ends of the range.

On the south side of the Carrabassett Valley, the splendor continues, as the neighboring Saddleback Range stretches south for an additional 30 miles. Seven more 4,000-foot summits rise out of this portion of the chain, including Sugarloaf (at 4,250 feet, Maine's highest point outside of Mount Katahdin), Abraham (4,050), and Saddleback itself (4,120). The summit ridge of Mount Abraham, which is nearly five miles long, includes a 350-acre treeless zone that is the second-largest alpine area in Maine, after only Mount Katahdin. A 6,600-acre state preserve protects the summit and north and east slopes.

Mount Abraham's summit is also reached by a Fire Warden's Trail, not to be confused with the trail of the same name on Bigelow Mountain, that begins along near Norton Brook west of Kingsfield and climbs at a moderate grade for 3 miles. It then rises at a steeper grade for a mile before emerging from the forests, ultimately reaching the summit at 4.5 miles. A full traverse of the Saddleback Range requires a rugged hike along the Appalachian Trail of more than 32 miles, with side trails leading to Mounts Sugarloaf and Abraham.

MOUNT
KATAHDIN

*Brilliant fall foliage and early snowfall mark the changing of the seasons at Mount Katahdin, one of New England's iconic peaks.*

**Closest Town:** Millinocket, ME

**Owner:** Baxter State Park, 207-723-5140

**Directions:** From Interstate 95 in Medway, take Exit 244 and follow ME 157 west for 11 miles to Millinocket. At a junction near the town center, follow the marked park road for 17 miles to the Togue Pond gatehouse. A $14.00 daily fee ($39 for a season pass) is charged for non-Maine residents. Visitors should contact the park in advance, as access to parking areas and trailheads is limited. Katahdin climbers should plan on an early morning arrival at the park.

Of the thousands of peaks of the Appalachian Mountains, few are as distinctive, fabled, and beloved as Mount Katahdin, or simply "Katahdin." As the northern terminus of the Appalachian Trail, its summit marks the ultimate goal sought by northbound "thru-hikers," or for those heading south, the starting point of their 2200-mile odyssey.

A mile-long plateau with six distinct peaks forms Katahdin's unique summit, which is capped by 5,267-foot Baxter Peak, the highest point in Maine. East of Baxter Peak are the 5,260-foot South and 4,919-foot Pamola Peaks, which are connected by a narrow ridge aptly known as the Knife Edge. Widely regarded by hikers as the most exhilarating, exposed, and potentially dangerous trail in New England, it narrows to barely a yard in places. Arcing to the north of Baxter Peak are 4,756-foot Hamlin Peak and the twin North and South Howes (4,706 and 4,740 feet respectively).

Katahdin's 1800-acre alpine zone, the second-largest alpine area in the East, is home to the world's only population of the Katahdin arctic, a medium sized, yellowish-brown butterfly that lives in exposed areas where granite boulders, grasses, and sedges overlap. Katahdin arctics are active and on the wing during the month of July on calm days, which can be few and far between at these wind-swept heights. Other uncommon wildlife includes the American pipit, a songbird of the tundra that in New England nests only atop Mount Katahdin and Mount Washington, and the northern bog lemming, a vole-sized rodent that is at the southern limit of its range in central Maine.

Though it is not as botanically diverse as the larger alpine zone of the Presidential Range, Kathadin's summit and ridges host a variety of high-elevation flora, including mountain cranberry, diapensia, alpine bilberry, mountain sandwort, and rosebay rhododendron. The latter is distinguished by its tiny, pink or purple bell-shaped flowers and thick evergreen leaves.

Below the summit are several giant glacial cirques, which are bowl-shaped ravines that glaciers scoured out of ancient valleys on the steep slopes. The best-known of these is the Great Basin on the east slopes, which is often regarded as the "heart of Katahdin." Flanked by Pamola Peak on the east and Hamlin Peak on the west, it has been a popular destination for hikers and campers since the mid-19th century. In the heart of the basin lies scenic Chimney Pond, which offers a dramatic perspective of the summit ridge from 2,000 feet below.

Waterfalls include Katahdin Stream Falls on the Appalachian Trail, where Katahdin Stream drops 60 feet across a series of step-like granite ledges. Further upstream lies a much higher, hidden waterfall on the mountain's upper slopes that is known as Katahdin Falls. These cascades are estimated at nearly 800 feet long, with a single drop of nearly 300 feet.

Katahdin and 46 neighboring peaks of the Longfellow Mountains are the centerpiece of 210,000-acre Baxter State Park. True to the "forever wild" decree mandated by former Maine Governor Percival Baxter, who was responsible for protecting this land, the park remains refreshingly free of development. The first recorded climb of Katahdin was by surveyor George Turner in 1804; Henry David Thoreau followed in 1846.

For today's hikers, Katahdin's summit trails present a variety of challenges in distance and terrain. From the southwest, the Abol Trail (3.8 miles one-way) is the shortest route to the top, but it also involves a climb of 4,000 feet over loose, constantly shifting rocks. The Hunt Trail, which is the northernmost segment of the Appalachian Trail and the final stage for "thru hikers" walking the fabled 2200-mile route in its entirety, offers a longer, 5.2-mile (one way) climb from the Katahdin Stream campground.

From the east, several popular routes begin at the Roaring Brook campground. The Chimney Pond trail ascends at a gentle grade for 3.3 miles to Chimney Pond and the Great Basin. Here one has the option of the 1.6-mile Cathedral Trail, which is quite rocky and steep and is recommended as a climbing but not as a descending route, or the longer but much easier 2.2-mile Saddle Trail. The Helon Taylor Trail branches off of the Chimney Pond trail, and follows the mostly open Keep Ridge for 3.4 miles to Pamola Peak. The Knife Edge trail is closed during high winds.

# MONADNOCKS
## chapter
## two

*These giant masses are holdovers from the region's last significant period of mountain formation more than 200 million years ago.*

*Formed of hardy, erosion-resistant bedrock, Mount Monadnock is one of several isolated mountains in central New England.*

*Like tall pyramids,* a handful of isolated mountains called "monadnocks" rise alone, high above the countryside of central New England. These giant masses, which are holdovers from the region's last significant period of mountain formation more than 200 million years ago, are comprised of stout bedrock that has resisted the continuous forces of erosion to a greater degree than their surrounding landscape, which has largely been reduced to low hills and valleys.

Although the elevations of the monadnocks are generally modest compared to the high peaks of northern New England, their isolation and height relative to the surrounding landscape affords visitors long, unbroken panoramic views. On clear days, hikers atop Mount Monadnock's 3,155-foot summit may glimpse portions of all six New England states, including Mount Washington and Boston's skyscrapers. There are striking views across central New England from the summits of Mounts Cardigan and Kearsarge in central New Hampshire, both of which are roughly 3,000 feet high. Wachusett Mountain in central Massachusetts barely exceeds 2,000 feet, but hosts views that extend the length of Massachusetts from Boston to the Berkshires.

In turn, the monadnocks themselves are prominent, easily identifiable landmarks.

Compiling a list of the places throughout New England where Mount Monadnock is visible would be a formidable but interesting undertaking. Mount Ascutney's pyramid-shaped profile serves as an especially useful point of orientation for the Connecticut River Valley for hikers in the White and Green Mountains and even some hilltops in central Massachusetts.

## MOUNT GREYLOCK

*The highest mountain in southern New England, Mount Greylock presides over a wildflower meadow in Williamstown.*

Closest Towns: North Adams and Williamstown, MA

Owner: Massachusetts Department of Conservation and Recreation, 413-499-4262

Directions: From US 7 in Lanesborough, 6.6 miles north of downtown Pittsfield, turn west on North Main Street, following signs for the state reservation, and continue for 1.5 miles to the visitor center and byway entrance. If coming via MA 2, from the junction of MA 2 and MA 8A in North Adams, follow MA 2 west for 1.3 miles, then turn left (north) on Notch Road and follow signs to the reservation and byway. A $2.00 parking fee is charged at War Memorial Park at the summit.

Historically, Mount Greylock, southern New England's highest mountain, has been a source of inspiration for many famous literary figures, including Henry David Thoreau, Ralph Waldo Emerson, Herman Melville, Nathaniel Hawthorne, and Oliver Wendell Holmes. Ironically, during their visits, the steep displayed the scars of heavy logging, which continued until the Mount Greylock State Reservation was established as the first state park in Massachusetts in 1898.

Mount Greylock differs from the other monadnocks detailed here in that it is part of a range; its 3,491-foot summit it is the second-highest summit of the Taconic Mountains after Equinox Mountain in southwestern Vermont. However, it has the characteristics of a monadnock in that it rises alone, high above the valley of the Hoosac River. Its prominent profile is visible from many distant viewpoints in New England, including the southern Taconic Mountains in northwestern Connecticut and Wachusett Mountain in central Massachusetts.

From the various overlooks at War Memorial Park on the summit, portions of five states are visible. To the north, the Green and Taconic Mountain chains extend across the Valley of Vermont. The park is also home to a tall concrete lighthouse, which was originally planned for the Charles River but was built here in 1932 as a memorial to World War I veterans, and the Bascomb Lodge, which offers food, lodging, and nature programs for visitors. Lookouts below the summit include Round Rock, where there are views to the Catskill Mountains, Jones Nose, which rises above an old pasture, and Robinson's Point, where there is a dramatic, bird's-eye view into the steep ravine known as "The Hopper."

Mount Greylock's long ridge, which includes the summits of 3,110-foot Mount Fitch and 2,951-foot Mount Williams, is home to the only boreal, sub-alpine forest community in Massachusetts. On the steep northern and western slopes are an estimated 200 acres of old-growth forest, including the world's oldest known red spruce grove, where some individual trees are more than 420 years old. These isolated groves survived the extensive lumbering that took place on the mountain through the 19th century.

A number of waterfalls and cascades are spread across these well-watered slopes, including picturesque March Cataract Falls, a 30-foot high cascade near the Sperry

*Scenic March Cataract Falls is one of many waterfalls and cascades on Mount Greylock's steep slopes.*

Campground. Nearby Deer Hill Falls is nearly hidden in a steep, rugged ravine lined with evergreen hemlock trees. On the north slopes below Mount Fitch, Money Brook drops more than 70 feet in a series of rock-strewn cascades at Money Brook Falls.

From strenuous full-day summit hikes to easy strolls to vistas and waterfalls from the auto road, there are a full range of options for visitors to the 11,000-acre reservation. The 16-mile scenic byway, which was renovated in 2008, winds to War Memorial Park at and passes a series of vistas below the summit. It also offers easy access to many trails, including the routes to Round Rock (1 mile loop) and Jones Nose (0.5 miles one-way). From the Sperry Road Campground, a fairly easy 0.5-mile (one-way) trail descends to March Cataract Falls, while a more rugged 2.2-mile loop follows the steep terrain along Deer Hill Brook, reaching the main falls in 0.5 miles. The 0.8-mile trail to Money Brook Falls begins on Notch Road, roughly 4 miles below the summit.

Base to summit hiking routes include the Cheshire Harbor Trail, a 6.6-mile round trip that climbs a total of 1,940 feet from West Mountain Road in Adams, and the Gould Trail, which ascends 2,120 feet over 6.4 miles, passing cascades along Peck Brook. A particularly interesting option for fit hikers looking to take in a number of the mountain's features is a 12-mile circuit (with a cumulative 2,400-foot elevation gain) that begins at the Haley Farm trailhead in Williamstown and comb.

## WACHUSETT MOUNTAIN

*The long views from Wachusett Mountain include Mount Monadnock, another fabled isolated peak.*

Closest Town: Princeton, MA

Owner: Massachusetts Department of Conservation and Recreation, 978-464-2987

Directions: From MA 2 in Westminster, take Exit 25 and follow MA 140 south for two miles. Following signs for the state reservation; turn right on Mile Hill Road, then bear left at a split on Mountain Road and continue to the parking area and auto road entrance on the right. A $2.00 fee is collected in season for those driving the auto road.

Among the many nineteenth-century visitors to Wachusett Mountain was Henry David Thoreau, who saw the masts of tall ships in Boston Harbor and fires burning on the slopes of Mount Monadnock in southern New Hampshire. Indeed, the long views from this isolated 2,006-foot summit, which is the highest point in Massachusetts east of the Berkshire Hills, have long attracted visitors to the countryside of central Massachusetts.

The summit vistas offer an interesting perspective of central New England's landscape. At first glance, the surrounding area appears to be level, broken only by the familiar profile of Mount Monadnock rising to the north. However, a closer look reveals the many layers of topography formed by the region's low hills, which are so numerous that they blend together. Other landmarks include the tall buildings of Boston to the east, Mount Greylock on the western horizon, and the hills of southern New Hampshire to the north. Elaborate hotels were present on the summit from 1882 until 1970, when the last structure was destroyed by fire.

Wachusett Mountain is one of the finest places in the Northeast to view migrating raptors, as it lies in the heart of a corridor that provides thermal lift for the birds as they travel to their southern wintering grounds. The peak viewing time is mid-September, when large flocks of broad-winged hawks are on the move, and the season continues into November. Other species that are regularly seen include bald eagles, osprey, and Cooper's and sharp-shinned hawks.

Though most of the mountain's forests were cut for use sheep pastures in historic times, several pockets of old-growth forest, a true rarity this far east in Massachusetts, are scattered across the rocky upper slopes. These include unusual stunted red oaks and yellow birches on the west slopes, whose diminutive size belies their age of 320 to 370 years old. South of the summit lies a grove of much larger hemlocks and red oaks that are around 300 years old.

The Wachusett Mountain State Reservation, which was established in 1900, encompasses the bulk of the mountain apart from the north slopes, which are part of a popular ski area. The trail network offers a choice of routes with possibilities for both long loop and short one-way hikes. The climbs are relatively easy for the most part, though the trails get steeper and rockier as they approach the summit. The main entrance on Mountain Road provides access to a visitor center, the auto road, and several trails, while other trailheads are situated on the roads along the perimeter of the mountains. The shortest route to the summit is the 0.5-mile Pine Hill Trail, while the Jack Frost and Old Indian Trails offer views of the old hemlock and stunted hardwood forests respectively. The summit may also be reached by the park auto road, which winds past overlooks and picnic areas. As this book went to press in 2012, renovations to the auto road and summit were in progress; contact the reservation for updated information.

# MOUNT ASCUTNEY

The highest point of the Connecticut River Valley, Mount Ascutney rises high above the Windsor-Cornish Covered Bridge on a foggy autumn morning.

Closest Town: Windsor, VT

Owner: Vermont Department of Forests, Parks, and Recreation, 802-674-2060

Directions: From Interstate 91, take Exit 8 and follow Route 5 north. Bear left on Route 44A at a sign to Ascutney State Park, and continue to the park entrance on the left.

The highest point along the entire 410-mile Connecticut River Valley is Mount Ascutney, which rises like a giant pyramid 2500 feet above the river above Windsor, Vermont's first township. This granite mountain, which was formed by an ancient volcano more than 120 million years ago, stands alone between the ridge of the Green Mountains, which rise 20 miles to the west, and the White Mountains, to which it is geologically related.

The rocks of Mount Ascutney have offered useful insight into the movement of glaciers during the last ice age in the form of "boulder trains," which are well-defined trails of glacial boulders. Pieces of the mountain have been found as far south as central Massachusetts. In much more recent times, several quarries were established on the slopes, providing stones for a handful of prominent buildings such as the Bank of Montreal.

Though Mount Ascutney's summit is wooded, an observation tower offers visitors sweeping views across the Connecticut Valley to the surrounding mountains. To the southwest rises Mount Monadnock, another well-known isolated peak. Below the summit is 2,940-foot West Peak, an open ledge that is a favored launch site for hang glider pilots for flights that travel as far as the New Hampshire and Massachusetts coasts and western Connecticut.

The mountain's unbroken forests and location in the heart of the Connecticut River Valley flyway makes it one of the region's best bird-watching destinations, especially during the spring and fall, when large flocks of migrating songbirds and hawks are on the move. These woodlands also offer cover for elusive black bears, bobcats, and fishers. On the lower south slopes is Cascade Falls, where seasonal Ascutney Brook drops 85 feet over steep granite ledges in a 30-foot wide ravine.

The trail network at Ascutney State Park includes several base to summit routes, including the 2.9-mile (one-way) Weathersfield Trail, which ascends the south slopes, passing Cascade Falls along the way. From the east, the scenic Brownsfield Trail provides an easy to moderate 3.2-mile route up the northeast slopes; hikers can combine this route with the Windsor Trail for a 7-mile loop by connecting the trailheads with a mile-long walk on Back Mountain Road. The auto road, which is open May to October ($3.00 toll), winds for 3.7 miles to a parking area below the summit. From here the summit is reached via the 0.5-mile Slab Trail or a 0.9 walk on the Hang Glider Trail via West Peak.

A nearby historical feature worth visiting is the Windsor-Cornish Covered Bridge, which spans the Connecticut River between Windsor and Cornish, New Hampshire. It is the world's longest wooden bridge and longest two-span covered bridge. From the east portal of the bridge in Cornish, there are excellent views of Mount Ascutney above the Connecticut River.

Looking west to the Green Mountains from the summit of Mount Ascutney.

*The spectacular Pumpelly Ridge Trail offers some of the finest views on Mount Monadnock, including this perspective of one of the world's most-climbed peaks.*

MOUNT
MONADNOCK

Closest Town: Jaffrey, NH

Owner: New Hampshire Division of Parks and Recreation, 603-532-8862

Directions: From the junction of US 202 and NH 124 in Jaffrey, follow NH 124 west, following signs for the park. Turn right on Dublin Road and continue past the Monadnock Bible Conference, then turn left on Poole Road and continue to the Toll House and parking area. A $3.00 fee per person is charged at the main entrance. Note that the reservation is a pet-free park.

Hard as it may be to believe today, there once was a time when Mount Monadnock's summit was forested and lacking the long, sweeping views that have made it one of the world's most-climbed mountains. While the exact sequence of events that swept the mountain's upper reaches clean remains unknown, it is believed that the process began in 1800, when a natural fire damaged the red spruce forest at the summit. These groves likely were further impacted by a strong hurricane that passed over southern New Hampshire in 1815. Five years later, a large blaze completely destroyed all of the vegetation and soils, creating the extensive open area that encompasses the mountain's upper 500 feet. According to many sources, this fire was set by farmers looking to eradicate wolves that had established dens into the tangle of damaged timber near the summit.

Regardless of their origin, the legacy of the fires was that they created one of New England's best-known natural attractions. It is often said that Mount Monadnock is the world's second most-climbed peak after Japan's Mount Fuji, and while such an assertion is nearly impossible to prove, the mountain is nevertheless a very popular destination for hundreds of thousands of visitors annually. From its 3,165-foot summit, portions of all six New England states are visible on clear days, including the Boston skyline and Berkshire Hills of Massachusetts, and Mount Washington and the highest summits of the White Mountains on the northern horizon. In turn, Mount Monadnock is one of New England's most prominent landmarks, and is visible from hundreds of viewpoints across New Hampshire, Vermont, Massachusetts, and even Connecticut.

Like many other New England mountains, Mount Monadnock's slopes were cleared for sheep pastures in colonial times, and logging continued into the 20th century. These forests were further impacted by the 1938 hurricane, which took an unusual inland track across southern New Hampshire, and the ice storm of December 2008. In

spite of these disturbances, the resilient forests continue to recover, with a mix of lowland species that transitions to red spruce at elevations above 2000 feet. Some of the wildflowers and shrubs that grow in pockets above and at treeline include high bush blueberry, mountain cranberry, and rhodora, a hardy species that is also common in bogs. In spring, colorful ephemerals such as painted trilliums thrive in the lower forests.

*Cotton grass rings a small pool on Mount Monadnock's summit.*

The well-traveled 40-mile trail network at Monadnock State Park offers a choice of options for hikers of all ages. The White Dot Trail offers an easy to moderate 2-mile climb to the top; many hikers combine this route with the White Cross Trail as a 4.2-mile circuit. These trails are often quite crowded, and those seeking solitude should consider the longer routes that begin at other trailheads, or visiting during weekdays.

For those seeking less crowded paths, a longer but especially rewarding option is the 4.5-mile (one-way) Pumpelly Trail, which follows a long ridge with many open views of the summit and the surrounding countryside. Another worthwhile option is the Marlboro Trail, which offers a rocky, periodically steep ascent up the west slopes. Though none of the routes are especially dangerous, hikers should be prepared for potential hazards above treeline, including high winds, lightning, and ice.

Stunted spruce trees and a fire tower rise out of the barren summit of Mount Cardigan, which was cleared by a great fire in 1855.

## MOUNT CARDIGAN

Closest Town: Canaan, NH

Owner: New Hampshire Division of Parks and Recreation, 603-823-7722

Directions: For the West Ridge trailhead, from the junction of NH 4 and NH 118 in Canaan, take NH 118 north for 0.5 miles to a marked right-hand turn for the mountain. Take this road and follow it for 4 miles to its end in the state forest. To reach Cardigan Lodge, take NH 3A north to Plymouth, then turn left on West Shore Road. After 1.9 miles, continue straight on Cardigan Mountain Road for 1 mile, then turn left on North Road. Follow North Road for 1 mile, then right on Alexandria Road. Bear right on Mount Cardigan Road and continue for 3.6 miles, staying left at Brook Road. Follow Shem Valley Road for 1.5 miles to the lodge.

Atop the barren summit of Mount Cardigan is a small solar-powered fire tower, where observers have long unbroken views in all directions across central New England. Ironically, this vista was the product of a great fire which swept across the top of the mountain in 1855, destroying the vegetation and soils, and exposing an extensive area of bedrock, earning the mountain the nickname "Old Baldy."

As was the case with Mount Monadnock, the fires also created one of New England's most popular mountains. Over the past 150 years, thousands of hikers have flocked to the 3,121-foot summit for sweeping views of the White and Green Mountains, the Connecticut River Valley, and the lakes, ponds, and hills of central and southern New Hampshire.

Also visible in the aftermath of the fires are exposed slabs of white "Kinsman quartz" granite, which are geologically similar to the rocks at Lost River Gorge at Kinsman Notch near Mount Moosilauke. The sparsely vegetated summit includes clumps of stunted, twisted spruce trees called "krummholz" (or "crooked wood") and blueberry bushes, which offer tasty fruits for wildlife and hikers during the summer. Ecologists classify this unique area as a "subalpine heath-krummholz rocky bald system."

North of the summit is Firescrew Mountain, a shoulder of Mount Cardigan so named because it offered striking views of the corkscrew-shaped columns of smoke that rose from the mountain during the 1855 fire. There are more fine views from its 3,040-foot summit.

The 5,600-acre Mount Cardigan State Forest offers 30 miles of well-traveled hiking trails. The easiest and most straightforward route is the popular West Ridge Trail, which offers a 1.5-mile ascent to the summit from the west. A longer but interesting option is a 5.5-mile circuit that combines several trails on the east side. From the Appalachian Mountain Club's Cardigan Lodge, follow the Holt Trail west to the Holt-Clark Cutoff, then take the Clark Trail to the summit. From the summit, follow the Moglis Trail for 0.6 miles to Firescrew Mountain, then descend via the Manning Trail, which is steep in places.

*Another New England monadnock that has been affected by fire is Mount Kearsarge, which offers long views from Vermont to Boston.*

# MOUNT KEARSARGE

Closest Towns: Warner and Wilmont, NH

Owner: New Hampshire Division of Parks and Recreation, Winslow State Park, 603-526-6168; Rollins State Park, 603-456-3808.

Directions: From Interstate 89 in Wilmont, take Exit 10 and follow the well-marked signs to Winslow or Rollins State Parks. A $3.00 fee is charged at both parks.

Like Mounts Cardigan and Monadnock, Mount Kearsarge is another New Hampshire monadnock where fires, in this instance a large blaze in 1796, have opened up views that belie its 2,937-foot elevation. It rises above the state's relatively level central region, west of Concord and roughly 30 miles southeast of Mount Cardigan. On clear days, one can see Mount Ascutney and the northern Green Mountains of Vermont to the west (distinct summits include Killington Peak, Camel's Hump, and the Monroe Skyline), Franconia Ridge, Mount Washington and the other jagged peaks of the White Mountains to the north, and Mount Monadnock, the hills of southern New Hampshire, and the Boston skyline to the south and east.

In addition to the sweeping views, the barren rocks offer visitors insight into the Ice Age in the form of many prominent scars and grooves. These markings, which are called "striations," were carved into the bedrock by glaciers as they passed over the top of the mountain more than 10,000 years ago. Even at this relative low elevation, the effects of wind on the isolated, unbuffered summit are evident in clusters of stunted red spruce trees, which have adapted to the inhospitable growing conditions. A short distance below the summit is a small alpine bog, where plants such as cotton grass grow.

The first Europeans to visit the mountain were explorers from Massachusetts who were searching for the source of the Merrimack River in 1652. They named it "Carasarga," likely after a Native word for "mountain of pines." There is another Mount Kearsarge in the White Mountains near Bartlett; exactly which of the two mountains the Navy ship *U.S.S. Kearsarge* was named for remains an issue of debate among historians.

The bulk of the mountain is protected by the Mount Kearsarge State Forest and Rollins and Winslow State Parks. The easiest route to the summit is via the Rollins Trail at Rollins State Park, which offers a quick, half-mile climb up the south slopes, with just 400 feet of elevation gain. Winslow State Park offers two longer routes that begin at the picnic area at the end of the auto road. The Winslow Trail makes a rocky, moderately steep 1.1-mile climb to the summit, while the Barlow Trail follows a more gradual 1.7-mile course that passes the bog and several vistas below the summit. These paths are easily combined as a 2.8-mile circuit.

# UNIQUE LOW MOUNTAINS
## chapter three

*Though the relentless forces of erosion over millions of years has reduced the stature of these eminences, many are home to unique features such as old-growth forests, high-elevation ponds, and cliffs and ledges.*

*Though only 650 feet high, the summit of Mount Sugarloaf offers commanding views of the Connecticut Valley to Mount Tom and the Holyoke Range.*

*While New England's 4,000-foot* mountains draw the bulk of the attention from climbers looking to "bag" the region's highest peaks, not to be overlooked are the region's many low mountains and hills. Though the relentless forces of erosion over millions of years has reduced the stature of these eminences, many are home to unique features such as old-growth forests, high-elevation ponds, and cliffs and ledges.

The mountains, hills, and ridges of the lower Connecticut Valley are part of the Metacomet Range, a chain of traprock outcroppings scattered over 100 miles from New Haven, Connecticut to Greenfield, Massachusetts. The range is the legacy of ancient volcanoes that erupted some 200 million years ago as the continents began to diverge. It features some of the world's finest examples of historic volcanic activity, including tall columns of basalt and round-shaped "pillows" that formed when lava was rapidly cooled by water. The term "trap rock" is derived from "trappa," a Swiss word for "step" that refers to the obvious formations eroded

into the basalt over millions of years. Today one can easily observe the legacy of the volcanoes at Chauncey Peak, Lamentation Mountain, and the Sleeping Giant hills in Connecticut, and Mounts Tom and Holyoke in Massachusetts.

Other distinctive low summits in southern New England include Bear Mountain and Mount Everett in the Taconic Mountains. This range, which stretches across the western edge of New England into central Vermont, was formed by continental collisions some 450 million years ago and once may have been as high as the Rockies or Himalayas are today. Groves of dwarf pitch pines, which are highly uncommon in the Northeast, crown both summits.

Many New England mountains, including Mount Everett and Tumbledown

and Borestone Mountains in Maine, feature high-elevation ponds, also called "tarns." These scenic water bodies, which are generally situated in depressions and basins scoured by glaciers, are fed by springs and/or the abundant precipitation in the mountain regions.

The effects of glaciation are also evident in the sheer cliffs of Tumbledown Mountain and the Cathedral and White Horse Ledges in New Hampshire's Mount Washington Valley. Moving ice tore apart the south-facing slopes of these and many other New England mountains, hills, and ridges. Meltwater also temporarily made Vermont's Mount Philo an island in a giant glacial lake in the Champlain Valley after the close of the last ice age.

## SLEEPING GIANT STATE PARK

*The trails of the Sleeping Giant offer close-up views of the traprock geology characteristic of the Metacomet Range.*

Closest Town: Hamden, CT

Owner: Connecticut Department of Forests and Parks, 203-287-5658

Directions: From Interstate 91 north of New Haven, take Exit 10 and follow signs to Hamden. At Hamden center, turn right (north) on CT 10 and continue to a right on Mount Carmel Avenue, following signs for the state park. The entrance is on the north side of the road, opposite the Quinnipiac College campus. A $10 (out of state) or $7.00 (resident) entrance fee is collected on weekends from April through November.

The "Sleeping Giant," a six-mile long chain of traprock hills whose profile loosely resembles a human figure on its back, lies at eternal rest amidst the northern suburbs of the greater New Haven area. Along with Totoket Mountain in Guilford, the Giant marks the southern terminus of the Metacomet Range of mountains formed by volcanoes 200 million years ago. Like the Holyoke Range in western Massachusetts, it has an unusual east-west orientation that stands apart from other mountain ridges, which are predominantly north-south. The extensive bare rock ledges of the hills were exposed by glaciers, which stripped away the vegetation and soils as they advanced across southern Connecticut.

The summits of the rocky hills, which range in stature from 350 to 740 feet, are named for the "Giant's" body. The sheer cliffs of the "Head" are arguably the most dramatic, as they rise almost vertically out of the west end of the chain. Atop 739-foot Mount Carmel (the "hip") is a rather medieval-looking, four-story stone observation tower that was built in 1936 as part of a WPA project and offers views across the hills to the New Haven skyline and Long Island Sound. The campus of Quinnipiac College lies at the base of the south slopes.

The vegetation of the hills reflects the variety of natural habitats. Well-adapted species such as red cedars and chestnut oaks grow atop the dry, exposed cliffs and ridges, while hemlocks favor shady, moist ravines. The rocks supply rich nutrients to the soils, supporting a number of plants that are regionally uncommon.

Historically, these hills and woodlands were an important spiritual place for native Americans of the Quinnipiac Tribe. According to legend, the giant, who they named "Hobomock," was a spirit who became angry at the mistreatment of his people and stamped his foot down, causing the Connecticut River to shift its course abruptly to the east at Middletown.

During the late 19th century, a number of cottages were built along the ridge by local residents. Since the 1920s, the Sleeping Giant Park Association has been working to protect the reservation by acquiring land and lobbying against quarrying on the slopes of the hills; 1,500 acres have been protected to date.

One of the highlights of the state park's 32-mile network of well-blazed footpaths is the White Trail, where a series of lookouts offer views of the "Head's" sheer cliffs, the New Haven skyline, Long Island Sound, Quinnipiac College, and the adjacent hills and forests. Another recommended route is the Blue Trail, which makes an east-west traverse of the hills, passing the observation tower and the dramatic cliff top views from the "Head." Those descending this trail over the "Head's" rocky southwest slope should be prepared for slow going and occasional tricky footing. For those with a half day or so, the White and Blue Trails can be combined as a strongly recommended 5.5-mile circuit of moderate difficulty; while there are few steep sections, both routes follow continually rolling, rocky terrain. For those looking for a shorter outing, a 1.6-mile (one way) dirt path offers a direct, easy to the observation tower at the "Hip."

## CHAUNCEY PEAK & LAMENTATION MOUNTAIN

*The ridge of Chauncey Peak offers a dramatic perspective of Crescent Lake below traprock cliffs.*

Closest Town: Meriden, CT

Owner: Town of Meriden (Giuffrida Park), 203-603-4259.

Directions: From Interstate 91 in Meriden, take Exit 20 and bear west (left from the north, or right from the south) on Country Club Drive and continue to the entrance to Guiffrida Park on the right-hand side of the road.

The twin ridges of Chauncey Peak and Lamentation Mountain, which rise high above the town of Meriden, offer some of the finest scenic views and examples of traprock geology in central Connecticut. Many rare plants and animals inhabit these dramatic basalt cliffs, which are a highlight of the recently dedicated New England National Scenic Trail.

The southernmost of the ridges is Chauncey Peak, which rises 300 feet above the east shores of narrow Crescent Lake, which is also known as the Hubbard Reservoir after the manufacturing company that built it in the late 19th century. From the 688-foot summit, there are sweeping views across the countryside to Long Island Sound, while the adjacent ridge offers dramatic perspectives of Crescent Lake nestled at the base of the steep, rocky cliffs. Though the west side of Chauncey Peak is protected, quarrying has impacted much of the east slopes.

Across the narrow valley at the lake's northern tip is the larger 3,600-foot long ridge of Lamentation Mountain, which crests at an elevation of 720 feet. It offers more long views of landmarks such as Mount Tom in western Massachusetts, the Sleeping Giant hills near New Haven to the south, Long Island Sound, nearby Silver Lake, and the foothills of the Connecticut Valley. In the valley between the ridges, the remains of a historic canal that was once cut through the basalt are still visible.

North of Chauncey Peak lies the twin ridge of Lamentation Mountain, which offers more fine views across the Connecticut Valley.

Among the many rare plants and wildlife that inhabit these cliffs are the falcate orange-tip butterfly, which emerges in early spring, as well as endangered eastern timber rattlesnakes and copperheads, which are elusive and rarely seen. Several regionally rare communities of stunted trees and grassy glades grow out of the thin, dry soils that characterize the ridge tops. The west sides of the ridges are generally steep, dramatic sheer cliffs, while the east sides are more gradual.

The 600-acre Guiffrida Park, which is managed by the town of Meriden, encompasses Crescent Lake and portions of both ridges. From a trailhead at the lake's southeast corner, a segment of the long-distance Mattabesett Trail, which is now part of the New England National Scenic Trail, offers a moderately steep half-mile climb to Chauncey Peak's summit. The trail continues north along the open ridge, then makes a rocky descent to the valley. The trail to Lamentation Mountain begins near the canal site and ascends at an easy to moderate grade to the ridge, reaching the crest at 2.1 miles. Most hikers double back for a 4.2-mile round trip; a repeat climb over Chauncey Peak can be bypassed by following the white-blazed trails along the shores of Crescent Lake.

## BEAR MOUNTAIN

*The summit of Bear Mountain is a highlight of the Riga Plateau, a scenic segment of the Taconic Mountains.*

Closest Town: Salisbury, CT

Contact: Appalachian Mountain Club Connecticut Chapter

Directions: To reach the Undermountain Trail, from Interstate 90 (the Massachusetts Turnpike), take Exit 2 and follow MA 102 west to US 7, then follow US 7 to the junction with MA 41 in Great Barrington. Follow MA 41 south to the Connecticut state line, then continue for approximately 1 mile to the parking area on the right (west) side of the highway. For the Lion's Head, from the center of Salisbury across from the town library, follow Bunker Hill Road for 1 mile to the marked parking area for the Lion's Head Trail.

The height of Bear Mountain, which rises out of the southern Taconic Mountains in Connecticut's northwestern corner, has long been a subject of interest for geographers and hikers alike. In 1885, a local resident named Robbins Battell commissioned a stone monument at its 2,316-foot summit after successfully disproving a claim in the Encyclopedia Britannica that there was no land in Connecticut higher than 1,000 feet. Through an arduous process, the large rocks were slowly hauled up the steep slopes. Today, the mountain is well-known for its unusual distinction of being the state's high peak but not its highest point of land, which is a 2,379-foot high slope on nearby Mount Frissell, the summit of which lies across the Massachusetts state line (this inevitably causes confusion for hikers looking to "bag" the state's highest mountain).

The panoramic views from Battell's stones include the ridge of New York's Catskill Mountains to the west, Mount Everett and the southern Berkshires to the north, and the Twin Lakes and countryside of the town of Salisbury to the east. The summit is also home to a rare forest of dwarf pitch pine trees, similar to that atop nearby Mount Everett *(see next entry)*. These ridge top communities are highly uncommon in the East, and the grove has been designated as a high priority by conservation groups and researchers. Several pockets of old hemlock and birch trees grow along the southeast slopes.

Another uncommon species of the southern Taconics is the eastern timber rattlesnake, which favors the isolated, rocky outcroppings characteristic of the region. The chances of encountering one are low, as they favor remote areas well off the beaten path and are able to detect footsteps at a long distance. Rattlesnake and copperhead populations in New England have declined significantly since colonial times due to hunting, collecting, and habitat loss.

Bear Mountain is part of a segment of the Taconic Range that is known as the Riga Plateau, which extends north to Mount Everett and the Jug End Reservation in Massachusetts. A nearby point of interest along this ridge, which is renowned for its unique natural communities and scenic views, is the Lion's Head, a 1,738-foot ledge that offers more fine views across the countryside. At the base of Bear Mountain's steep, rugged north slopes is Sage's Ravine, a deep gorge with old forests and waterfalls *(see Gorges chapter)*.

The most popular route for Bear Mountain day hikers is a 6.7-mile round trip that begins at the trailhead on Route 41. Here the Undermountain and Paradise Lane Trails serve as a link to the Appalachian Trail, which then climbs at an easy to moderate grade to the summit. Another possible approach is from the north via Sage's Ravine *(see Gorges chapter)*, where the Appalachian Trail offers a short but steep, 0.6-mile climb that traverses rocky outcroppings. A one-way traverse of the Riga Plateau requires a 17-mile hike and a car shuttle. The Lion's Head can be reached by following the Appalachian Trail south from Bear Mountain for 3 miles, or via an easy 2.3-mile (one way) trail that begins on Bunker Hill Road near the center of Salisbury and winds through fields (respect private property here) before making a quick, moderate climb to the rocky ledges.

MOUNT
EVERETT

Closest Town: Mount Washington, MA

Owner: Massachusetts Department of Conservation and Recreation, 413-528-0330

Directions: From the Massachusetts Turnpike (I-90) in Lee, take Exit 2 and follow MA 102 west for 4.7 miles to Stockbridge. Turn left on US 7 south and continue 7.7 miles to Great Barrington. After passing through the town center, bear right on MA 41/23 and continue west for 4.9 miles to South Egremont. For the Race Brook Falls trailhead, bear left on MA 41 south and continue for 5.5 miles to the parking area on the west side of the road. For the auto road, bear left on MA 41, then immediately right on Mount Washington Road, which becomes East Street, and continue for 7.4 miles to Mount Everett Road on the left.

*A rare forest of old pitch pines at the summit of Mount Everett, the highest mountain in the southern Berkshires.*

Once known as the "Taconic Dome," Mount Everett, the highest summit in the southern Berkshire region, rises high out of the north end of the Riga Plateau. Like the surrounding areas of the southern Taconics, it is a treasure trove of natural attractions, including an old forest with rare trees, one of southern New England's highest-elevation ponds, tall waterfalls and cascades, and overlooks with sweeping views.

Out of the sparse soils atop the wind-swept, 2,608-foot summit grows a rare 20-acre grove forest of dwarf pitch pine trees, which are found at only a handful of other locations in the Northeast, including nearby Bear Mountain. These trees have long been established here, as their average age is nearly 90 years and the oldest specimens are roughly 180 years old, which is their full life cycle. The shrubby character of the summit has been cited in historical descriptions dating as far back as 1749, and the first person to specifically identify the pitch pines was Edward Hitchcock in 1841. Pitch pines are hardy trees that thrive in marginal growing conditions, such

as mountaintops and ridges, inland sand plains and barrens, and coastal areas. Many of the trees at the summit, which also include scrub oaks, red maples and red oaks, grow in unusual forms, shaped by wind and storms.

Amid the trees are rocky vistas that offer views across the southern Berkshires to Mount Greylock, which rises to the north, some forty miles distant. To the west rise are the summits of the Catskill Mountains of neighboring upstate New York, while the neighboring peaks of the Taconic chain, including Race Mountain and Bear Mountain, are visible to the south. Several fire towers have been built at the summit; the last was removed by helicopter in 2003 due to concerns about safety and impact on the forest.

Below the summit on the mountain's northwest shoulder is scenic Guilder Pond, which is surrounded by groves of old hemlocks and mountain laurel. At an elevation of 2042 feet, it is the second-highest pond in Massachusetts, after Berry Pond in the Pittsfield State Forest. The pond's outflow forms Guilder Brook, which drains down the

west slopes to meet other waterways below Bash Bish Falls.

On the steep east slopes, Race Brook plunges toward the base of the mountain in a long series of cascades collectively known as Race Brook Falls. At the Lower Falls, which are roughly a half mile upstream from the valley, the brook plunges a total of 50 feet, changing direction as it flows over ledges and pools. The higher, 80-foot Upper Falls are a quarter-mile upstream, near the Appalachian Trail crossing.

The Mount Everett State Reservation's seasonal, 0.5-mile long auto road, accessed from East Street on the mountain's west side, leads to a parking area at Guilder Pond. From here, trails offer a quick 0.75-mile climb to the summit, and a pleasant 0.7-mile loop around the pond. For a longer outing that is one of the classic hikes of the Berkshires, the Race Brook Falls Trail begins along Route 41 and parallels the falls and cascades at a moderately steep grade for two miles. After passing the Upper Falls, it meets the Appalachian Trail, which continues north for 0.8 miles to the summit. Hikers can backtrack for a 5.6-mile round trip, or make a longer one-way outing by spotting cars.

Race Brook churns down the steep east slopes of Mount Everett in a series of waterfalls and cascades.

*Steep sheer cliffs form Monument Mountain's distinctive summit ridge. Mount Greylock is visible on the horizon.*

# MONUMENT MOUNTAIN

Closest Town: Great Barrington, MA

Owner: The Trustees of Reservations, 413-298-3239

Directions: From the Massachusetts Turnpike (I-90) in Lee, take Exit 2 and follow MA 102 west for 4.7 miles to the junction with MA 7 in Stockbridge. Bear left and follow MA 7 south for 3 miles to the parking area and trailhead on the right, 4 miles north of the center of Great Barrington.

One of the most distinctive eminences of the Berkshire Hills, Monument Mountain has long been a popular destination for explorers and artists. Authors Nathaniel Hawthorne and Herman Melville began a long-standing friendship after meeting on the summit in 1850, and the mountain was also the subject of early landscape paintings and poems penned by artists such as Asher Durand and William Cummings Bryant. Today, an estimated 20,000 people visit the mountain annually, drawn by its unique peak and relatively easy trails.

The main attraction for most of these visitors is the mountain's steep, jagged quartzite rock ridge, which stands apart from the surrounding rolling hills of the Housatonic River Valley. These steep cliffs include a rock face that loosely resembles the former Old Man of the Mountain in New Hampshire's White Mountains. From atop 1,640-foot Squaw Peak, the true summit, there are fine views of Mount Everett to the southwest, the Catskill Mountains to the west, and Mount Greylock

to the north. The nearby Devil's Pulpit lookout offers views of an unusual narrow rock pillar that rises high out of the forest below, and a scenic perspective of the Housatonic Valley. Common ravens nest along these cliffs, which are also an excellent area for viewing hawk migrations in late autumn.

The unbroken character of the mountain's forests today belies centuries of use by humans. Timber was once cut from the slopes to supply industries such as iron foundries and tanneries in the valley. Stone walls mark old sheep pastures, and there are many miles of old roads and trails that were once used by Native Americans, horses and carriages, and even early automobiles.

*The Devil's Pulpit Overlook offers views of a unique rock column and the upper Housatonic Valley.*

Today visitors to the 503-acre Monument Mountain Reservation have a choice of two trails to the summit, which is 720 feet above the trailhead off of Route 7 in the valley. The most direct route is the Hickey Trail, which ascends the south slopes at a moderate grade for 0.8 miles, passing a small seasonal waterfall along the way. A longer and gentler option is the 1.3-mile Indian Monument Trail, which leads west along the base of the mountain before following an old road up the west and north slopes. The 0.6-mile Squaw Peak Trail, which is often used as a connecting path between the two trails, winds along the summit and offers the best vistas. Visitors should use caution near the edges of the cliffs.

# MOUNT TOM & MOUNT HOLYOKE RANGES

The traprock ridge of Mount Tom is one of the world's finest examples of an ancient volcano.

Closest Towns: Easthampton, Holyoke, and South Hadley, MA

Owner: Massachusetts Department of Conservation and Recreation, 413-534-1186 (Mount Tom State Reservation); 413-586-0350 (Skinner State Park)

Directions: For the Mount Tom State Reservation's Holyoke entrance, from Interstate 91 (northbound), take Exit 17A and follow US 5 north for 4 miles to the entrance on the left. For the Easthampton entrance, from Interstate 91 northbound take Exit 17B and follow MA 141 west for 4 miles to the reservation entrance at the road's height-of-land. For the Skinner State Park visitor center, from Amherst follow MA 116 south to the parking area at the height-of-land in the notch between Bare Mountain and Mount Norwottuck.

While most of the volcanoes that shaped the mountains and hills of the Metacomet Range were relatively gentle, a series of stronger eruptions in the Connecticut Valley of western Massachusetts formed the spectacular long ridges of Mounts Tom and Holyoke. The hardy basalt rock of these twin mountains has resisted the forces of erosion that have leveled the surrounding landscape of the valley over the past 200 million years. Both mountains have an unusual east-west orientation that resulted from a series of geologic processes as the earth shifted along a fault line in the aftermath of the volcanoes.

The ridge of Mount Tom, which rises above the west side of the valley, offers especially interesting and dramatic views of the traprock geology, including steep, sheer basalt cliffs, slides, ledges, and rock columns, some of which are detached from the main cliff. Many of the rocks at the crest of the ridge have smooth tops that were polished by glaciers during the last ice age. At the true 1,202-foot summit, which lies just outside of the Mount Tom State Reservation boundary, are the remains of an old hotel that burned in 1929 and many antennas and communication towers. Other peaks of the ridge include 1,110-foot Deadtop and 1,014-foot Whiting Peaks.

The Metacomet-Monadnock Trail, which is now part of the federally designated New England National Scenic Trail, follows the crest of Mount Tom's ridge and offers outstanding views of the cliffs and the surrounding countryside. From inside the Mount Tom State Reservation, day hikers can access the trail where it crosses Smith Ferry Road, and head south along the ridge. After crossing the Quarry Trail, the trail makes a steep but short climb to Whiting Peak, then continues along the ridge over Deadtop to the summit, which is two trail miles from Smith's Ferry Road. Another option is to park at the Route 141 entrance and follow a connecting path to the M-M Trail below the summit.

Across the valley, the ridge of Mount Holyoke stretches for an additional dozen miles. The 874-foot summit of Mount Holyoke itself is home to an overlook made famous by Thomas Cole's 1836 painting *The Oxbow,* and a historic hotel that now serves as a state park visitor center. Along the ridge to the east are a series of minor rolling peaks known as the "Seven Sisters," followed by 1,005-foot Mount Hitchcock, and 1,014-foot Bare Mountain, which offer more views across the countryside. Across a narrow gap called "The Notch" is 1,106-foot Mount Norwottuck, where rock caves below the summit were used as hideouts by western Massachusetts farmers during Shay's Rebellion. Once largely cleared for pastures, these ridges are now reforested with groves of hemlock, birch, and beech on the north slopes, while oaks and hickories thrive on the warmer, sunlit south faces.

The Metacomet-Monadnock/New England National Scenic Trail and numerous side trails offer options ranging from a full, 10-mile traverse of the Holyoke Range to short hikes to the individual summits. Though the elevations are modest, the ridge trails follow continually rolling terrain over the traprock, and some of the climbs traverse steep areas. The summit of Mount Holyoke can also be reached by an auto road, which begins on Mountain Road off of Route 47 in South Hadley. The most direct access to Bare Mountain and Mount Norwottuck at the eastern edge of the range is via the Skinner State Park entrance on Route 116 in the Notch.

The historic hotel atop Mount Holyoke's summit now serves as a park visitor center.

*The village of Sunderland lies in the valley
between Mount Sugarloaf and Mount Toby.*

## MOUNT SUGARLOAF

Closest Town: Sunderland, MA

Owner: Massachusetts Department of Conservation and Recreation, 413-665-2928

Directions: From Interstate 91 in South Deerfield, take Exit 24 and follow MA 116 south for 1.1 miles to a 4-way intersection at the traffic night just north of the Sunderland Bridge. Turn left on Sugarloaf Street, then make an immediate right into the park entrance. A $2.00 fee is charged for the auto road.

The rather modest, 652-foot south summit of Mount Sugarloaf belies the fact that it hosts one of the finest vistas in western Massachusetts, a panoramic overview of a quintessential New England scene. To the east, the village of Sunderland, capped by its white church steeple, lies nestled at the base of the forested ridge of Mount Toby and the rolling Pelham Hills. The Connecticut River winds its way south through the upper Pioneer Valley, gliding past a maze of farmlands and woodlots toward the distant ridges of Mounts Tom and Holyoke on the horizon. To the west are the rolling Connecticut Valley foothills and the Berkshire Hills.

South Sugarloaf is one of two twin summits that collectively form Mount Sugarloaf. Its steep south cliffs, which make for a marked contrast with the surrounding rolling hills of the Connecticut Valley, mark the southern terminus of the Pocumtuck Ridge, which stretches north along the valley for 11 miles to Greenfield and is the northernmost sliver of the overall Metacomet Range. A short distance to the north rises the mostly wooded summit ridge of North Sugarloaf, which crests at 791 feet and offers westerly views of South Deerfield and the surrounding hills from rocky ledges.

Mount Sugarloaf differs from other Metacomet Range summits such as Mounts Holyoke and Tom in that it is comprised of arkose sandstone rock, rather than basalt. The rocks at the top of the mountain are similar to those of Mount Toby, which rises across the east side of the valley, which those in its middle are characteristic of the adjacent Pocumtuck Ridge.

South Sugarloaf's summit is easily reached in season via the auto road, which winds for slightly less than a mile to the top. The road is also a good option for walkers and photographers seeking early morning or evening light. The most direct hiking route is via the first segment of the Pocumtuck Ridge Trail, which begins next to the auto road gate and offers a half-mile ascent up the steep south cliff. An easier option is the West Side Trail, which follows the reservation boundary before turning sharply to cross the auto road. From here, a brief steep climb along the Pocumtuck Ridge Trail leads to the summit, 1.1 miles from the entrance.

## MOUNT PHILO

Closest Town: Charlotte, VT

Owner: Vermont Department of Forests, Parks, and Recreation, 802-425-2390

Directions: From the junction of US 7 and VT F5 in Charlotte, follow US 7 south for 2.5 miles, then turn left (east) on State Park Road and continue for 0.5 miles to the entrance.

Home to scenic vistas, unique geology, and abundant flora and wildlife, Mount Philo rises gently out the Champlain Valley south of Burlington. It is well-known known for its outstanding panoramic views across Lake Champlain and the surrounding farms, fields, barns, and woodlots to the Adirondack and central Green Mountains.

Following the end of the last ice age around 10,000 years ago, this same view was almost entirely dominated by water. For a time, Mount Philo was an island in Lake Vermont, a massive lake formed by meltwater from glaciers as they retreated from the Champlain region. Evidence of the lake, which once filled the valley and even covered the low foothills of the Green Mountains, includes marks left on the mountain's slopes by waves, and sand and beach gravel deposits along its base. In 1845, the remains of a beluga whale were discovered near Charlotte in the valley below.

Like other mountains in western New England, Mount Philo features nutrient-rich soils that host a wide variety of plant life. In spring, the slopes are alive with the blooms of colorful wildflowers, including pink and white showy trilliums, which thrive along the margins of the

*A favored destination for rock climbers, tourists, and walkers, the sheer cliffs of Cathedral Ledge offer views across the Mount Washington Valley.*

## CATHEDRAL & WHITE HORSE LEDGES

Closest Town: North Conway, NH

Owner: New Hampshire Division of Parks and Recreation Echo Lake-Cathedral Ledge State Park.

Directions: From the junction of NH 16 and River Road in North Conway, drive west on River Road for 1.5 miles, then follow signs for Cathedral Ledge and Echo Lake State Parks.

The steep, sheer cliffs of the Cathedral and White Horse Ledges are among the most dramatic attractions of the Mount Washington Valley. These twin ledges, which rise above the west banks of the Saco River near the center of North Conway, are a popular attraction for tourists, who enjoy striking views across the valley from the top of the ledges, and rock and ice climbers, who enjoy challenging scrambles up their high walls.

These ledges are excellent examples of what geologists call "sheep's backs" (also known as "*rouches moutonees*"), which refers to mountains and hills with glacially shaped smooth, gentle northwest slopes and steep, abrupt southeast faces. As the glaciers flowed up and over the north slopes, open water was compressed against the south faces, where it eventually froze. As the ice continued away from the ledges, it pulled apart the rocks on the south slopes, causing substantial erosion and forming the sheer cliffs.

At 1149 feet, Cathedral Ledge is the most-visited of the two, thanks to an auto road that offers a safe, easy passage to the overlook at the top of the cliffs. On its north slopes are a long series of cascades known as Diana's Baths, where Lucy Brook drops a total of 60 feet over granite ledges, then winds past the site of an old mill as it flows toward its confluence with the Saco River. To the south rises the higher, 1,450-foot White Horse Ledge, which has an 800-foot high cliff. At the base of the ledges is Echo Lake, a 16-acre pond with a swimming beach that offers fine views of the cliff faces from its east shores.

One doesn't have to be a rock climber, or even a hiker for that matter, to enjoy the views at Cathedral Ledge, as the mile-long auto road climbs up the gentle back slopes to a parking area adjacent to overlooks at the top of the cliffs. One can drive the road, or park at the base of the ledge and walk to the overlook. An easy footpath circles Echo Lake, offering a different perspective of the ledges from below. Visitors should use caution at the top of the cliffs, as fatalities from falls have occurred.

*Once an island in glacial Lake Vermont, Mount Philo is renown for its abundant wildflowers and views across the Champlain Valley.*

auto road. The quartzite rocks at the summit are unique in that they are older than the rocks at the base of the mountain; they were shuffled up to the top along a geologic fault line.

Thanks to its location along the heart of the Champlain Valley flyway, Mount Philo is an excellent place to watch flocks of migrating raptors in late summer and autumn. The peak viewing occurs during mid-September, when large groups of broad-winged hawks are on the wing, though the season continues into November.

During the early 20th century, the Mount Philo Inn hosted visitors to the summit, who arrived by horse via a carriage road that was built in 1903. In 1924, Frances Humphries donated 150 acres of the mountain to the state, forming Vermont's first state park. The inn still stands today, just outside of the park boundary, and portions of the original road are still visible from the present auto road.

The road, which is open seasonally from May to October, offers an easy route to the summit. The House Rock Trail begins at the lower parking area and offers a moderately steep but short 0.9-mile climb up the northwest slopes that passes a cluster of large glacial erratics for which the trail is named. This trail may be walked as an out-and back hike, or combined with the Devil's Chair Trail and/or the auto road as a slightly longer circuit.

## MOUNT CHOCORUA

**Closest Town:** Tamworth, NH

**Owner:** White Mountain National Forest, Saco Ranger District, 603-337-5448

**Directions:** For the Champney Falls Trail, from the junction of NH 16 and NH 112 in Conway, follow NH 112 (the Kancamagus Highway) west for 11.5 miles to the trailhead. For the Brook and Liberty Trails, from the junction of NH 113 and 113A in Tamworth, follow NH 113A for 3.5 miles, then turn right on Fowler's Mill Road and continue 1.2 miles to another right on Paugus Fire Road. Continue another 0.8 miles to the parking area and trailhead, where a White Mountain National Forest parking permit ($3.00 for day-use) is required.

Of all the mountains and hills of New Hampshire's White Mountain region, few are as recognizable as Mount Chocorua, thanks to its distinctive summit cone. Though its 3,475-foot elevation is modest – more than 60 surrounding peaks are higher – the striking views both of and from the cone have made the mountain a very popular destination for hikers, photographers, and artists. Indeed, it is believed to be the region's most-climbed peak, perhaps second in New Hampshire only to Mount Monadnock.

Chocorua's barren summit, which is the largest area exposed granite outside of Acadia National Park, is the legacy of historical fires. It is the highest point of land for several miles, and, as such, is exposed to frequent lightning strikes. On the northern ridges of the mountain grow stands of jack pine, a northern species that thrives following fires or logging. It is uncommon in New Hampshire, and is at its overall southern range limit in the White Mountains (a rare lowland site is Lake Umbagoag). The mountain is the eastern terminus of the Sandwich Range, a 30-mile sliver of the southern White Mountains that rises above the lakes of central New Hampshire.

The views from the exposed "horn" are spectacular. To the south are the hills and lakes of the lakes region, east are the mountains and lakes of western Maine, and to the north and west are the surrounding White Mountain peaks and ridges, including

*Fires, likely caused by lightning, have exposed the granite summit of Mount Chocorua.*

Mount Washington and the Presidential Range. Near the base of the mountain are several scenic lakes, including Chocorua Lake in Tamworth and Silver Lake in Madison, that offer outstanding views of the range.

The mountain's trail network offers a choice of routes that are generally easy to moderate in difficulty, with some brief minor scrambling over the exposed rocks at the top. Two of the most popular approaches are the Piper Trail (9 mile round trip) from the east, and the 7.6-mile Champney Brook Trail, which begins on the Kancamagus Highway and passes Champney Falls, a seasonal waterfall that is picturesque during rainy periods but often dry in summer, en route to the summit. For those looking to avoid the inevitable warm-weather weekend crowds, the Brook and Liberty Trails offer less-traveled routes from the southwest. The latter is considered the mountain's easiest trail, as it follows an old bridle path for 3.8 miles to the top. Hikers often combine the Liberty and the slightly steeper Brook Trail as a 7.4-mile circuit.

*Mount Chocorua, one of the most familiar landmarks of the White Mountains, rises high above a foggy Chocorua Lake.*

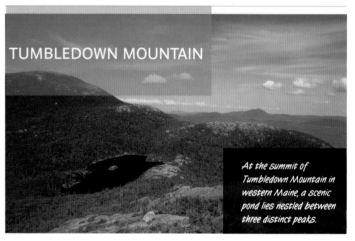

## TUMBLEDOWN MOUNTAIN

*At the summit of Tumbledown Mountain in western Maine, a scenic pond lies nestled between three distinct peaks.*

**Closest Town:** Weld, ME

**Owner:** Maine Department of Conservation/Mount Blue State Park, 207-585-2347

**Directions:** From ME 4 in Wilton, follow ME 156 to Weld. At the crossroads, follow ME 142 for 2.4 miles to Weld Corner, then turn left on West Side Road at a sign for Mount Blue State Park. Continue for a half mile, then bear right onto a dirt road and continue for another 2.3 miles past the Mountain View Cemetery. Bear right on the next dirt road to Byron Notch and continue for 1.6 miles to the parking area for the Brook Trail, or continue along the road to the Loop Trail parking area.

With three distinct peaks, steep sheer cliffs, and a picturesque alpine pond, Tumbledown Mountain has one of the most unusual summits of any New England mountain. It lies at the end of a ridge that rises above the northwest shores near Webb Lake, opposite pyramid-shaped Mount Blue, which stands alone to the east. The summit's half-mile long open ridge is capped by the twin East and West Peaks, which offer views from the summit pond below to the surrounding mountains, hills, and lakes of western Maine, and, on clear days, the White Mountains in the distance to the southwest. The nearby North Peak, which is the true summit at 3,090 feet, can only be reached by bushwhacking.

Like many other mountains that were shaped by glaciers, the south face of Tumbledown has a much steeper profile than the north slopes, with sheer 700-foot high cliffs that are favored by rock climbers. As the ice sheets moved down slope from the summit, they broke apart large sections of the rock, a process known as "plucking." Further evidence of the glaciers are grooves called "striations" that are visible along the exposed ridge, including the rocks at East Peak.

Nestled at the base of the three peaks is Tumbledown Mountain Pond (also known as Crater Lake or Beaver Pond), which offers hikers a sheltered picnic area and the opportunity to enjoy a refreshing swim during the warm months. The pond's outflow forms Tumbledown Brook, which cascades down the southwest slopes.

Thanks to the efforts of several conservation groups and a number of concerned citizens, some 26,000 acres have been protected in this area through land purchases and easements, including the summit, the hiking trails, and portions of nearby Little Jackson Mountain and Mount Blue State Park. The easiest route to Tumbledown Mountain's summit is the Brook Trail, which roughly parallels the Tumbledown Brook as it makes a gradual ascent along a rocky old logging road for one mile, then steepens as it approaches the summit pond that it reaches at 1.5 miles. From the pond, the Ridge Trail continues for 0.4 miles to the East Peak, and 0.7 miles to the West Peak. A more rugged and adventurous option is the Loop Trail, which traverses steep areas below the summit and requires some scrambling over boulders as it rises for 1.9 miles to its junction with the Ridge Trail between East and West Peaks. Many hikers combine the Brook and Loop Trails with a walk along Byron Notch Road for a 5.6-mile circuit.

# BORESTONE MOUNTAIN

*This steep cliff is part of the unique ridge of Borestone Mountain, which rises out of the industrial timberlands of central Maine.*

In a high valley on the mountain's upper southwest slopes are a series of interconnected ponds that are fed by springs. This was once the site of the Borestone Mountain Fox Ranch and Fish Hatchery, where large numbers of foxes were bred for their pelts, which were sold in New York and other markets during the early 20th century. Some of the captives escaped and bred with wild foxes, producing mixed breeds with distinctive colors. Long after the ranch ceased operations, generations of the unique foxes continued to roam the mountain.

The founder of the ranch, Robert T. Moore, also commissioned an Adirondack lodge that was built on the shores of Sunset Pond, the northernmost of the chain, and a dam was built at Sunrise Pond to manage water levels at the fish hatchery. No fish live in the ponds, but they do offer habitat for a variety of other wildlife including beavers, frogs, dragonflies, and damselflies. Moore donated the property to the Maine Audubon Society in 1958.

Rising 700 feet above the ponds is an exposed granite summit ridge, capped by the twin East and West Peaks. The 360-degree views include the ponds in the valley below, and the nearby lakes, mountains, and hills of central Maine; one of the eminences to the north blocks a view to Mount Katahdin. These steep cliffs are ideal habitat for breeding peregrine falcons, which have made a strong recovery after suffering greatly from the effects of pesticides during the mid-20th century.

The 1600-acre Borestone Mountain Audubon Sanctuary includes a seasonal visitor center on the southeast shores of Sunrise Pond. Hikers can reach the ponds via either the mile-long Base Trail, which winds through the mountain's northern hardwood forests, or the 1.3-mile dirt road, which is closed to public vehicle access. From the visitor center, the one-way Summit Trail continues on a steep, rocky ascent to the ridge, reaching the West Peak at 0.7 miles and the East Peak at 1 mile from the nature center.

Closest Town: Monson, ME

Owner: Maine Audubon, 207-781-2330, 207-631-4050

Directions: From the junction of ME 15 and Elliotsville Road in Monson, follow Elliotsville Road north for 8 miles. After crossing the bridge at Big Wilson Falls, bear left and continue for 0.2 miles to the parking area on the left, opposite the mountain's entrance gate. A $4.00 fee ($2.00 for students, seniors, and nonprofits) is collected at the nature center at Sunrise Pond.

While scrambling over rocks along an exposed, wind-swept summit ridge and enjoying panoramic wilderness views across central Maine, it's hard to imagine that Borestone Mountain boasts a relatively modest elevation of 1,956 feet. Renown for its ridge and scenic high-elevation ponds, the mountain rises high above Lake Onawa in the Piscataquis River Valley near Monson, a short distance from the southern terminus of the "100 Mile Wilderness," a famed corridor of the Appalachian Trail.

*Also see: Monadnocks chapter, Squam Lake & Rattlesnake Mountain (Lakes chapter), Moosehead Lake/Mount Kineo (Lakes chapter), Mount Agamenticus (Coastal Northern New England), Camden Hills (Coastal Northern New England), Cadillac Mountain (Coastal Northern New England).*

# MOUNTAIN PASSES

## chapter four

*These narrow passes are among the most dramatic examples of the impacts of glaciers in the Northeast.*

*Brandon Gap in the central Green Mountains is a classic example of a U-shaped glacial valley.*

*In addition to alpine peaks,* another distinctive feature of New England's mountains are the high-walled mountain passes that are known in local parlance as "notches" in New Hampshire and western Maine, and as "gaps" and "notches" in Vermont. These narrow passes are among the most dramatic examples of the impacts of glaciers in the Northeast.

Prior to the ice age, many of these valleys sported narrower, angular V-shaped profiles that were carved by ancient rivers. When the glaciers entered the region and covered the mountains, tongues of moving ice were pressed down and through the valleys, where they rounded the floors and straightened and widened the walls into a distinctive U-shape.

One can easily observe the effects of this process from overlooks such as the Great Cliff of Mount Horrid in Vermont, Mount Willard and the Frankenstein Cliffs in Crawford Notch, Cannon Mountain in Franconia Notch, and Table Rock at Grafton Notch in Maine. Several other passes, most notably Smuggler's Notch in Vermont and Dixville Notch in New Hampshire, still have a V-shape.

The steep walls of these valleys are often home to associated natural features such as high waterfalls and cascades, gorges, rare plants, and rock caves and outcroppings. Many of the familiar waterfalls of the White Mountains are situated in mountain passes, and Grafton Notch in Maine is home to three

of the state's only gorges and the tall cascades of Step Falls.

Historically, the passes served as important routes through the heart of the rugged Appalachian Mountains, which were a formidable barrier to early travelers and traders. The discovery of Crawford Notch by early settlers was motivated by a reward from the governor of New Hampshire for finding a passable route through the northern White Mountains. Vermont's Smugger's Notch served as a route to Canada for contraband smugglers and slaves escaping the country. Today, these same routes are popular attractions for tourists and hikers, who come for views of the spectacular scenery.

# THE VALLEY OF VERMONT

*The summit of Equinox Mountain is the highest peak of the Taconic Mountain Range, which extends along the edge of western New England.*

**Closest Towns:** Arlington and Manchester, VT

**Contact:** Carthusian Order Monastery (Equinox Mountain), 802-362-1114; Vermont Department of Forests and Parks (Emerald Lake State Park), 802-362-1655

**Directions:** For Mount Equinox, from the junction of US 7 and VT 11/30 in Manchester, follow VT 30 west for 1.5 miles to the village center. Bear left on VT 7A and continue for 5.8 miles to the Skyline Drive entrance ($8.00 toll). For Emerald Lake, from the junction of US 7 and VT 30 in Manchester, follow US 7 north to North Dorset, and watch for the state park entrance and roadside pullouts on the left (west) side of the highway.

The Valley of Vermont, a southerly extension of the Lake Champlain Valley, is a long, scenic corridor that stretches for 85 miles from Bennington to Brandon in the state's southwest corner. It is renowned for its extensive deposits of high-quality marble, which has been used in structures such as the Washington Monument, United States Supreme Court building, and the New York Public Library.

The valley divides the ridges of the Taconic Mountains, which extend along the western edge of New England, and the southern Green Mountains. The relationship and formation of the two ranges has long been one of the most interesting mysteries of the New England landscape. Geologists surmise that the Taconics originally rose to the east of the Green Mountains, then shifted to the west during a series of upheavals, literally sliding off the top of the Green Mountains in the process. The rocks at the top of the Taconics are younger than those at the bottom of the range. The Valley of Vermont then was likely scoured by water flowing off the slopes of both ranges.

One of the narrowest and most interesting portions of the valley is the area near Manchester, where Equinox Mountain presides over the surrounding countryside. Its 3,816-foot summit is the highest peak of the Taconic Mountain Range, which stretches along western New England south to Connecticut, and it is the tallest eminence in Vermont outside of the Green Mountains. A series of overlooks at and near the summit offer excellent perspectives of the region, including the Berkshire Hills of Massachusetts, the surrounding ridges of Taconic and Green Mountains, the Battenkill River Valley and the Adirondack Mountains of New York, and even the White Mountains in the distance to the far northeast.

The forests on the mountain's lower slopes are mostly comprised of northern hardwood maple, birch, and beech trees, with a transition to evergreen spruces and firs at elevations above 2,800 feet. These woodlands provide habitat for wildlife such as moose, bobcats, fishers, and migratory songbirds, while peregrine falcons inhabit the rugged cliffs.

Historically, early settlers established roads, farms, and pastures on the mountain's lower slopes to avoid the swampy areas of the valley and potential Native American raiders. A rough road to Lookout Rock, which offers views of Manchester in the valley below and the Green Mountains to the east, was built during the late nineteen century. In the mid-20th century, acclaimed chemist Joseph Davidson purchased the bulk of the mountain, then turned it over to the Carthusian Order Monastery before his death in 1969. The Skyline Inn was built atop the summit during the 1950s and hosted visitors until it was abandoned due to maintenance concerns.

The mountain's auto toll road, which opened in 1947, offers a scenic climb to the summit, gaining 3,235 feet from the toll house on Route 7A. From the parking area near the inn site, an easy 0.5-mile trail leads to Lookout Rock. The main base to summit hiking route is the moderately strenuous Burr Burton Trail, which begins at the seminary of the same name and ascends the east slopes along an old logging road. Below the summit, it meets the trail to Lookout Rock. The round-trip, including both the summit and Lookout Rock, is 6.8 miles.

North of Equinox Mountain is scenic Emerald Lake, which lies nestled in the narrowest portion of the valley beneath the steep slopes of Dorset Mountain. Named for the green-tinted hues of its waters, the lake offers fine views of the surrounding mountains from its shores. At its southern tip is a four-acre natural area where a grove of old hemlock-hardwood forest rises out of a steep bank. The 20-acre lake is part of a 430-acre state park with campsites and a swimming beach.

*The shores of Emerald Lake, seen here on an early October morning, offer a fine perspective of the narrowest portion of the Valley of Vermont.*

## BRANDON GAP

*A summer storm crosses over Brandon Gap in the central Green Mountains, as seen from the Great Cliff of Mount Horrid.*

Closest Towns: Brandon and Rochester, VT

Owner: Green Mountain National Forest, 802-767-4261

Directions: From the east, from the junction of VT 100 and VT 73 in Rochester, follow VT 73 west for 9 miles to the gap. From the west, from the junction of US 7 and VT 73 in Brandon, drive west on VT 73 for 8 miles.

The sweeping views from atop of the cliffs include a fine perspective of the gap and the surrounding landscape of central Vermont. To the east is the valley of Brandon Brook, the hills of the White River Valley, and the distant White Mountains. To the west, Lake Champlain and the Adirondack Mountains are visible on clear days. There's also a striking perspective of the beaver pond at the base of the cliffs in the valley below – those with binoculars or a spotting scope may enjoy a unique perspective of a moose or beaver.

Route 73 leads through the heart of the gap, cresting at an elevation of 2,170 feet as it passes below the Great Cliff. A roadside lookout near the height-of-land offers a good view of the cliffs and the beaver pond, which is frequented by moose and other wildlife. For those who wish to hike to the top of the cliffs, the Long Trail crosses the highway at a parking area just west of the overlook and offers a fairly quick, moderately steep 0.7-mile climb to a blue-blazed side trail that leads to the rocky lookout. The cliffs may be closed to hikers during the spring and summer if nesting falcons are present; contact the Vermont Fish and Wildlife Department for updated information.

Out of the north wall of Brandon Gap, a narrow valley in the central Green Mountains, rises the Great Cliff of Mount Horrid, a 700-foot sheer cliff that is one of Vermont's most dramatic natural features. Peregrine falcons nest atop these ledges, reaching speeds of 175 miles per hour as they dive to hunt smaller birds in the valley below. The 3,126-foot summit of Mount Horrid is roughly a half mile to the north of the cliffs, while across the valley is 3,297-foot Goshen Mountain, which forms the south wall of the gap.

The effect of glaciers is evidence in both the shape of the cliff and the gap itself. After the moving ice flowed up and across the north slopes and summit of Mount Horrid, it froze to the rocks on the south slopes and pulled them apart as the sheets moved down the mountain's slopes, forming the steep cliff face. This process, known as "plucking," is evident in many other mountains and hills in New England. The reason that the effect is less evident on north slopes is because the ice was unable to break apart rocks when it moved upslope. As the ice was channeled through the narrow valley, it widened and smoothed the floor into the distinctive U-shape characteristic of other mountain passes, including those in the nearby White Mountains.

*The beaver pond at the base of the Great Cliff is home to a variety of wildlife, including moose.*

## MONROE SKYLINE: APPALACHIAN & LINCOLN GAPS

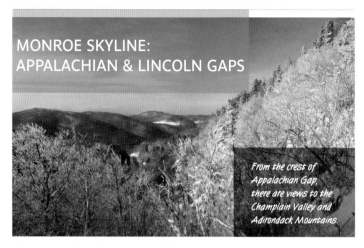

*From the crest of Appalachian Gap, there are views to the Champlain Valley and Adirondack Mountains.*

Closest Towns: Waitsfield, Lincoln and Warrens, VT

Owner: Green Mountain National Forest, 802-767-4261

Directions: For Appalachian Gap, from the junction of VT 100 and VT 17 in Irasville, follow VT 17 west for roughly six miles the gap. For Lincoln Gap, from the junction of VT 100 and the Lincoln-Warren Road in Lincoln, follow the latter west for 3.7 miles to the crest of the gap and 7 miles to Lincoln.

One of the most scenic segments of the Green Mountains is the "Monroe Skyline," the portion of the range that stretches from Middlebury Gap north to the Winooski River. The prominent peaks include Camel's Hump, Mount Ellen, and Mount Abraham, which are among the handful of 4,000-foot mountains in Vermont. It is regarded by many Long Trail hikers as the heart of the 270-mile route.

Offering an especially scenic passage through the heart of the Skyline is Appalachian Gap, a narrow, winding passage between 3,362-foot Stark and 2,863-foot Baby Stark Mountains in the Camel's Hump State Forest near Waitsfield. At its 2,375-foot crest is one of Vermont's finest roadside mountain overlooks, where there are dramatic views of the gap's rock ledges, cliffs, and forests. In the distance to the west, the Adirondack Mountains rise above the Champlain Valley. At the base of the overlook is a high-elevation wetland ringed by maple and evergreen spruce trees. The popular Mad River Glen ski area is just south of the gap, on the northeast slopes of nearby Stark Mountain.

Route 17 offers a steep but safe passage over the gap, which is the highest paved mountain pass in the Green Mountains. The highway is open year-round, offering the opportunity to view unique snow and ice formations on the rocks and trees during the winter.

*Sugar maples and spruce trees ring a high-elevation beaver pond just below the crest of Appalachian Gap.*

Roughly 10 miles to the south lies Lincoln Gap, a narrow passage at the south end of the Monroe Skyline between Mount Abraham *(see Alpine Mountains chapter)* and the lesser-known Mount Grant, which is Vermont's 24th-highest summit at 3,623 feet. Though the roadside views aren't quite as dramatic as some of the other passes detailed here, there are excellent views of the mountains from the farm fields along the back roads near Lincoln on the west side of the gap. The seven-mile long Lincoln-Warren Road climbs through the heart of the gap, passing the Long Trail crossing. Though the portion of the road at the gap's height-of-land is closed during the winter, visitors may park at the gates and hike to the Long Trail, or ski, snowshoe, or sled along the road.

## SMUGGLER'S NOTCH

*Narrow, V-shaped Smuggler's Notch is walled by steep, rugged cliffs that are inhabited by peregrine falcons.*

Closest Town: Stowe, VT

Owner: Vermont Department of Forests, Parks, and Recreation, 802-253-4014

Directions: From Interstate 89, take Exit 10 and follow VT 100 north to its junction with VT 108 in the center of Stowe, then follow VT 108 north for 6 miles to the notch. The road is closed to vehicles in winter, though visitors may park near the gate and hike, snowshoe, or ski the road.

Befitting its name, Smuggler's Notch, the narrow gap between Mount Mansfield and the neighboring Sterling Range, has a long and rather colorful history. During the War of 1812, contraband smugglers used this boulder-strewn passage to transport cattle and goods to Canada during a trade embargo, and in the years preceding the Civil War, slaves also used the route to escape the country. As recently the 1920s, alcohol was imported from Canada during the height of Prohibition. Today, the notch is the site of the popular, 4000-acre Smuggler's Notch State Park, which is frequented by visitors who arrive via a much smoother, albeit rather twisty passage along Route 108.

Geologists theorize that the notch was carved by a river formed by glacier meltwater, as it has a narrow, winding V-shape that contrasts with the well-defined U-shape characteristic of valleys that were scoured by glaciers. In the process, a unique landscape of high cliffs, caves, and boulders was formed. At the notch's height-of-land are rock caves that may have been as hideouts by the various characters during their travels. Another distinctive formation is the Elephant's Head, an outcropping on the shoulder of Spruce Peak that offers fine views from the east side of the notch.

These high cliffs are ideal habitat for nesting peregrine falcons, which have returned to Vermont after being absent for several decades due to the devastating effects of DDT, a pesticide (illegal since 1972) that affected the integrity of the reproductive eggs of several species. A handful of uncommon plants, including alpine woodsia, butterwort,

The rock caves of Smuggler's Notch have sheltered a variety of colorful travelers over the years.

liverworts, marble sandwort, and purple mountain saxifrage, also grow in the cool, moist environment of the cliffs. Several seasonal waterfalls and cascades are visible along the well-watered slopes.

The steep cliffs of the notch are also prone to rock slides. In 1910, a 6000-ton boulder now known as King Rock broke loose from the cliffs and crashed to the floor of the notch. Another giant boulder came down in October 2007, temporarily closing the road through the notch.

The original carriage road through the notch was built in 1894, and opened to automobiles in 1920. Today scenic Route 108 offers easy access to the state park viewing areas and trailheads. At the parking area at the height-of-land, one can explore rock caves and enjoy views of the jagged cliffs high above. For those looking to stretch their legs, the long-distance Long Trail crosses the notch and ascends (northbound) along an old rock slide on the east side of the valley, reaching the Elephant Head of Spruce Peak in 2.3 miles. Southbound, from the lower portion of the notch it makes a moderately steep, 2.3-mile climb to the summit of Mount Mansfield, Vermont's highest peak *(see Alpine Mountains chapter)*. Another nearby attraction worth visiting is the gorge and falls at Bingham Falls, which is just south of the park boundary *(see Gorges chapter)*.

FRANCONIA NOTCH

*The aerial tram at Franconia Notch State Park offers a 10-minute ascent to the 4,077-foot summit of Cannon Mountain.*

Closest Town: Lincoln, NH

Owners: New Hampshire Division of Parks and Recreation, 603-745-8391; White Mountain National Forest, 603-536-6100

Directions: Take Interstate 93 to Lincoln, then continue to follow Interstate 93/US 3 (the Franconia Notch Parkway) north through the notch. The various attractions and trailheads are well-marked. There are $14.00 ($11.00 children) fees for the Flume Gorge and Cannon Mountain tram; a pass for both is $24.

The story of Franconia Notch, one of the best-known areas of the White Mountains, began millions of years ago, when an ancient river flowed across a relatively level, gentle valley that bore little resemblance to the rugged landscape of today. After the White Mountains rose up out of this plateau some 100 million years ago, this valley remained as a narrow gap between the towering ridges of Mount Lafayette and Franconia Ridge on the east, and Cannon Mountain and the peaks of the Kinsman Range to the west. The most recent significant event that shaped the eight-mile long notch as we know it today was the last ice age, when the glaciers smoothed and rounded out the valley and the steep cliffs.

The 4,077-foot summit of Cannon Mountain offers an excellent overview of the U-shaped valley and the mass of Mount Lafayette to the east. Also visible are the distant mountains of northern Vermont, including the Green Mountain ridge and the distinctive profiles of Mounts Pisgah and Hor above Willoughby Lake in the Northeast Kingdom region. Nestled in a high-elevation valley on the lower south slopes is popular Lonesome Lake, somewhat of a misnomer given the crowds that are often present during warm-weather weekends. This scenic mountain tarn offers a striking view of the upper slopes of Mount Lafayette across the valley.

At the base of Cannon Mountain, scenic Profile Lake serves as the headwaters for the Pemigewasset River, which follows the ancient valley as it flows south through the heart of the notch. Along the way, it passes by The Basin, a giant colorful granite pothole shaped by flowing water. The cliffs above Profile Lake were once home to the Old Man of the Mountain, a series of rocky ledges that resembled the profile of a human face. Long regarded as one of the iconic landmarks of the White Mountains, the Old Man finally collapsed in May 2003, after many attempts to preserve and reinforce it. Though proposals to restore the "Great Stone Face" were rejected, construction work on a memorial at scenic Profile Lake began in the summer of 2010. The steep cliffs of the notch are susceptible to erosion, and a number of other landslides have occurred on Franconia Ridge.

The numerous attractions and trailheads of the 6440-acre Franconia Notch State Park are easily accessible from marked exits along the Franconia Notch Parkway, including the Flume Gorge *(see Gorges chapter)*, and Mount Lafayette and Franconia Ridge *(see Alpine Mountains chapter)*. Cannon Mountain's summit is easily reached by an aerial tramway, which whisks visitors to the top in less than 10 minutes. A scenic hiking route is the Hi-Cannon trail, which branches off the Lonesome Lake trail after 0.4 miles and climbs steeply to a ridge with fine views across the notch, then continues to the summit via the Kinsman Ridge Trail 2.8 miles from the trailhead. The Lonesome Lake Trail offers a moderately steep, 1.3-mile climb to

*Scenic and popular Lonesome Lake offers striking views across Franconia Notch to Mount Lafayette.*

CRAWFORD NOTCH

The valley of Crawford Notch offers a narrow passage
through the heart of the northern White Mountains.

**Closest Town:** Harts Location, NH

**Owner:** New Hampshire Division of Parks and Recreation (Crawford Notch State Park), 603-374-2272

**Directions:** From the south or west, follow combined Interstate 93/US 3 north through Franconia Notch, then take Exit 36 and follow US 3 north to its junction with US 302. Turn right and follow US 302 east to the notch, following signs to Crawford Notch State Park. From the Conway area, from the junction of NH 16 and US 302, follow US 302 west to the notch.

During the 18th century, the governor of New Hampshire offered a reward for any person who could uncover a route through the heart of the White Mountains, which were a formidable barrier to trade between the towns of the upper Connecticut Valley and the ports along the coast. In 1771, hunter Timothy Nash was tracking moose when he happened upon a narrow path that traversed the rock-strewn gap between Mounts Willard and Willey and Mount Webster. After convincing the governor that the route was suitable for a road – a process that involved coaxing a confused and scared horse across the rugged terrain – Nash received his reward in the form of gold and a land grant, and within a few years a passable turnpike was opened.

Shortly after its discovery, the notch was named was named for the Crawford family, which settled in the area in 1790 and provided lodging and guide services for visitors. In 1819, Abel and Ethan Allen Crawford created the Crawford Path, which is the southern route up the Presidential Range and is the country's oldest maintained hiking trail. The notch was the site of a well-known tragedy in 1826, when seven members of the Willey family and two helpers were killed by a landslide; the home from which they fled was untouched. The increasing popularity of tourism as the 19th century progressed prompted the construction of a railway through the rugged terrain. In 1913, the state of New Hampshire established Crawford Notch State Park, which encompasses 5,770 acres of the notch.

In the northern portion of the notch, one of the best views of the valley and its glacial U-shape is from the 2,804-foot summit of Mount Willard, which is reached by a relatively easy, 1.4-mile hiking trail that

begins near the Appalachian Mountain Club's Highland Center. Another good vista is the "Elephant Head," a tall rock slab that resembles the trunk of an elephant when viewed from below; it is easily reached via a 0.3-mile walk along a trail that begins just south of Saco Lake. At Willey Pond, which lies in the valley across from the Willey House historic site, there are more good views of the cliffs and trails and the Saco River, which flows through the heart of the notch.

Rising above the southern portion of the notch are the dramatic, rugged Frankenstein Cliffs, where 2450-foot high ledges offer more commanding views of the valley. The steep, rocky Frankenstein Cliff Trail is often combined by hikers as a 4-mile loop that also passes Arethusa Falls, the highest waterfall in New Hampshire. Arethusa Falls is one of many waterfalls spread throughout these steep slopes; see Waterfalls chapter for more details.

Route 302 leads through the notch, offering easy access to the many viewing areas and trailheads. For a unique perspective of the notch, the privately owned Conway Scenic Railroad offers train rides that follow the historic rail line along the west slopes of the valley. The trains stop at stations between Conway to Crawford Depot at the north end of the notch; visit their Web site for full details.

PINKHAM
NOTCH

Capped by Mount Washington, the Presidential Range, seen here from
Mount Prospect, is New England's highest mountain range.

Closest Towns: North Conway and Gorham, NH

Owners: Appalachian Mountain Club (Pinkham Notch Visitor Center), 603-466-2721;
White Mountain National Forest, 603-536-6100

Directions: To reach the Pinkham Notch visitor center from North Conway, follow
NH 16 north for 18 miles to the entrance on the left side of the highway.
From the north, from the junction of US 2 and NH 16 in Gorham, follow NH
16 south for 10 miles.

Flanked by the bulk of 6280-foot Mount Washington and the ridge of the Presidential Range, Pinkham Notch boasts the highest wall of New England's mountain passes. Motivated by the increasing popularity of the region, a group of designers led by Daniel Pinkham, for whom the pass is named, conceived the route through the notch during the 1830s. August 1861 saw the opening of the popular Mount Washington Carriage Road, now the auto toll road, which offered an easy eight-mile passage from the notch to the summit. The Appalachian Mountain Club's Pinkham Notch Center, which offers a visitor center, accommodations and meals for hikers, and access to several popular Presidential Range trails, opened in 1920.

Pinkham Notch sports a less-defined glacial profile than Crawford and Franconia Notches, due to a variety of factors including topography, the resistance of the rocks, and the height of the Presidential Range. Its east wall is 4222-foot Wildcat Mountain, which, thanks to its spectacular views of Mount Washington's east slopes, is widely regarded as one of

the country's most scenic ski mountains. Though Wildcat's summit is wooded with limited views, the mountain's hiking trails lead to fine cliff top views of nearby Carter Notch and the Carter Range.

Jutting out of Wildcat Mountain's slopes is Square Ledge, a 400-foot high rock ledge with more fine views across the notch. It rises above Lost Pond, which offers another good view of Mount Washington from rocks along its east shores. The pond and its associated wetlands are frequented by moose, beavers, and other wildlife. The trails to the Square Ledge and Lost Pond begin across the highway from the Pinkham Notch visitor center; the Square Ledge trail branches to the left and climbs for 0.6 miles to the main overlook, while the Lost Pond Trail continues for an easy, occasionally rocky mile to the pond.

There are also good views of the notch from pullouts along Route 16. From the Great Glen Trails parking area on the east side of the highway opposite the auto road entrance, one can see several features of Mount Washington, including Tuckerman's Ravine and the Lion's Head, as well as the northern summits of the Presidential Range. The highway also offers easy access to the Crystal Cascade and Glen Ellis Falls (see Waterfalls chapter).

## DIXVILLE NOTCH

Closest Town: Dixville, NH

Owner: New Hampshire Division of Parks and Recreation (Dixville Notch State Park), 603-538-6707

Directions: From the junction of NH 26 and NH 16 in Errol, follow NH 26 north for approximately 10 miles to the notch. From the west, from the junctions of US 3 and NH 26 in Colebrook, follow NH 26 south for 11 mile.

*Distinctive rocky crags form the walls of Dixville Notch, the narrowest of the White Mountain passes.*

The jagged rocky crags of Dixville Notch, the northernmost and narrowest of the White Mountain passes, make for a scene that is perhaps more reminiscent of the western badlands and canyons than New England. This distinctive passage, which divides Sanguinary and Gloriette Mountains sports a more defined and abrupt V-shape than the more rounded valleys of Crawford, Franconia, and Pinkham notches, thanks to hardy layers of rocks that were more resistant to the smoothing action of the glaciers. The notch divides the watersheds of the Androscoggin and Connecticut Rivers, two of New England's longest and most significant waterways.

Jutting out of the cliff face of Mount Gloriette is Table Rock, a narrow, rock ledge that protrudes high above the valley floor at an elevation of 2,720 feet. Hikers who are comfortable with exposure are rewarded with excellent views of the notch and The Balsams resort. A short but very steep 0.4-mile state park climbing trail begins at a pullout on Route 26 just west of the road's height-of-land and offers a good sampling of the rugged, rocky terrain. A longer but much gentler hiking trail begins at another roadside pullout west of the state park boundary. This

path begins at a moderately steep grade, then levels as it approaches the rock, 1.2 miles from the trailhead.

The 127-acre Dixville Notch State Park encompasses the notch and its features along both sides of Route 26, which winds through the heart of the gap. Several trails ascend

the mountains on both sides of the notch, offering possibilities for loop hikes.

Waterfalls in the eastern portion of the notch include the Huntingdon Cascades, where Cascade Brook makes plunges of 50 and 18 feet as it drops down the lower slopes of Mount Gloriette. On the opposite side of the valley is the Flume, a 600-foot long gorge carved by Flume Brook, which drops 25 feet as it flows between the bedrock walls. Both falls are easily reached from short walks from the parking areas near the east entrance.

A well-known landmark adjacent to the notch is the Balsams, an exclusive resort motel characteristic of the 19th century inns that were once prominent throughout the region. The motel is the site of the village of Dixville Notch's claim to fame, the annual midnight presidential vote held at the inn that gives it the distinction of being the first town in the United States to report election returns.

A short distance south of the east entrance is a wildlife viewing blind on Route 26 that offers visitors the opportunity to see moose, deer, and a variety of woodland warblers.

*Cascade Brook drops past the roots of an old tree at the Huntingdon Cascades in Dixville Notch.*

EVANS
NOTCH

*Home to the picturesque cascades of Kees Falls and an open summit plateau, Caribou Mountain is a highlight of Evans Notch.*

**Closest Town:** Gilead, ME

**Owner:** White Mountain National Forest, 603-536-6100

**Directions:** From the junction of US 2 and ME 113 in Gilead, Maine (just east of the New Hampshire line), follow ME 113 south through the notch. The Mount Caribou parking area is 4.8 miles south of the junction. The highway is closed through the notch during winter.

Though most people associate the White Mountains with New Hampshire, the northernmost portion of the chain extends into the highlands of western Maine. Straddling the state line is Evans Notch, a narrow valley that divides East and West Royce Mountains on the west, and Caribou and Speckled Mountains to the east. The latter two form the centerpiece of a 41,000-acre reserve that is the largest of five designated wilderness areas within the White Mountain National Forest. In these areas, regulations restricting activities such as timber harvesting and road and dam construction have preserved the region's wild character.

Caribou Mountain's signature feature is its long, mostly open summit plateau, which offers sweeping views across the White Mountains and the lakes and hills of western Maine that belie its 2828-foot elevation. Abundant blueberry bushes offer nourishment for hikers and other wild creatures here, while rare flora such as White Mountain silverlings and mountain sandworts cling to a

precarious existence in the fragile xeric habitats of the granite ledges. On the western slopes, Morrison Brook drops 25 feet over a rock ledge into a small, emerald pool at picturesque Kees Falls. The Mud Brook and Caribou Trails combine to form one of the most pleasant and interesting hikes in the notch, a long but relatively easy 7-mile loop that crosses over the summit and passes by the brook and falls.

Across the valley rises 3116-foot East Royce Mountain, which is the highest point of the notch and northernmost peak of the Baldface Range. From the summit, there are more fine views south and west to the Presidential Range. The Cold River, which is one of several waterways that flow through the base of the notch, originates on the mountain's east slopes. Hikers have several options here, including the 1.75-mile East Royce Trail, which follows an old road along the Cold River, then bears right to reach the summit after climbing 1,700 feet from the floor of the notch. Another is the Laughing Lion Trail, which begins at a trailhead short distance to the south, and climbs through mixed forests to the summit trails.

GRAFTON NOTCH

*The mass of Old Speck Mountain, the forth-highest summit in Maine, rises above a wildflower meadow in Grafton Notch.*

**Closest Towns:** Newry and Bethel, ME

**Owner:** Maine Bureau of Parks and Lands (Grafton Notch State Park), 207-824-2912

**Directions:** From the junction of US 2 and ME 26 in Newry, just east of Bethel, turn north on ME 26 and follow it to the notch and state park. The various trailheads and parking areas are well marked; the Old Speck Mountain parking area and trailhead is 6.7 miles from the park's southern boundary. A $2.00 self-service fee is charged at some parking areas.

In the uplands north of the Androscoggin River Valley lies one of Maine's most dramatic natural features, the steep-walled mountain pass known as Grafton Notch. Here the rugged mountains of the Mahoosuc Range, a 25-mile long chain that marks the northern terminus of the White Mountains, rise above a series of waterfalls and gorges in the narrow valley of the Bear River.

The mass of Old Speck Mountain, which at 4,180 feet is the highest peak of the Mahoosucs and the fourth-highest in Maine, forms the west wall of the notch. At its summit is an old fire tower that offers 360-degree views of Mount Washington and the Presidential Range to the southwest, the isolated, cone-shaped summit of Mount Blue in the distance to the east, and the surrounding mountains and hills of western Maine. On the northeast slopes is the "Eyebrow," a rock ledge that offers a bird's-eye

perspective of the notch and its U-shaped floor from 1,000 feet above the parking area. The Appalachian Trail offers a 3.8-mile (one-way) route up Old Speck that is rather steep at the onset, but moderates as it approaches the summit. The Eyebrow Trail is a spur off the Appalachian Trail; from their upper junction it's a short 0.1-mile walk to the vistas.

Across the valley is Baldpate Mountain, so named for its partially treeless, 3812-foot East Peak, from which there are more fine views. Table Rock extends out of the lower slopes, offering views of the notch and the surrounding mountains from 800 feet above the valley. Beneath Table Rock are a series of tall, narrow caves.

Though gorges are a rarity in Maine – only a handful are scattered across its vast wilderness areas – three lie within Grafton Notch, carved by the waters of the Bear River. The southernmost and most-visited of the trio is the gorge below Screw Auger Falls *(see Waterfalls chapter)*. A short distance to the north is Mother Walker Falls, a small V-shaped gorge, roughly 40 feet wide and 1,000 feet long, where river drops nearly 100 feet as it flows between the walls. The third and smallest of the group is adjacent to the nearby Moose Cave, a large opening in a rock above a brook that is named for an unfortunate animal that was once reputedly trapped there.

One of the most interesting (or notorious, depending on one's perspective), features of the Mahoosuc Range is Mahoosuc Notch, a narrow gap between Fulling Mill and Mahoosuc Mountains that lies just south of Old Speck Mountain and the state park boundary. This passage is widely regarded as the most challenging mile of the entire Appalachian Trail, as it obliges hikers, often encumbered with backpacks, to negotiate their way around and even beneath giant boulders that have rolled off the mountains. The temperature is noticeably cooler in this rocky gap, where snow may linger well into summer.

Once home to a lumbering camp, the notch is now the centerpiece of the 3,000-acre Grafton Notch State Park. Route 26 leads through the notch and offers access to the various natural features and hiking trails. Screw Auger Falls and the gorges are roadside attractions are easily accessed from marked pullouts along the highway.

*Also see: Mount Abraham, VT (Alpine Mountains chapter); Mount Mansfield, VT (Alpine Mountains chapter); Franconia Ridge and Mount Lafayette (Alpine Mountains chapter); Mount Washington and the Presidential Range (Alpine Mountains chapter); Moss Glen and Texas Falls (Waterfalls chapter), Franconia Ridge Falls (Waterfalls chapter); Crawford Notch Falls (Waterfalls chapter); Pinkham Notch Falls (Waterfalls chapter); Screw Auger and Step Falls (Waterfalls chapter); Bingham Falls (Gorges chapter); Somes Sound (Coastal Northern New England chapter).*

GORGES
AND CHASMS
chapter
five

Thanks to their wild, rocky character which often made access impractical for loggers, some gorges have served as shelters for old forests.

*The steep, 135-foot high walls of the French King Gorge line a fault where the North American and African continents nearly broke apart millions of years ago.*

New England's gorges vary considerably in size, shape, and setting. Gulf Hagas, Quechee Gorge in Vermont, and the French King Gorge in western Massachusetts are long with high walls that rise more than 100 feet above their floors. The Flume Gorge is notable for its narrow width, which is barely a dozen feet in places. Chesterfield Gorge in southern New Hampshire and Bingham Falls in Vermont are examples of smaller, more compact gorges.

Thanks to their wild, rocky character which often made access impractical for loggers, some gorges have served as shelters for old forests. The Ice Glen ravine in western Massachusetts is home to one of New England's finest examples of an old-growth forest, and other gorges with old trees include Quechee Gorge, Bingham Falls, Purgatory Chasm in Massachusetts, and Gulf Hagas. The high, moist walls also provide habitat for uncommon botanical communities comprised of species that are well-adapted to the rocky outcroppings and marginal soils.

Though similar physically to gorges, "chasms" differ in they were not carved by flowing water over thousands of years, but instead were rapidly formed when massive pressure from glacial or ocean water caused a sudden split in the rock. The water then drained out, leaving behind a dry floor. Purgatory Chasm in south-central Massachusetts is a well-known example of this phenomenon.

*Gorges and chasms*, which are also generally known as "canyons," are steep ravines between cliffs that are most often carved by rivers. The wild, often rugged character of these areas has historically inspired foreboding names such as "Purgatory Chasm" and "Gulf Hagas," which translates to "Evil Place."

Gorges are much more common in arid regions such as the American West than in well-watered areas such as the Northeast, because dry regions offer a more favorable environment for the weathering process that forms them. While none of New England's gorges approach the grandeur of the famous Grand Canyon of the Colorado River, scattered across the region's landscape are a handful of distinctive canyons that are often associated with other unique features such as old-growth forests, waterfalls, rock caves, and mountain passes.

The first step in the formation of most gorges is when glacial meltwater, rivers, or streams encounter an opening or weak area within a section of bedrock. Over time, the cutting power of the flowing water gradually erodes a channel through the rock. Frequent freezing and thawing of ice may also cause the walls to crack and crumble, further widening the canyon.

Gorges differ from waterfalls in that their profile is largely horizontal, longer, and more stable in geologic time, while waterfalls are vertical and short-lived; they gradually level off or migrate upstream as their underlying bedrock is eroded away. Sage's Ravine in Massachusetts, the Flume Gorge in the White Mountains, and Screw Auger Falls and Gulf Hagas in Maine are places where gorges and waterfalls can be observed together.

*The Farmington River carves a path through basalt cliffs of the Metacomet Range at Tariffville Gorge in the hills of northwestern Connecticut.*

## TARIFFVILLE GORGE

**Closest Town:** Simsbury, CT

**Owner:** Private, part of New England National Scenic (Metacomet) Trail

**Directions:** From Interstate 91 near Windsor Locks, take Exits 38A-B and follow Exit 38B onto Day Hill Road. Follow Day Hill Road for 3.7 miles, then bear right on CT 187. After 1.4 miles, take the ramp for CT 189 North and follow it to Tariffville. From the junction of CT 189 and CT 315 in the village, continue on CT 189 north to the bridge across the Farmington River. Cross the bridge and park on the east side of the road where the Metacomet Trail crosses the road.

In the Connecticut Valley foothills north of Hartford lies the high-walled Tariffville Gorge, where the Farmington River passes beneath tall basalt cliffs that are part of the Metacomet Range *(see Unique Low Mountains chapter)*. Though these rock ledges emerged from the earth roughly 200 million years ago during a series of volcanic eruptions in the Connecticut Valley, the creation of the gorge is a relatively recent event that was prompted by the close of the last ice age.

As glaciers retreated across northwestern Connecticut more than 10,000 years ago, their meltwater and debris deposits formed a series of lakes and dams along the region's waterways. One of the dams caused the Farmington River to shift its course east toward the Metacomet Range, where it encountered a large basalt formation near the present-day site of Tariffville, a village on the Simsbury/East Granby town line. Over thousands of years, the river's relentless cutting activity gradually opened and widened a passage through the rock, forming the Tariffville Gorge.

The walls of the gorge are a geologist's delight, as they offer an opportunity to view basalt columns that represent millions of years worth of processes, including the ancient volcanoes. From the lookout atop the gorge, there's a fine perspective of the Farmington River as it winds through the valley below against the backdrop of the distant Connecticut Valley foothills.

The Farmington River originates from branches in the southern Berkshire Hills of Massachusetts, which meet at New Hartford to form the main stem. It flows a total of 80 miles to its mouth at the Connecticut River near Windsor. A 14-mile portion of the West Branch is a designated Wild and Scenic River, one of only six in New England. The river has several white water areas that have been used for Olympic and national competitions, including a section at Tariffville Gorge that is potentially dangerous for the unprepared.

The top of the gorge is easily reached by a 0.6-mile hike along a short segment of the long-distance Metacomet Trail, which is now part of the New England National Scenic Trail. From the parking area on the north side of the Route 189 bridge over the Farmington River, the trail follows fisherman's paths along the banks, then makes a quick climb through the woods to the overlook. This out-and-back hike can be completed in less than an hour.

*Mossy boulders, waterfalls, and old-growth*
*forests characterize Sage's Ravine, one of many*
*unique habitats of the southern Taconics*

SAGE'S
RAVINE

CHESTERFIELD
GORGE
(MA)

*The tall granite walls of Chesterfield Gorge rise high above the*
*Westfield River, a designated Wild and Scenic River.*

**Closest Town:** Mount Washington, MA

**Owners/contacts:** Various public and private, including Massachusetts Department of Conservation and Recreation and National Park Service (Appalachian Trail)

**Directions:** From the junction of MA 41 and MA 23 in Egremont, follow MA 41 south at Mill Pond and turn right on Mount Washington Road, which becomes East Street in Mount Washington. Continue on East Street past the Mount Everett auto road and the Mount Washington State Forest headquarters. Beyond the headquarters, the road becomes dirt and continues for another 3.4 miles to a parking area on the Massachusetts-Connecticut state line.

**Closest Town:** Chesterfield, MA

**Owner:** The Trustees of Reservations, 413-532-1631

**Directions:** From the junction of MA 9 and MA 143 in Williamsburg, follow MA 143 southeast through Chesterfield and West Chesterfield. After crossing the bridge over the Westfield River, turn left on Ireland Street and continue 0.8 miles to a left on River Road, following signs for the gorge. The entrance, marked with a Trustees of Reservations sign, is on the left.

In contrast to the open, sunlit summits and ridges of the surrounding southern Taconic Mountains, Sage's Ravine is a dark, secretive environment of shady hemlock trees, hidden waterfalls and cascading streams. Situated on the Massachusetts-Connecticut state line, this deep, mile-long valley divides Bear Mountain, the highest summit in Connecticut, and Mount Race, a shoulder of Mount Everett.

The ravine was carved by Sage's Ravine Brook, a tributary of the Housatonic River that drops roughly 400 feet as it flows through the gorge. Several seasonal streams tumble down these steep, rugged walls, while brown trout congregate in pools beneath the cascades. The variable light that reaches this environment is reflected in subtle vegetation changes: hemlocks and red maples generally favor the dark south slopes, while beech and hay-scented ferns thrive in the lighter north side of the ravine. The oldest hemlocks, birches, and pines, which were protected from logging in historic times because of the rugged topography, range in age from 250 to more than 400 years old.

The easiest access to the ravine for day hikers is from the end of East Street in the town of Mount Washington, where a 0.75-mile connecting trail leads to a junction with the Appalachian Trail near the base of Bear Mountain. Here the Appalachian Trail (northbound) descends steeply for 0.3 miles to the base of the ravine, then continues along the south bank of the brook. It ultimately crosses the brook at the end of the gorge and climbs out of the ravine toward Bear Rock Falls. Hikers can backtrack from this point or continue to the falls and the summits of Mounts Race and Everett, which are 4 and 5.8 miles from the junction below Bear Mountain respectively.

Several campsites are available in the ravine, including a first-come, first-served area. Campers should be sure to secure food here, as black bears have been notorious for raiding sites.

Torrents of glacial meltwater originally carved the dramatic Chesterfield Gorge in the picturesque Berkshire foothills of western Massachusetts, where granite walls as high as 70 feet rise above the riverbed. Today, the East Branch of the Westfield River, one of America's designated Wild and Scenic Rivers, continues the cutting process as it winds toward its confluence with the Connecticut River.

A dark canopy of eastern hemlock, a long-lived, fire-intolerant species that thrives in the moist environments along rivers and streams, grows along and atop the gorge walls, along with ashes, oaks, and pine. Abundant wildflowers thrive in this rich, fertile setting, and a variety of wildlife including waterfowl and colorful butterflies and dragonflies are also present. The waters of the Westfield River are rich in trout and Atlantic salmon, and the area is a popular destination for anglers.

At the northern, upper end of the gorge, stone abutments mark the location of the High Bridge, which was built across the river in 1762 as part of the Boston-Albany Post Road. After their defeat at Saratoga in 1777, British troops crossed this bridge while retreating to eastern Massachusetts during the close of the American Revolution. A toll gate was built at the east end of the bridge, which served horses and stagecoaches until it was lost to an extensive flood in 1835, which also damaged a number of mills in the valley.

The gorge is now the centerpiece of a 166-acre preserve managed by the Massachusetts Trustees of Reservations. An easy, half-mile long footpath follows the top of the walls along the south banks, offering safe views of the river from behind a sturdy cable railing. The preserve is part of an extensive network of conservation lands along the river, and one can continue downstream along River Road (the East Branch Trail) to explore the adjacent state forest and wildlife management areas, and the Knightville flood control dam.

FRENCH
KING
GORGE

Closest Towns: Gill and Erving, MA

Contact: Northfield Mountain Recreation and Environmental Center, 800-859-2960

Directions: From the junction of MA 2 and Interstate 91 in Greenfield, follow MA 2 east for 5.5 miles to the French King Bridge. The entrance to the Barton Cove campground is on the south side of Route 2 in Gill, 2.3 miles west of the bridge.

*The Millers River discharges into the Connecticut River at the base of the French King Bridge, one of New England's best-known highway landmarks.*

When the bridge across the French King Gorge was completed in 1932, tens of thousands of visitors attended its dedication, drawn by the spectacular views from 135 feet above the Connecticut River. As anyone who has driven Route 2 (the famous "Mohawk Trail Highway") during an autumn weekend can attest, the gorge remains one of the region's most popular attractions.

Approximately 200 million years ago, shifting of the earth's tectonic plates almost made this area part of the Eastern seaboard. During this time, the North American and African continents nearly broke apart along a tear known as the Border Fault. The fault became the Connecticut River Valley, and the rocks on the east side of the gorge are millions of years older than those on the west. Ultimately, of course, another fault near Boston was responsible for separating the two continents and forming the Atlantic Ocean. Along the Border Fault within the gorge are the two deepest known areas of the Connecticut River. Just below the base of the bridge is the French King Hole, which is 120 feet deep. A short distance downstream is King Phillip's Abyss, a 125-foot underwater cliff where uncommon marine plants such as white sponges grow.

The gorge and bridge are named for the once-prominent French King Rock, a large boulder at the gorge's north end that was "claimed" in the name of their King by the French in the early 1700s when they arrived in the area from Quebec. This eminence, which is still a potential hazard to unwary boaters, was largely flooded following completion of the nearby Turners Falls Dam in the mid-19th century. At the base of the bridge, the Connecticut River is joined by the Millers River, its largest tributary in central Massachusetts.

The gorge is easily viewed from above from a walkway on the bridge, which has received a number of engineering awards. For a complete perspective, be sure to include a boat tour or paddling trip. From June to late October, interpretive cruises are held aboard the *Quinnetucket II*, a tour boat operated by the Northfield Mountain Recreation Center. The trips begin at the north end of the gorge and continue downstream to Barton Cove, an excellent birding area where bald eagles, osprey, large flocks of waterfowl, and regionally uncommon species such as cackling geese, red-headed woodpeckers, and whistling swans are often seen. For those with their own watercraft, boat launches are available at both Barton Cove and the Riverview Picnic Area near the north end of the gorge.

## PURGATORY CHASM

A narrow nature trail winds through the heart of Purgatory Chasm, a "dry ravine" in the hills of central Massachusetts.

Closest Town: Sutton, MA

Owner: Massachusetts Department of Conservation and Recreation, 508-234-3733

Directions: From the junction of MA 146 and US 20 south of Worcester, follow MA 146 south for 7.5 miles. Take the Purgatory Road exit in Sutton, and follow signs to the reservation parking areas.

Unlike the other canyons detailed here, Purgatory Chasm is a "dry ravine," as no water flows through its 60-foot wide floor. Though the exact process by which this quarter-mile long chasm formed also remains unclear – it was a mystery even to the noted state geologist Edward Hitchcock during the 19th century – one plausible theory is that it formed when water from a massive glacial lake carved a gap through the granite bedrock, then subsequent freezing and melting of ice further eroded the walls. Adorning the 70-foot high walls are towering old hemlock trees that were never logged because of the rugged terrain. Within the chasm are numerous gaps, cracks, rock slabs, and caves, including one narrow passage appropriately known as "Fat Man's Misery."

The trails at the 960-acre Purgatory Chasm State Reservation include the half-mile long Loop Trail, a footpath that leads walkers through the heart of the chasm. It then climbs to follow the top of the rocky east walls; short side paths lead to "Fat Man's Misery" and the "Devil's Corncrib." Visitors should use caution near the overlooks, as several accidents have occurred here. For those with additional time, other trails, including Charley's Loop Trail, wind through the woodlands surrounding the gorge; in early spring, listen for the chorus of wood frogs calling from vernal pools.

Exactly how Purgatory Chasm received its colorful name remains unclear, but several sources credit the Quakers, who viewed this rocky ravine in the hills south of Worcester as a place between Heaven and Hell, for the title. Indeed, within the chasm are features with names such as "Devil's Pulpit" and "Devil's Corncrib." Fortunately, this nomenclature hasn't deterred visitors from enjoying one of the most popular natural areas in central Massachusetts.

## QUECHEE GORGE

A complex series of geological processes after the last ice age created Quechee Gorge, one of Vermont's best-known attractions.

Closest Town: Quechee, VT

Owner: Vermont Department of Forests, Parks, and Recreation, 802-295-2990

Directions: From the junction of Interstates 91 and 89 at White River Junction, take Interstate 89 north to Exit 1, then follow VT 4 west for 2.5 miles to the gorge and parking areas. The visitor center is on the east side of the bridge, opposite the gift shop.

With high walls that rise as high as 165 feet above the Ottauquechee River, Quechee Gorge is one of Vermont's most dramatic and popular natural attractions. It's hard to imagine that at one point in geologic time, the river's course led it away from the giant mass of bedrock at the present gorge site, but a fascinating series of processes combined to create the gorge over thousands of years.

As the last ice age drew to a close across west-central Vermont some 13,000 years ago, the river emerged from beneath the glaciers and resumed flowing toward the nearby Connecticut River Valley. Here it drained into a corner of Lake Hitchcock, a giant glacial lake that once stretched along the Connecticut River Valley from northern Vermont to a debris dam in Connecticut. As the river entered the lake, it shaped a ridge that would alter its future course.

After Lake Hitchcock abruptly drained after the failure of the dam, the Ottauquechee began flowing south along its new course, which led it to the bedrock at the gorge site. At the same time, a giant waterfall began to gradually migrate north up the Connecticut River and its tributaries from the old dam site. When the waterfall finally reached central Vermont and the Ottauquechee Valley, it combined with the river to wear down the bedrock and open up the gap that is the present gorge.

In more recent times, from 1869 to 1952 the river provided power for a successful woolen mill that operated at the base of the gorge. The mill provided employment for hundreds of area residents, and a number of technical and clothing inventions were pioneered on the grounds. Because the rugged terrain was impractical for logging, the gorge is home to an old forest that is comprised of eastern hemlock, a fire-intolerant species that thrives in such cool, moist areas, a stand of old-growth red pine, and northern hardwoods such as American beech and sugar maple.

The first bridge across the gorge was built in 1875 as part of the Woodstock Railroad line. It was replaced in 1911 by the present steel arch bridge, which was converted to a highway bridge when Route 4 replaced the railway in 1933.

While most visitors enjoy the dramatic overview of the gorge and river from the bridge, the well-maintained trails at Quechee Gorge State Park offer a variety of additional perspectives. The main path is the Quechee Gorge Trail, which can be accessed behind the Quechee Gorge Gift Shop or by a short, universally-accessible connecting trail at the state park visitor center. From the Route 4 crossing, the trail leads north along the wall of the gorge for 0.3 miles to an overlook of an old dam, and 0.6 miles to Dewey's Mill Pond. Southbound, it descends for 0.4 miles to the base of the gorge and riverbed.

## CLARENDON GORGE

*The famous Long Trail offers this unique perspective of Clarendon Gorge from a long suspension bridge.*

Closest Town: Clarendon, VT

Owner: Vermont Department of Forests, Parks, and Recreation, 802-786-3858

Directions: From the junction of US 7 and VT 103 in Clarendon, follow VT 103 west for 2 miles to a parking area where the Long Trail crosses the highway.

One of the most unusual segments of Vermont's famous Long Trail is the 30-foot long suspension bridge that spans the walls of the Clarendon Gorge. Here hikers enjoy an elevated perspective of the Mill River as it churns between high walls, passing a series of rock ledges, cascades, potholes, and colorful green and yellow-hued pools.

The gorge, which formed as the Mill River carved a path through a soft layer of Champlain Valley bedrock on the lower west slopes of the Green Mountains near Rutland, exists in two sections that total two-and-a-half miles. The shorter, upper area is roughly one-third of a mile long and is home to a series of pools connected by small waterfalls and cascades. The lower portion, which narrows to only 10 feet in places, features walls that rise as high as 80-100 feet above the river. These ledges are home to uncommon botanical communities that forge an existence in the calcium-rich bedrock characteristic of the region. Within the riverbed is a large pool that is a popular local swimming area during the summer; a mile upstream from the pool are a series of waterfalls.

To protect the head of the gorge, improve access, and control litter and trashing dumping, the state of Vermont established the Lower Clarendon Gorge State Forest following land purchases in 2002 and 2004, adding a 75-acre buffer of forest. From the parking area on Route 103, it's a short, easy walk of 0.1 miles south along the Long Trail to the suspension bridge. Hikers can backtrack from the gorge, or continue to follow the trail for another 0.8 miles as it rises to the Airport Lookout, where rock ledges offer views across the valley west to the Adirondacks.

## BINGHAM FALLS GORGE

*The unique gorge at Bingham Falls lies in a narrow valley at the base of Mount Mansfield and Smuggler's Notch.*

Closest Town: Stowe, VT

Owner: Vermont Department of Forest Parks, and Recreation
(Mount Mansfield State Forest)

Directions: From Interstate 89, take Exit 10 and follow VT 100 north to its junction with VT 108 in Stowe. Follow VT 108 north for 5.5 miles to the Mount Mansfield toll road, then continue another 0.75 mile to the roadside parking areas for the falls; the trailhead is on the right (east) side of the road.

In a narrow valley at the base of Mount Mansfield's southeast slopes and the cliffs of Smuggler's Notch lies the compact gorge, cascades, and old forests of Bingham Falls, which has also been historically known as Lewis Falls, Grotto Cascade, and Orpha Falls. Fed by a series of brooks that drain the slopes of Mount Mansfield and Spruce Peak, the West Branch of the Waterbury River passes through a narrow channel as it enters the head of gorge, which is roughly 20 feet deep. Here it winds its way around a jumble of rock columns that have been carved and hollowed by the flowing water, then passes by a small pool and deep potholes.

As it winds through the gorge, the river then drops a total of 90 feet in a series of five cascades and plunges. The last waterfall, which was historically known as Roaring Falls, is also the highest, at 25 feet. At the base of this drop is an especially attractive emerald green pool. Adorning the gorge are groves of old evergreen eastern hemlock trees, some of which have been dated at more than 400 years old. They are the largest old trees on Mount Mansfield's slopes.

From the base of the gorge, the West Branch meanders south through the popular resort village of Stowe en route to its confluence with the Winooski River. The river is renowned among anglers for its healthy populations of brook, brown, and rainbow trout.

From roadside parking areas along Route 108, the short trail to the falls leads to a good view upstream of the rocks in the upper gorge. It then continues downstream to a viewing area at the main falls, which it reaches in 0.3 miles after descending 150 feet. The gorge is easily combined with a visit to Smugger's Notch, which is just up the road.

*The highest of the cascades at Bingham Falls is the 25-foot drop at the lower end of the gorge.*

## CHESTERFIELD GORGE (NH)

Like its namesake in the hills of western Massachusetts, the Chesterfield Gorge of southwestern New Hampshire is carved by water ultimately bound for the Connecticut River. From headwaters at two small ponds in the uplands between Keene and Brattleboro, Vermont, the waters of Wilde Brook churn through this small canyon en route to their confluence with nearby Partridge Brook and the Connecticut River, which is 10 miles downstream.

Because Wilde Brook's course is relatively irregular with numerous sharp bends, steep walls, and no major falls or cascades, it is considered to be relatively young in geologic time. Older waterways, which have been eroding and shaping their underlying bedrock for longer periods of time, generally follow a smoother, more regular course.

The ravine is shaded by a forest of large eastern hemlock trees that are more than 200 years old; the largest specimens grow as high as 100 feet. Hemlocks favor these moist, shady environments, which were sheltered from fires in historic times. In the dryer, more open environment near the parking area grow oaks and pines, which thrive in sunlit areas. These trees motivated local farmer George White to buy the land encompassing the gorge to protect it from logging during the 1930s. White subsequently sold the property to the Society for the Protection of New Hampshire Forests, who in turn donated it to the state.

The gorge is now part of a 13-acre natural area that is easily accessed from the state wayside on Route 9. An easy, 0.7-mile nature trail, which is excellent for families, begins at the edge of the parking lot and descends at a gentle grade into the hemlock ravine. It then forks a short loop that follows the top of the walls on both sides of the gorge, crossing two wood bridges over Wilde Brook. After completing the loop, backtrack to the parking area.

Closest Town: Chesterfield, NH

Owner: New Hampshire Division of Parks and Recreation, 603-363-8373

Directions: From Interstate 91 in Brattleboro, take exit 3 and follow NH 9 east for 8 miles to the parking area on the left (north) side of the highway.

A forest of large old hemlock trees grows above the walls of Chesterfield Gorge.

FLUME
GORGE

Closest Town: Lincoln, NH

Owner: New Hampshire State Forests and Parks, 603-745-8391

Directions: From Interstate 93 in Lincoln, follow the highway north to the notch, where it joins US 3 and becomes the Franconia Notch Parkway. Take Exit 34A and follow signs for the Flume Gorge and visitor center. A $12.00 fee is charged for the Flume trail, which is open from mid-May through October.

*The narrow Flume Gorge has long been one of the most popular attractions of the White Mountains.*

Legend has it that during 1808, a 93-year old woman named Aunt Jess Gurnsey discovered the narrow canyon now known as The Flume while fishing at the base of Mount Liberty in Franconia Notch. This 800-foot long gorge, which is only 12-20 feet wide and is walled by towering 90-foot cliffs, subsequently became one of the signature attractions of the White Mountains.

Long before Aunt Jess's discovery, the Flume formed when molten lava filled cracks in a mass of ancient Conway granite, forming a series of dikes that eroded away over time. The largest of these gaps was the gorge itself, which was subsequently widened by the waters of Flume Brook and frequent freezing and thawing of ice over thousands of years. In 1883, a significant rainstorm caused a landslide that made the gorge deeper and also washed away a giant boulder that once was once wedged between the narrow walls.

This storm also created Avalanche Falls, where Flume Brook drops 45 feet as it enters the head of the gorge. After coursing through the narrow passage, it then glides across an area of smooth granite called Table Rock, then empties into the Pemigewasset River, which flows south through the heart of Franconia Notch.

In addition to the Flume, many other attractions are spread along this unique valley. Another scenic waterfall is Liberty Gorge, where Cascade Brook plunges toward its confluence with the Pemigewasset River. Just above the meeting of these waterways is a large, 40-foot deep pool on the Pemigewasset River, walled by cliffs that rise as high as 130 feet. The Sentinel Pine, a giant, 175-foot white pine that was one of New Hampshire's tallest trees, once grew out of the gorge walls here. After it was blown down by the great hurricane of 1938, its timbers were used to build the Sentinel Pine Covered Bridge, which spans the river above The Pool. A series of large glacial boulders are spread along the Wildwood Path on the west banks of the river.

All of these attractions are easily accessed and viewed by a popular 2-mile loop trail that begins at the Franconia Notch Visitor Center, which includes exhibits, a gift shop, and videos detailing the history of the notch. After passing by the historic Flume Covered Bridge (c. 1886) over the Pemigewasset River, this path leads east along Flume Brook and Table Rock to the base of the gorge. A boardwalk offers a safe passage through the narrow canyon, ending at Avalanche Falls and the Bear's Cave, which are 0.7 miles from the trailhead. Visitors can backtrack for a 1.4-mile round trip, or continue to follow the main loop, which passes a number of attractions including Liberty Gorge, Stairs Falls, the Sentinel Pine Covered Bridge, The Pool, and a view of Mounts Liberty and Flume.

*The historic Flume Covered Bridge (c. 1886) spans the Pemigewasset River at the Flume Gorge.*

These trees are more than 200 years old and grow as high as 130 feet. Some were branded with the King of England's mark for use as naval ship masts during the 18th century, but were never subsequently cut. These marked trees are prized finds for old-growth forest enthusiasts.

The Gulf Hagas Rim Trail, a 5.2-mile spur off the Appalachian Trail, offers a variety of perspectives of the gorge and its various features. Short, well-marked side paths lead to close-up views of the falls, rocks, and overlooks such as Hammond Street Pitch, where there's a fine overview of the gorge. At the canyon's west end, ledges offer another overview of the river, Billings Falls, and a large pool near the Head of the Gulf. This route follows constantly rolling terrain, though none of the climbs are especially steep or long. Many hikers make an 8-mile circuit by combining the Rim Trail with Pleasant River Road, an old logging road that offers an easy, level return route through the woods. Those seeking a shorter outing can do an out-and-back hike to Screw Auger Falls and one or two of the overlooks, then backtrack.

In spite of the gorge's relative isolation, it is a popular destination in warm months, especially the river is warm enough for swimming. Note that a crossing of the wide but shallow Pleasant River is required at the onset of this hike; an extra pair of footwear such as sandals or old shoes is recommended. Moose are common throughout the area and regularly seen along the roads, particularly near timber harvests.

Closest Town: Millinocket, ME

Owners and contacts: North Maine Woods/KI-JO Mary Forest, 207-435-6213; Maine Appalachian Trail Club, National Park Service.

Directions: From ME 11 five miles north of Brownville Junction, turn left at the sign for Katahdin Iron Works and continue seven miles to the gate, where an $8.00 toll is collected, and maps of the area are available. Bear right, cross the Pleasant River, then continue for 6 miles from the Iron Works to a junction. Turn left here and continue for another mile to the parking area.

For centuries, the gorge at Gulf Hagas has inspired dramatic nomenclature: it was first named "Hagas," or "Evil Place," by the Abenaki Indians, and today it is popularly known as "Maine's Grand Canyon." In 1969, this four-mile long canyon in the heart of Maine's interior timberlands was designated as a National Natural Landmark by the National Park Service.

Though the exact origin of Gulf Hagas is unclear, it is believed to have been carved by a glacial meltwater stream at the close of the last ice age. Today, the West Branch of the Pleasant River courses between the slate walls, which rise as high as 125 feet. As it flows through the gorge, the river drops a total of 500 feet. The many waterfalls and cascades include Screw Auger Falls (not to be confused with the popular falls of the same name in Grafton Notch), where Gulf Hagas Brook drops 25 feet over the steep walls into a deep pool at the river's edge, a narrow passage known as The Jaws, and Buttermilk, Stairs, and Billings Falls.

Near the east end of the gorge is the Hermitage, a 35-acre former camp site that includes a five-acre grove of towering old white pines.

WATERFALLS
chapter
six

The character of waterfalls often changes notably throughout the seasons. As the snow melts in late winter and early spring, many thunder with a high volume.

*From tall*, graceful drops of seasonal woodland streams to thundering, block-like cascades along roaring rivers, more than 500 waterfalls of all sizes and shapes are spread throughout New England's landscape. The region's highly variable topography and abundant precipitation offer an ideal setting for these popular and often dramatic attractions. The majority of the falls are located in the mountain and hill regions, though they may be found anywhere where there's elevation change.

In geologic time, waterfalls are actually relatively short-lived and mobile. With every pebble that is carried away from its lip or scoured out of its base by the relentless cutting of a flowing river or stream, a waterfall is gradually transformed over tens of thousands of years. The pools at the bottom of the drops are areas where a substantial amount of energy is often dissipated, causing the base of the falls to erode (a process known as "undermining"). Ultimately, the area above the base breaks apart, causing the waterfall to migrate upstream as the process begins again or level off, depending on the resistance and shape of the surrounding bedrock.

A handful of general classifications are often used to describe the shape and characteristics of waterfalls. Some of the most common in New England are "plunges," where water makes a thin, vertical drop off an overhanging ledge, "fans," where a narrow flow at the lip widens as it spreads across a rock face, and "blocks," where the drop is roughly as wide as it is tall.

The character of waterfalls often changes notably throughout the seasons. As the snow melts in late winter and early spring, many thunder with a high volume. As the spring and summer progress, those along smaller streams and brooks slow significantly and may dry up completely. They are often recharged by late summer and autumn storms, including the soaking tropical storms that periodically pass over New England. In winter, unique ice formations often form along falls and their associated ravines.

*The carving power of waterfalls, which are short-lived in geologic time, is evident at Royalston Falls in central Massachusetts.*

## KENT FALLS

*The lower falls are the largest of the 20 individual cascades that collectively form Kent Falls.*

## CHAPMAN FALLS

*Spring rains recharge the volume of the Eight Mile River, which drops 60 feet at Chapman Falls.*

Closest Town: Kent, CT

Owner: Connecticut Forests and Parks (Macedonia Brook State Park), 860-927-3238

Directions: From the junction of US 7 and CT 341 in Kent, follow US 7 north for 5 miles to the state park entrance on the east side of the highway. On weekends and holidays from Memorial Day until the end of October, there is an admission fee of $9.00 for Connecticut residents and $15.00 for out-of-state residents.

Closest Town: Millington, CT

Owner: Connecticut Department of Forests and Parks (Devil's Hopyard State Park), 860-345-8521

Directions: From the junction of CT 82 and CT 158 in East Haddam, follow CT 82 east for 0.2 miles, then turn left on Hopyard Road and continue for 3.5 miles to the state park entrance on the right.

With no less than 17 individual cascades spread over a quarter-mile, Kent Falls is one of southern New England's longest and highest waterfalls. The steep slopes of the Housatonic River Valley in Connecticut's scenic northwest hill region serve as the setting for this popular attraction, which has been featured on television shows and in advertisements.

From an upland wetland in the town of Warren, the waters of Falls Brook drop a total of 250 feet over the valley's steep limestone cliffs, culminating with a 70-foot plunge at the base that is the highest of the numerous cascades. After the main falls, the brook levels off, passes under a hiker's covered bridge at the entrance to Kent Falls State Park, and continues to its confluence with the Housatonic River roughly four miles downstream from Cornwall Bridge.

Waterfalls with multiple cascades such as Kent Falls generally reflect a mixture of both soft and erosion-resistant bedrock; the brook drops through fractures in the rock. Spread throughout the falls are numerous artifacts of the cutting power of water over thousands of years, including geologic potholes, which are small depressions that have been scoured into the bedrock by pebbles in pockets of swirling water. Also visible are columns that have been shaped and smoothed by the flowing brook.

The falls are safely viewed by a well-maintained trail at Kent Falls State Park, which is part of a network of conservation areas along the scenic Housatonic River corridor. From the entrance on Route 7, this path leads visitors across the covered bridge and through the large grassy picnic area adjacent to the base of the falls. It then ascends along the south bank of the brook for 0.3 miles to the head of the falls, passing a series of observation decks that offer close-up views of the cascades, potholes, and rocks.

Exactly how the portion of the Eight Mile River Valley known as "Devil's Hopyard" acquired its colorful name is unclear, but it is nevertheless the subject of several entertaining myths and legends. One popular fable claims that the potholes at the base of Chapman Falls were created by the devil's footprints as he hopped across the rocks; another, somewhat less lively account asserts that the area was named for a farmer named Dibble who grew hops in a nearby field.

Today, Chapman Falls, where the Eight Mile River drops 60 feet over a high ledge and past the potholes, is the main attraction at popular Devil's Hopyard State Park. The considerable power of the falls powered a gristmill that operated here until the 1820s, and then a sawmill that shut down in 1895. The cascades are located in the northern portion of the park, a short distance downstream from a wetland on the north side of Foxton Road. The Eight Mile River is not named for its length, but instead because it meets the Connecticut River eight miles north of the Connecticut's mouth at Long Island Sound. Sadly, many of the eastern hemlock trees along the riverbanks have been decimated by the hemlock woolly adelgid, a forest pest that migrated north into southern Connecticut during the mid-1980s.

The state park encompasses 860 acres of the river's watershed. The falls are easily accessed and viewed from the main park entrance, and there is also a parking area above the falls along Foxton Road. A recommended route for hikers looking to further explore this area is the Vista Trail, which offers a mostly easy three-mile circuit along the east side of the valley. This pleasant path includes a section along the riverbanks and a short climb to a lookout with an overview of the forested valley.

## CAMPBELL FALLS

Nearly hidden in a remote, quiet valley on the Massachusetts-Connecticut state line are the roaring 60-foot cascades of Campbell Falls, one of the region's highest-volume waterfalls. From the lip atop a tall gorge, the Whiting River funnels through a narrow chasm and falls into a small pool, then changes direction and makes a second, wider drop to the base of the gorge. It then winds to its confluence with nearby Ginger Creek. These falls are often roaring with a high flow, especially during the spring or after a summer or autumn rainstorm.

Rippled patterns in the rocks adjacent to the falls indicate areas where softer minerals of the granitic gneiss rock have been eroded away by the flowing river. During the spring, colorful red columbine wildflowers, which thrive in rocky areas such as gorge walls and hillsides, grow out of cracks in the bedrock, where there's just enough soil to sustain them.

Protecting the falls and surrounding woodlands are Campbell Falls State Parks in both Massachusetts and Connecticut. The falls lie within the tiny three-acre Massachusetts park, just 100 yards from the state line. Here a short path slopes downhill from the roadside parking area for 0.2 miles to the base of the falls, dropping 150 feet along the way. Across the state line, the larger park in Connecticut encompasses a portion of the watershed of Ginger Creek. A 0.4-mile long trail begins at the parking area on Tobey Hill Road and descends through hardwood forests to the falls, passing a stone monument that marks the state boundary.

Closest Towns: New Marlborough, MA and Norfolk, CT

Owners: Massachusetts Department of Conservation and Recreation, Connecticut Department of Environmental Protection, 860-482-1817

Directions: For the Massachusetts park, take MA 57 to the center of New Marlborough, then turn south on New Marlborough-Southfield Road and follow it to Southfield, then bear left at a fork and follow Norfolk Road south for 4.4 miles. Turn right on Campbell Falls Road and continue for 0.3 miles to the parking area. For the Connecticut park, follow Norfolk Road to the state line, where it becomes CT 272. Turn right (or left if coming from the south) on Tobey Hill Road (marked as Old Spaulding Hill Road on some maps) and continue to the parking area on the right.

At the rocky lip of Campbell Falls, the Whiting River squeezes through this narrow gorge.

## BASH BISH FALLS

*The famous twin cascades of Bash Bish Falls are one of the signature attractions of the Berkshire Hills.*

the slopes of Mount Washington, the waters of Bash Bish Brook descend 200 feet to the valley below, culminating with the final drop at Bash Bish Falls, where the brook is split by a large, angular boulder. From the pool at the base of the falls, the brook churns through a narrow gorge, then follows a much gentler course west toward its confluence with the Hudson River.

Like New England's other waterfalls, Bash Bish Falls is relatively young in geologic time. It formed at the close of the last ice age roughly 10,000 years ago when glacial meltwater broke through a debris dam on the mountain's slopes. The falls and brook draw their names from an ancient Mohican legend involving a woman who, after being condemned to death for adultery, vanished without a trace into the pool. According to lore, her spirit is believed to still be present in the gorge. In 1858, French acrobat Charles Blodin, who had previously crossed Niagra Falls, walked a tightrope across the rocky gorge.

The falls lie within the Mount Washington State Forest, which encompasses 4,500 scenic acres of the Taconics near the Connecticut and New York state lines. The shortest approach to the falls is from the main parking area on Falls Road, where the blue-blazed Bash Bish Falls Trail descends steeply for a quarter-mile through groves of hemlock and yellow birch trees to the base of the falls. A short path at the edge of the lot offers a quick climb to an overlook with a fine westerly view across the valley towards New York State. A slightly longer but gentler option is to park at the lower lot on Falls Road at the Massachusetts-New York state line, and follow the trail upstream for a half mile to the falls.

In addition to the falls, the state forest offers an additional 30 miles of hiking trails, including an easy three-mile trail to the top of Alander Mountain, where the scenic South Taconic Trail offers long views across three states from an open ridge. Bash Bish Falls is just two trail miles from Alander Mountain's summit, and one can combine these two attractions in one outing as a long out-and-back hike or shuttle cars between the trailheads.

Closest Town: Mount Washington, MA

Owner: Massachusetts Department of Conservation and Recreation, 413-528-0330

Directions: From the Massachusetts Turnpike (I-90) in Lee, take Exit 2 and follow MA 102 west for 4.7 miles to Stockbridge. Turn left on US 7 south and continue 7.7 miles to Great Barrington. After passing the town center, bear right on MA 41/MA 23 and continue 4.9 miles to South Egremont. Follow MA 41 left where the routes split, then bear right on Mount Washington Road for 7.5 miles. Turn right on Cross Road, then right on West Street for 1 mile. Turn left on Falls Road and follow it for 1.5 miles to the main parking area.

In spite of their location in a remote, rugged valley of the southern Taconic Mountains near the New York state line, the distinctive twin cascades of Bash Bish Falls are one of the best-known attractions in Massachusetts. Fed by a series of springs, streams, and brooks on

# SAVOY MOUNTAIN:

## TANNERY & ROSS BROOK FALLS

*Just a few hundred feet upstream from its confluence with Ross Brook, Tannery Brook drops 80 feet over jagged ledges.*

Closest Town: Savoy, MA

Owner: Massachusetts Department of Conservation and Recreation (Savoy Mountain State Forest), 413-663-8469

Directions: From MA 2 on the Charlemont-Savoy town line, drive west for 1.5 miles and turn left (south) on Black Brook Road. Follow Black Brook Road for 1.4 miles, then turn right on Tannery Brook Road and continue for 0.7 miles to the parking area at Tannery Pond. If the upper portion of Tannery Brook Road is impassable during winter, park at the end of the maintained area at the state forest boundary and walk along the road to the trailhead.

In a high, steep-walled ravine in the Savoy Mountain State Forest in the northern Berkshire Hills are not one, but two dramatic waterfalls where a pair of mountain brooks simultaneously cascade over steep ledges. The nomenclature of these falls varies by the source and is rather confusing: the falls on Ross Brook are known as both Ross Brook Falls and Tannery Falls, while the adjacent cascades along Tannery Brook are known as Tannery Brook Falls and Parker Brook Falls.

The falls on Tannery Brook are distinguished by the steep, jagged cliffs at the head of the ravine. Fed by the outflow of nearby Tannery Pond, this seasonal waterway cascades a total of approximately 80 feet through long diagonal cracks in the bedrock ledges that likely formed when the walls on the west bank shifted downslope.

Roughly 100 feet away are the falls on Ross Brook, which are nearly 70 feet high. The brook originates at the base of Lewis Hill in the center of the state forest and winds north and east toward the ravine. From the lip of the falls, it makes plunges of 30 and 25 feet onto rock shelves, then

changes direction slightly and makes a final short drop to a large pool at the base of the falls.

Below the Ross Brook Falls pool, the two brooks converge to form a single waterway that flows a short distance to its confluence with the Cold River at the state forest's eastern boundary. The river parallels Route 2, the famous Mohawk Trail Highway, as both wind through a steep valley of the Hoosac Range, which is a southerly extension of the Green Mountains of Vermont.

*Picturesque Ross Brook Falls is one of two waterfalls that share the same ravine in the heart of the Savoy Mountain State Forest.*

The Savoy Mountain and Mohawk Trail State Forests combine to protect nearly 20,000 acres of this especially scenic region. The quarter-mile long trail to the falls begins at a dirt parking area across from Tannery Pond. After following a narrow ridge between the brooks, where several cascades are visible, it reaches a set of stairs that offer a safe passage to the base of the ravine. Tannery Falls is to the right of the stairs, while Ross Brook Falls is around the corner to the left.

A recommended hike for visitors with additional time is the Busby Trail, which begins near the state forest headquarters and offers an easy 1.5-mile climb to the 2566-foot summit of Spruce Hill, where there are commanding views that range from nearby Mount Greylock and the Hoosac River Valley to Mount Monadnock and Wachusett Mountain on the eastern horizon.

*At Doane's Falls, the wide, roaring waters of
Lawrence Brook pass through a series of cascades
and pools as they drop to Tully Lake.*

TULLY
VALLEY:

ROYALSTON
&
DOANES
FALLS

*Once surrounded by farm fields and a casino, Royalston Falls today lies
in a quiet wooded valley in north-central Massachusetts.*

Closest Town: Royalston, MA

Owner: The Trustees of Reservations, 978-921-1944

Directions: From MA 2 in Athol, take Exit 17 and follow MA 32 north to the junction
with MA 2A. Turn left on MA 32/2A, then right on MA 32 north. Cross the bridge
over the Millers River and follow MA 32 to Tully Lake. For Royalston Falls, continue
on MA 32 north to its junction with MA 68, then continue for 1.7 miles to the
entrance on the right adjacent to Newton Cemetery. For Doanes Falls, after
passing Tully Lake, turn right on Doane Hill Road and continue past the Tully
Lake Campground to a pullout on the right near the lower falls, or continue up
the hill to a parking area at the bridge over Lawrence Brook.

The Tully River Valley, a less-known but highly scenic region of
low mountains, rivers, wetlands, and abundant wildlife in north-central
Massachusetts, is the heart of a 120,000-acre bio-reserve that is one
of only five such designated areas in the state. Two of its distinctive
attractions are Royalston Falls and Doanes Falls, both of which are situated
along tributary streams of the Tully River.

Though it is rather narrow and seasonal, Falls Brook offers ample
evidence of the cutting power of water over thousands of years. As
it flows south from the New Hampshire state line, the brook passes
potholes, pools, sculpted rocks, and a small natural bridge, then reaches
the head of the high gorge at Royalston Falls. Here it drops roughly
60 feet, then winds beneath the steep cliffs as it continues toward its
confluence with the East Branch of the Tully River.

The remote, wild character of the falls today belies its past,
when it was the site of town events, festivals, and a casino. From
the trailhead on Route 32, the combined Tully and Metacomet-

Monadnock Trails descend the valley at a moderate grade, reaching the brook and a wood bridge at 0.5 miles. After the crossing the trails split; to reach the falls bear right and follow the yellow-blazed Tully Trail south for 0.3 miles. The natural bridge is a short distance upstream from the bridge.

The nearby Doanes Falls have a much different character; Lawrence Brook, a much larger tributary of the East Branch, drops nearly 200 feet in a quarter-mile long series of roaring cascades. At the upper falls, the brook drops beneath an old stone bridge, then continues down the valley in a chain of cascades. After curving through a narrow chasm, it reaches the block-shaped lower falls, then empties into the northeast corner of Tully Lake, which was created for flood control in 1949. The moderately steep trail that parallels the cascades can be accessed by parking areas near the top and base of the falls; the lower portion of this route is universally accessible. Visitors should obey posted signs, as several fatal accidents have occurred here.

LYE
BROOK
FALLS

Closest Town: Manchester, VT

Owner: Green Mountain National Forest (Lye Brook Wilderness), 802-363-2307

Directions: From the junction of US 7 and VT 11/30 in Manchester, follow VT 11/30 for 0.4 miles to a right on East
   Manchester Road. Follow East Manchester Road for one mile, then turn right on Glen Road. Bear right at a
   fork on the gravel Lye Brook access road and continue to the parking area at the road's end; use caution as
   this road may be in poor condition.

*A long chain of ledges and cascades form Lye Brook Falls, one
of the highest waterfalls of the Green Mountains.*

Once known as the Trestle Cascade, thanks to an old logging railway that passed over a bridge below the falls, Lye Brook Falls is one of Vermont's highest and most dramatic waterfalls. Here Lye Brook drops more than 125 feet over a series of step ledges in a narrow, steep ravine. The brook is seasonal, and as a result the falls assume a variety of characteristics as the year progresses. At the end of winter and following heavy storms, they thunder with a high volume, but they rapidly transition to a thin, veil-like ribbon or series of trickles during dry periods.

*Overview of the Lye Brook Wilderness from the crest of
Lye Brook Falls.*

The falls are situated at the edge the western slopes of the Green Mountains, in the uplands east of Manchester and the Valley of Vermont. Protecting nearly 18,000 acres of this scenic area is the Lye Brook Wilderness, which encompasses the watershed of the brook and the surrounding northern hardwood-spruce woodlands, streams, ponds, and bogs. Much of the preserve lies on a high plateau with elevations of 2,500 feet or more.

The falls are reached by a mostly easy 2.3-mile (one way) trail that follows portions of the old railroad bed past an overlook with a view of the valley and several stream crossings. It then rises to a marked junction at 1.8 miles, gaining 750 feet from the trailhead. Here the half-mile long side trail to the falls forks to the right and descends roughly 150 feet along the ravine to the base of the cascades and a series of rock ledges and cliffs.

# HAMILTON FALLS

Closest Town: Jamaica, VT

Owner: Vermont Department of Forests, Parks, and Recreation (Jamaica State Park), 802-874-4600

Directions: For Jamaica State Park and the West River Trail, from Brattleboro, follow VT 30 north to its junction with VT 100 near the Townshend-Jamaica town line, then continue on VT 30 /100 to the Jamaica town common. Turn east on Depot Street and continue for a half mile to the entrance, following signs for the state park. To access the falls directly, take VT 30 to West Townsend. Turn right (north) on Windham Hill Road and continue 4.1 miles, then turn left on Burbee Pond Road and follow it 0.8 miles to another left on West Windham Road. Continue on West Windham Road for nearly 3 miles to the parking area and Switch Road Trail on the left.

*At Hamilton Falls, Cobb Brook carves narrow channels through rock ledges as it plunges 125 feet towards the West River Valley.*

The picturesque West River Valley in the southern Green Mountains serves as the setting for Hamilton Falls, one of Vermont's tallest and most distinctive waterfalls. On the steep north slopes of the valley, Cobb Brook, one of the river's tributaries, drops a total of 125 feet as it flows across a series of rock ledges.

At the top of the falls are a series of deep, wide potholes, which were scoured by the frothing, swirling water. As it glides across the exposed bedrock, the seasonal brook follows a series of narrow, well-defined channels, then forks into a prong for the final drop. From the pool at the base of the base of the falls, the brook continues down the slopes of the valley for a mile to its confluence with the West River.

From headwaters in southeast Rutland County, the West River flows 50 miles to its confluence with the Connecticut River at Brattleboro. In pre-colonial times, Native Americans used the river as a key trade corridor between the Lake Champlain and Connecticut River Valleys. European settlers subsequently cleared much for the land for agriculture, and established a number of sawmills along the river. A railway was constructed through the valley during the 1880s, but was constantly plagued by flooding before finally being destroyed in 1927. In 1961, the Ball Mountain and Townshend Dams were established along the river for flood control.

Today, Jamaica State Park, located just east of the Green Mountain National Forest boundary along the section of river between the dams, protects 772 acres of this scenic valley. The Hamilton Falls Natural Area encompasses the falls and a 50-acre forest buffer. Though the falls can be easily reached from Windham Road, a more interesting option is to begin at the state park entrance and follow the West River recreational trail along the river's edge for two miles to the bend known as the Oxbow. The moderately steep, one-way trail to Hamilton Falls, which follows an old switch road, begins here and parallels Cobb Brook for one mile upstream to the falls. Another side trail branches off the recreational trail and offers an easy walk to the ledges of Little Ball Mountain, where there are views across the countryside.

FALLS OF LANA

As Sucker Brook drops down the lower slopes of 2640-foot Mount Moosalamoo in the west-central Green Mountains, it winds and twists through a series of cascades, chutes, and pools that collectively form one of New England's most unique waterfalls. During the mid-19th century, noted Army General John E. Wool came across these cascades while leading a group of explorers through the Middlebury area. The group named the falls "Ilana," the Spanish word for "wool," in his honor; over time one of the "I's" was dropped.

Each of the main cascades has its own character. In the upper section, the brook squeezes tightly between large sections of exposed bedrock and drops into a large pool. It then makes a sharp turn and falls through a long, narrow diagonal chasm at the edge of the cliffs. At the base of the chasm, it switches direction yet again and falls to the valley in two drops around an angular section of bedrock. From the last falls, the brook flows a short distance west to its confluence with popular Lake Dunsmore at Branbury Beach State Park.

From the parking area on Route 53, the trail to the falls, which is part of a network of hiking routes on Mount Moosalamoo, ascends at an easy grade for 0.5 miles to the cascades. Side paths lead to the rocky ravine and its viewpoints; while none of are especially dangerous, the ravine is steep and caution should be used around the rocks.

After exploring the falls, hikers can backtrack to the trailhead, or continue to features such as the Rattlesnake Cliffs, where rock ledges offer views across Lake Dunsmore to the Adirondack Mountains.

*Sucker Brook changes direction and form multiple times at the distinctive Falls of Lana on the west slopes of the Green Mountains.*

Closest Town: Middlebury, VT

Owner: Green Mountain National Forest, 802-388-4362

Directions: From the junction of US 7 and VT 73, follow VT 73 east for 3 miles to Forest Dale, then turn right (north) on VT 53 and continue 5.3 miles to the parking area on the east side of the road.

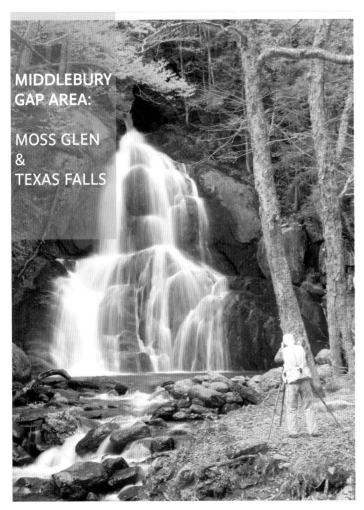

## MIDDLEBURY GAP AREA:

## MOSS GLEN & TEXAS FALLS

Though the cascades of nearby Texas Falls aren't quite as dramatic, the waters of Texas Brook make for a picturesque sight as they drop a total of 35 feet in a series of small cascades through a narrow gorge formed by glaciers. The falls are located at the eastern portion of Middlebury Gap, halfway between Route 100 and the gap's height-of-land between Worth and Boyce Mountains. An easy, mile-long nature trail crosses the falls and gorge on a wood bridge, then follows a portion of the brook before looping back along the ravine to the trailhead. As of late 2010, a portion of this trail was temporarily closed for repairs to the bridge, which was damaged by a recent flood.

*A compact gorge, two cascades, and pools form Texas Falls on the east side of Middlebury Gap.*

*The tall cascades of Moss Glen Falls near Granville are a popular destination for photographers and tourists in all seasons.*

Closest Towns: Hancock and Granville, VT

Owner: Green Mountain National Forest, 802-747-6700

Directions: For Moss Glen Falls, from the junction of VT 100 and 125 in Hancock, follow VT 100 north for 6.7 miles to the roadside viewing area on the west side of the highway, 3 miles north of Granville village. For Texas Falls, from the junction of VT 100 and VT 125, follow VT 125 west for 3 miles to the entrance on the right (north) side of the road.

Thanks to its photogenic qualities and roadside location along Route 100, the well-known scenic highway that follows the ridge of the Green Mountains for nearly the entire length of Vermont, Moss Glen Falls is one of the state's most-visited natural attractions. Large crowds of tourists are present during the autumn foliage season and even the coldest February days often see visitors drawn to the distinctive ice formations. In spite of its popularity, it still shares a name with (and is not to be confused with) another scenic Moss Glen Falls near Stowe.

The source of this Moss Glen Falls is Deer Hollow Brook, which flows through a narrow gap and then fans across the steep schist rock ledges as it drops 35 feet into a small pool along the edge of the highway. Surrounding the falls is the Granville Gulf Wilderness, an 1171-acre state preserve that includes a small block of old-growth spruce-hemlock forest. A wooden platform and short boardwalk allow easy, safe viewing of the falls and an adjacent series of cascades from several perspectives.

*As Dry Brook approaches the floor of Franconia Notch, it drops over the granite steps of Stairs Falls.*

*Scenic Cloudland Falls is the largest of the waterfalls and cascades on the west slopes of Franconia Ridge.*

Closest Town: Lincoln, NH

Owners: New Hampshire Division of Parks and Recreation, White Mountain National Forest, 603-803-5563

Directions: From Lincoln, follow Interstate 93 north to Franconia Notch State Park, where the highway becomes the Franconia Notch Parkway. Continue past Exit 34A and The Basin, then exit the highway at a sign marked "Trailhead Parking," where there is parking and access to the Falling Waters and Old Bridle Path trails.

It's little wonder that the 8.8-mile circuit over Mount Lafayette and Franconia Ridge *(see Alpine Mountains chapter)* is regarded as one the finest hikes in all of New England. Not only does this route traverse an open ridge capped by two 5,000-foot peaks with spectacular views and alpine wildflowers, but it also leads past a chain of waterfalls along Dry Brook that are worth a visit in their own right. They include Cloudland Falls, one of the most scenic cascades in the White Mountains.

As the brook drops down the steep west slopes of the ridge, it passes over three main falls and a number of lesser cascades. The lowest of these is 20-foot Stairs Falls, which is well-named for the many step-like formations that the brook has eroded out of a broad granite ledge. A short distance upstream is the taller and narrower Swiftwater Falls, where the brook makes a 60-foot plunge across a rock face at a trail crossing.

Roughly 1,000 feet above the floor of the notch is picturesque Cloudland Falls, where the brook spreads into a wide fan as it plunges 80 feet over the granite rock face. From the lip of the falls, there's an

open view across the valley toward Mount Moosilauke, which rises in the distance to the west. Many smaller cascades are visible adjacent to and below these falls as well.

The aptly named Falling Waters Trail parallels the brook as it ascends from the trailhead in Franconia Notch to Little Haystack Mountain and Franconia Ridge. The lower portion of this route follows easy to moderate terrain for a mile to Stairs Falls. After crossing the base of Swiftwater Falls, it becomes steeper and rockier as it rises to Cloudland Falls, 1.6 miles from the trailhead. Hikers have the option of backtracking from Cloudland Falls for a 3.2-mile round trip, or continuing the moderately steep climb to the ridge. Two especially pleasant times to walk this route are in May, when wildflowers such as painted and red trillium are in bloom and the volume of the falls is high, and October, when colorful foliage adorns the mountain slopes.

# CRAWFORD NOTCH:

## ARETHUSA & RIPLEY FALLS

*Hikers enjoy a respite beneath a low-volume Arethusa Falls on a late summer afternoon.*

Closest Town: Harts Location, NH

Owner: New Hampshire Division of Parks and Recreation (Crawford Notch State Park), 603-374-2272

Directions: From Interstate 93, take Exit 36 and follow US 3 North, to its junction with US 302. Follow US 302 East to the notch, following signs to Crawford Notch State Park. From the Willey House historic site in the state park, follow US 302 east for 1 mile to the Ripley Falls parking area and 3.3 miles to Arethusa Falls.

Crawford Notch *(see Mountain Passes chapter)* encompasses some of the most dramatic mountain scenery in New England. These steep slopes of this narrow mountain pass, which was shaped by glaciers, are home to some of the tallest and most distinctive waterfalls in the White Mountain region.

Though the exact height of Arethusa Falls varies from 125 to 200 feet depending on what source one consults (160-170 feet is a reasonable

estimate), it is nevertheless one of the highest falls in all of New England. While narrow Bemis Brook rarely provides a great volume, its light flow often produces a series of graceful cascades as the water glides and fans over the exposed rock. Downstream from the main falls are a series of smaller cascades, including Bemis and Coliseum Falls, and the Fawn Pool. The trail to Arethusa Falls follows easy to moderate terrain along the brook before reaching the falls at 1.4 miles. Many hikers incorporate the route to the falls as part of a rugged 4-mile circuit that includes a steep climb to the nearby Frankenstein Cliffs, where there are fine views of the southern portion of Crawford Notch.

A short distance to the north is Ripley Falls, where the waters of Avalanche Brook drop 100 feet over steep ledges in the ravine between Mounts Willey and Bemis. From the lip of the falls, the brook glides across a series of steps, then spreads into a long, smooth slide across exposed granite. These falls are easily reached via a 20-minute, half-mile walk that begins on the combined Appalachian and Ethan Pond Trails at a well-marked trailhead in the notch. This path quickly rises to a junction where the blue-blazed Ripley Falls Trail branches to the left and follows the brook's ravine before dropping to the base of the falls.

Arethusa and Ripley Falls can be visited individually by following the aforementioned trails, or combined in a single outing via the 2.1-mile (one-way) Ripley and Arethusa Falls Trail, which branches off of the Ripley Falls Trail. While walking these trails, keep an eye out for black bears and moose, particularly early and late in the day.

Other significant falls in the notch include the Silver and Flume Cascades, which are roadside attractions easily viewed from Route 302, and Nancy Cascade on the upper slopes of Mount Nancy *(see Old Forests chapter)*.

*Avalanche Brook glides over smooth granite at Ripley Falls, one of many cascades on the steep slopes of Crawford Notch.*

# PINKHAM NOTCH:

## CRYSTAL CASCADE & GLEN ELLIS FALLS

*As it flows down Mount Washington's lower slopes towards Pinkham Notch, the Ellis River drops 100 feet at the Crystal Cascade.*

Closest Town: North Conway, NH

Owner: White Mountain National Forest, 603-536-6100

Directions: The Pinkham Notch Visitor Center is located on the west side of Route 16, 18 miles north of North Conway, and 10 miles south of Gorham. The parking area for Glen Ellis Falls is 0.6 miles south of the visitor center, also on the west side of the highway. A national forest parking pass ($3.00 daily, $5.00 1-7 days) is required for the Glen Ellis Falls parking lot.

As Mount Washington hikers begin their long, arduous ascent along the Tuckerman Ravine Trail to the summit of the highest mountain in the Northeast, the first attraction they pass by is the Crystal Cascade. Here the Ellis River, which originates on the east slopes of the mountain and merges with the Cutler River, drops a total of 100 feet in two distinct steps, the larger of which is the fan-shaped upper falls. These falls are easily reached by a 0.3-mile walk from the Appalachian Mountain Club's Pinkham Notch Visitor Center.

Not content with shaping one attraction, the Ellis River continues downstream along the base of Mount Washington into the southern portion of Pinkham Notch, where it drops an additional 65 feet at Glen Ellis Falls. From the narrow lip at the height of falls, the river makes a long, narrow plunge through a steep ravine shaped by glaciers. At the base of the drop is a deep, emerald green pool. Unlike many of New England's other falls, it has a relatively high flow throughout much of the year. The 0.3-mile trail to the falls begins at a parking area on Route 16, follows a tunnel under the highway, then makes a 100-foot descent over stairs to the base of the falls.

When water levels are relatively low, it is possible to visit both falls in a single hike by using the Lost Pond Trail as a connecting path.

From the Pinkham Notch Visitor Center, visit the Crystal Cascade, then backtrack to the center. Cross Route 16 and follow the Lost Pond Trail to its junction with the Wildcat Trail near Lost Pond. Just beyond this junction is a crossing of the Ellis River that can be hazardous during high water. If conditions are safe, cross the river and continue a short distance to Glen Ellis Falls.

# GRAFTON NOTCH:

## SCREW AUGER & STEP FALLS

*Named for a logging tool, Screw Auger Falls is one of several natural features carved by the Bear River in Grafton Notch.*

Closest Town: Newry, ME

Owners: Maine Bureau of Parks and Lands (Screw Auger Falls), 207-624-6080; The Nature Conservancy (Step Falls), 207-824-2912

Directions: From the junction of US 2 and ME 26 in Newry, turn north on ME 26 and continue for 8 miles to the state park boundary. The trailheads and parking areas are well marked. A $2.00 fee is charged at the Screw Auger Falls parking area. The parking area for Step Falls is on the east side of the road just south of the state park boundary; watch for a sign marking "Wight Brook."

The cutting power of water over thousands of years is evident throughout Grafton Notch *(see Mountain Passes chapter)* in the mountains of western Maine. Within this narrow valley between Old Speck and Baldpate Mountains are three gorges, the only two known natural bridges in Maine, and two of the region's most distinctive waterfalls. In the lower portion of the notch is Screw Auger Falls, arguably Maine's most accessible and visited waterfall. Here the Bear River makes a sheer drop of about 20 feet, then churns through a miniature gorge, passing a series of pools and potholes. Named after a twisty logging tool, the cascades here once powered a log saw in the days when Grafton Notch was home to a small lumbering community. Above the falls, the river glides across an open, smooth rock face. This Screw Auger Falls is not to be confused with the waterfall of the same name at Gulf Hagas in central Maine.

Though the rather diminutive Bear River is the waterway that churns through the gorge and falls today, geologists believe that a much larger stream formed by meltwater from glaciers was responsible for originally scouring out the canyon. Indeed, markings of a much higher flow are evident along the walls of the riverbanks.

At the nearby Step Falls, Wight Brook drops more than 250 feet down the lower slopes of Baldpate Mountain in a long, rocky, wide series of cascades and pools as it flows toward its confluence with the Bear River. Geologic potholes mark areas of soft rocks that were eroded by the swirling water. The large, rocky opening created by the wide brook affords fine views south to the mountains on the opposite side of the notch. These falls are part of a 24-acre preserve just outside of Grafton Notch State Park that is managed by the Nature Conservancy. The easy, 0.5-mile (one way) trail to the falls begins at the parking area on Route 26 leads to the base of the cascades, then ascends along the east bank of the brook to its end at the reservation boundary.

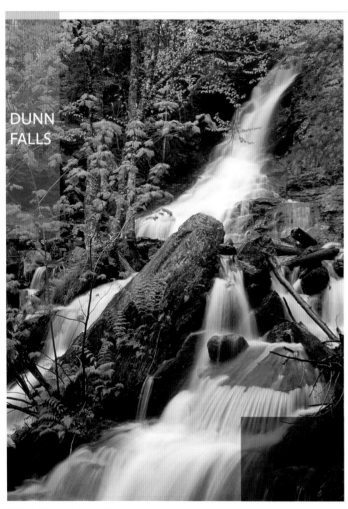

DUNN FALLS

*The Appalachian Trail passes a long series of cascades at Dunn's Falls in the western Maine mountains.*

As the Appalachian Trail winds north of Grafton Notch through the mountains of western Maine, it passes by a hidden valley of cascading rocky streams, gorges, and waterfalls at Dunn Falls. Here the West Branch of the Ellis River drops more than 150 feet in a long series of cascades, including two high waterfalls.

The Lower Falls are especially dramatic, as the water makes an 80-foot plunge through a tall, narrow canyon with steep, 100-foot high walls. From the top of this gorge, there are views across the wild, steep valley. A short distance upstream is the Upper Falls, where the river drops 70 more feet in a horsetail and fans, then flows through a pair of large pools. In spring, colorful woodland wildflowers such as foamflowers, blue violets, pink lady's slippers, and red and painted trilliums thrive in the moist soils of the ravine. Moose are common here as well; their sign is often visible along the trails.

The Cascade and Appalachian Trails combine to form a moderately difficult, two-mile circuit that explores the various features of the valley. From the parking area on East B Hill Road, the blue-blazed Cascade Trail branches off the Appalachian Trail and follows a series of small cascades, crossing the river twice. After the second crossing, the one-way side trail to the Lower Falls forks to the right and continues along the river's edge for 0.2 miles to the base of the gorge. The main trail continues to the top of the gorge and crosses the narrow lip of the falls, then arrives at a four-way junction with the Appalachian Trail and the side trail to the upper falls. After exploring the upper falls, backtrack to the junction and bear left on the Appalachian Trail to complete the loop with a moderate climb to the trailhead.

Closest Town: Andover, ME

Contact: Maine Appalachian Trail Club

Directions: From the junction of ME 120 and ME 5 at the general store in Andover, bear left (west) on Newton Street (also known as East B Hill Road) and continue for 8.2 miles to a pullout where the Appalachian Trail crosses the road. The trail to the falls is on the left (south) side of the road.

ANGEL
FALLS

*Nearly hidden in western Maine's uplands is Angel Falls, one of the state's tallest and most picturesque waterfalls.*

With a bit of imagination, when water levels are high one can visualize the angel-like shape that is the namesake of Angel Falls, which is one of Maine's tallest and most scenic waterfalls. Here Mountain Brook drops 90 feet over the walls of a steep canyon, the jagged walls of which rise as high as 115 feet. Above the main falls, and out of view from the overlook, the brook drops an additional 35 feet as it churns through the rugged terrain of western Maine's highlands. A series of subtle diagonal ledges in the cliff face give the falls their distinctive appearance.

From the base of the falls, the brook continues to its confluence with Bordeen Stream, which in turn discharges into the Swift River north of Byron. The falls and gorge are nearly hidden in a remote valley in "Township D" near Houghton, roughly five miles south of Mooselookmeguntic Lake in the Rangeley Lakes region *(see Lakes chapter)*, and a similar distance east of the old-growth forest on Old Blue and Elephant Mountains *(see Old Forests chapter)*.

Although Angel Falls and Moxie Falls near Jackman have traditionally been acknowledged as the highest waterfalls in Maine, this distinction is now believed to be a much larger cascade of 700-800 feet that is hidden on the upper slopes of Mount Katahdin in Baxter State Park.

Getting to the Angel Falls trailhead can be a bit of a challenge, as the dirt Bemis Road is rutted and slow going in places. From a roadside pullout, the one-way, red-blazed trail to the falls follows a dirt road downhill for 0.2 miles to a gravel pit, then continues in the woods on the far side of the clearing. After crossing the brook (which can be difficult when water levels are high), it ends at an overlook with a fine view of the falls, 0.8 miles from the trailhead.

Closest Town: Houghton, ME

Owner: Private

Directions: From the junction of US 2 and ME 17 near Rumford Falls, turn north on ME 17 and continue to a left turn on Houghton Road, which is 4 miles north of a general store and a roadside park. Cross the bridge over the Swift River, then bear right on Bemis Road, a dirt road which may be in poor condition; drivers should be prepared for ruts and take it slowly. Follow Bemis Road for 3.4 miles to a pullout at the junction with a woods road that slopes downhill on the left. The red-blazed trail to the falls follows this road.

MOXIE
FALLS

Closest Towns: The Forks and Jackman, ME

Owner: Maine Bureau of Public Lands, 207-287-3821

Directions: From the Skowhegan area, follow US 201 north along the Kennebec River for 50 miles to The Forks. At a rest area and information sign before the Kennebec River bridge, turn right on Moxie Falls Road (which is also known as Lake Moxie or Moxie Pond Road) and continue for 2.3 miles to the parking area on the left.

*Framed by northern hardwood and spruce trees, Moxie Brook drops 90 feet through a high-walled gorge at Moxie Falls in the Kennebec River Valley.*

With its wide, roaring single drop and steep, high-walled gorge, Moxie Falls is one of Maine's highest and most dramatic waterfalls. Fed by the outflow of Moxie Pond, Moxie Stream drops toward its confluence with the Kennebec River in a series of cascades, culminating with the main, 90-foot plunge into a pool at the base of the narrow slate gorge. Along with Angel Falls and a cascade on the upper slopes of Mount Katahdin, it is one of Maine's tallest single-drop falls.

The wild, remote upper Kennebec River Valley, an area popular with white-water rafters, serves as the setting for the falls, which are located in the hills south of Jackman.

The falls are roughly a half mile upstream from the confluence of Moxie Stream and the Kennebec, which is an area known among anglers for its brown trout pools and runs. The exposed rocks visible at the gorge are classified by geologists as "The Forks Formation of Silurean Age" and "Devonian gray slate." Granitic dikes are visible at the falls and at other locations along the stream. Plants along the stream include tiny diatoms, which forge an existence amidst the flowing water by attaching themselves to exposed rocks, while northern hardwood and spruce trees adorn the gorge wall.

The easy trail to the falls begins at the parking area and descends at a gentle grade for 0.6 miles, passing straight through a marked 4-way intersection. Wooden platforms offer safe, close-up views of the lip of the falls, a front-on perspective of the falls, and the high walls of the gorge. There are also views of a series of cascades just above the main falls.

*Also see: Beaver Brook Cascades, Mount Moosilauke, NH (Alpine Mountains chapter); Katahdin Stream Falls, Mount Katahdin, ME (Alpine Mountains chapter); Race Brook Falls, Mount Everett, MA (Unique Mountains chapter); Diana's Baths, Cathedral Ledge, NH (Unique Mountains chapter); Mount Nancy, NH (Old Forests chapter); Chesterfield Gorge, NH (Gorges chapter); Flume Gorge, NH (Gorges chapter); Gulf Hagas, ME (Gorges chapter).*

# LAKES
## chapter
## seven

Profiled here are some of New England's largest and most distinctive lakes, including Lake Champlain in Vermont, Lake Winnipesaukee in New Hampshire, and Maine's Moosehead Lake.

*Mount Morgan and the summits of the Squam Mountains offer spectacular views across New Hampshire's lakes region.*

*Within the bounds of New England* are some of the country's largest and most picturesque lakes. With a high average annual precipitation and a landscape with countless basins scoured by glaciers, the region is an ideal environment for freshwater lakes and ponds. There are nearly 300 waterbodies in central New Hampshire's modest-sized Lakes Region alone, and several thousand more scattered across Maine. Thanks to their scenery and abundant wildlife, the lakes have long been a popular attraction for tourists and sportsmen alike.

The terms "lake" and "pond" are used somewhat interchangeably at times, as a number of rather modest-sized ponds are called lakes. The technical difference between the two is that a lake is deep enough so that sunlight cannot reach portions of its base and, as a result, there is a lack of aquatic plants. In contrast, ponds are shallower and generally host more diverse plant and animal communities.

Many artificial lakes and ponds have also been built along the region's waterway in recent centuries, for purposes such as industrial use, drinking water reservoirs, and flood control. The two largest freshwater lakes in southern New England are the Quabbin and Wachusett Reservoirs in central Massachusetts, which were built as a water source for the greater Boston area during the early 20th century.

Perhaps no wild creature symbolizes a large, healthy lake more than the common loon, whose loud, laughing call is one of the classic sounds of the wild. Familiar birds of prey include bald eagles and osprey, both of which are making strong recoveries after being largely eliminated by pesticide use during the mid-20th century. During the spring and fall, lakes serve as important rest areas for large flocks of migratory

waterfowl, including mergansers, ring-necked ducks, and buffleheads.

Sustaining the birds and human anglers are a variety of fish that favor lake habitats, including brown, brook, and lake trout, chain pickerel, northern pike, sunfish, smallmouth bass, and walleye. Other creatures that use lakes and their adjacent habitats include moose, river otters, mink, wading birds, turtles, dragonflies, and damselflies.

Profiled here are some of New England's largest and most distinctive lakes, including Lake Champlain in Vermont, Lake Winnipesaukee in New Hampshire, and Maine's Moosehead Lake, which are the region's three largest waterbodies. Though it is not natural, Quabbin Reservoir is included because of its size and importance to a variety of wildlife.

# QUABBIN RESERVOIR

*A winter moon lights Quabbin Reservoir, the largest lake and expanse of protected land in southern New England.*

Closest Towns: Belchertown and Ware, MA

Owner: Massachusetts Department of Conservation and Recreation, 413-323-7221 (Quabbin Park)

Directions: To reach the Quabbin Park visitor center, from the junction of MA 9 and MA 202 in Belchertown, follow MA 9 east for 3 miles to the marked entrance road on the north side of the highway. If coming from the Massachusetts Turnpike, take Exit 8 and follow MA 32 north to the junction with MA 9 in Ware, then follow MA 9 west for 4.3 miles to the auto road east entrance.

Those familiar with the history of water supply in Massachusetts may raise an eyebrow at the inclusion of Quabbin Reservoir in a listing of "natural wonders," as it was created during the 1930s as a water source for the greater Boston area. However, in the process, southern New England's largest freshwater lake and largest conservation area were formed, providing a 40 square-mile wilderness that offers habitat for a wide variety of wildlife. Indeed, though it lies in the heart of a highly populated state just 70 miles from Boston and an hour from Worcester, the reservation has a feel similar to northern New England.

The reservoir was created by flooding of the Swift River Valley in central Massachusetts, where the topography was ideal for the creation of an artificial lake. In the process, four towns were abandoned, 3500 residents were forced to relocate, and the valley was cleared of vegetation. It took seven years to fill to its 512-billion gallon capacity, which it reached in 1945. The many sources of Quabbin include the East, Middle, and West Branches of the Swift River, the East and West Branches of Fever Brook, and other smaller streams that meet in the valley.

Surrounding the reservoir, and helping to ensure water quality, is a large buffer of protected land. Mixed forests of oak, maple, birch, hemlock, and other species are predominant, and other habitats include the low rolling hills of the valley, beaver wetlands, ponds, swamps, old fields, and rocky outcroppings. The diverse wildlife includes an ever-growing moose population, black bears, bobcats, coyotes, fishers, bald eagles, and common loons.

In addition to its natural features, artifacts of history are evident throughout the reservation. One of the most interesting sites is the former town common of Dana, which was not flooded but was abandoned because of its proximity to the watershed. Though the buildings are gone, the cellar holes, stone walls, and roads remain visible. Another point of interest is the historic Keystone Bridge, a stone arch bridge that spans a former town road. Other features include mill sites, railroad beds, roads, and old fields, some of which are maintained today as wildlife habitat.

With more than 50 access points (called "gates") in seven towns, there is a wealth of options for explorers. Public recreation use is limited to hiking and nature study at many gates, though several are open to on-road bicycling. A recommended starting point is Quabbin Park in Belchertown and Ware, where there is a visitor center and a 5.3-mile auto road that is open year-round. The road passes many attractions, including the trails across the Windsor Dam and Goodnough Dike, the spillway, the Enfield Lookout, the observation tower atop Quabbin Hill, and a series of open meadows, where deer, wild turkeys, bluebirds, and a variety of other wildlife are regularly seen. Dana Common is reached by an easy 1.8-mile walk from Gate 40 on Route 32A in Petersham.

Bordering the reservoir are additional conservation lands that further protect the source waters, including the Federated Women's Club State Forest in Petersham and New Salem, the Swift River Reservation and Brooks Woodland Preserve in Petersham, and the Bear's Den, a gorge and waterfall along the Middle Branch in New Salem.

*Quabbin Reservoir is home to a wide variety of wildlife, including this white-tailed deer buck.*

LAKE
CHAMPLAIN

The marshy edges of Lake Champlain
provide cover for resident and
migratory waterfowl.

Closest major town: Burlington, VT
Directions: The main approaches are via Interstate 89 from the south and east, or US
7 from the Rutland area. To reach the islands, from Interstate 89 in Colchester,
take Exit 17 and follow US 2 west.

Because of its relatively modest width and finger-like shape, Lake
Champlain's size can be somewhat deceiving. Though it is just 20 miles
at its widest point and narrows to less than a mile in places along its
south shores, Champlain is in fact the sixth-largest freshwater lake in the
United States, and the largest outside of the Great Lakes. It fills a broad,
fertile valley between the Green and Adirondack Mountain Ranges, and
has a long and rich geologic and human history.

Roughly 12,500 years ago, this same valley was home to the even larger
glacial Lake Vermont, which was nearly 600 feet higher than the present
Champlain and stretched all the way south to Rutland. Mount Philo near
Charlotte was once an island in this massive lake, and marks carved by
waves are visible on its slopes. The present-day sites of communities such
as Burlington and Saint Albans were deep under water during this time.

After the glaciers retreated from northwest Vermont, their meltwater
formed the Champlain Sea, which temporarily connected the lake to the
Saint Lawrence estuary and the Atlantic Ocean. Marine creatures such as
whales, seals, fish, and clams were present in its waters, and many fossils,
including the skeleton of a beluga whale that was found near Charlotte

in 1849, have been uncovered in deposits in the valley. Roughly 8,000
years ago, the lake reverted back to fresh water as the waters subsided.
It now has a maximum depth of about 400 feet.

In more recent times, Native Americans of the Iroquois and
Algonquin tribes inhabited the valley. Samuel de Champlain, for whom
the lake is named after, and his explorers were the first Europeans to
visit the area in 1609. Following settlement, the valley, particularly the
port of Burlington, subsequently developed into a center for lumber
trade. The lake offered travelers an easier passage year-round between
the Saint Lawrence and Hudson Valleys than the rough mountain
roads. Significant naval battles were fought on its waters during the
Revolutionary War and the War of 1812.

*Sailboats line the waterfront of Burlington, which was a key trade port of the Champlain Valley.*

Despite its northerly location, the Champlain Valley features the mildest climate and most fertile agricultural lands in Vermont. The nearby Adirondacks mitigate westerly storms by creating a "rain shadow" that lessens precipitation in the valley. The valley is a key migratory corridor for a variety of birds including snow geese, large flocks of which pause to rest in the agricultural fields while traveling to and from Arctic breeding grounds.

Though protected land and parks are somewhat small and scattered here, a number of opportunities exist for explorers. One of the most interesting destinations is Button Bay State Park *(see Artifacts of History chapter)* on the south shores, where a 250-acre bluff includes ancient fossils and old-growth trees. Nearby Kingsland Bay State Park offers more easy walking trails that offer good views of the lake and surrounding mountains. Within the greater Burlington area, a handful of preserves managed by the Winooski Valley Parks District allow exploration of the mouth of the Winooski River. The northern islands are easily reached via Route 2 north of Burlington; there are good views from the causeway to South Hero Island. A handful of state parks here offer primitive camping, swimming, picnicking, and boating facilities.

Some of the best views of the lake and valley are from Mount Philo and Snake Mountain, which rises above the Dead Creek Wildlife Management Area near Addison. For a different perspective, the Missiquoi National Wildlife Refuge in Swanton encompasses a variety of habitats at the rich floodplain where the Missiquoi River discharges into the lake.

WILLOUGHBY
LAKE

Closest Town: Barton, VT

Owner: Vermont Department of Forests, Parks, and Recreation, 802-748-8787

Directions: From Interstate 91 north of Saint Johnsbury, take Exit 23 and follow US 5 north for 9.5 miles to West Burke, then bear right and follow VT 5A north for 5.6 miles to the Mount Pisgah trailhead on the left.

Surrounded by steep cliffs that are often described as fjord-like in appearance, Willoughby Lake is a landscape unlike any other in Vermont. Set in the heart of the state's wild "Northeast Kingdom" region, this narrow lake, which is nearly five miles long but less than a mile wide for much of its length, sits nestled in a valley flanked by the thousand-foot high cliffs of 2756-foot Mount Pisgah on the east and 2656-foot Mount Hor to the west.

This narrow valley was originally formed millions of years ago by an ancient river that carved a path along a fault in the bedrock. During the ice age, glaciers widened this gap into a deep valley, and shaped the steep slopes of Mounts Pisgah and Hor. Today, the Willoughby River, which flows north out of the lake's northern tip, is renown among anglers for its rainbow trout.

In addition to their scenic characteristics, the rocky cliffs are home to a number of rare and uncommon flora and fauna. In 1985, Mount Pisgah hosted the first documented pair of breeding peregrine falcons to nest in Vermont following their near extinction during the mid-20th century due to pesticides. Some of the well-adapted, hardy, and uncommon plants that grow along the rocky ledges are bird's-eye primrose, mountain saxifrage, and butterwort. This unique ecosystem includes a 3000-acre area that was designated as a National Natural Landmark in 1967.

The Willoughby State Forest protects approximately 8,000 acres of this unique setting, including Mounts Pisgah and Hor and the surrounding forests. Arguably the most scenic and dramatic route for hikers here is the South Trail on Mount Pisgah, which begins by following a boardwalk across Swampy's Pond, then ascends the south slopes at a moderately steep grade to a striking vista at Pulpit Rock at 0.9 miles. A mile further along is a rocky opening just below the height-of-land with a view south to the White and Green Mountains, and as the trail begins to descend side trails lead to more overlooks. Hikers can double back from here for a 4-mile round-trip, or make a 7-mile circuit by descending via the North Trail, then walking 3 miles along Route 5A back to the parking area.

Across the valley, the Hawkes and East Branch Trails of Mount Hor lead to more overlooks, including the North Lookout on the East Branch Trail, which offers fine views of the Northeast Kingdom region and the distant mountains and lakes of Quebec. Those not inclined to hike can enjoy fine views of the lake from Route 5A, which follows the east shores along the base of Mount Pisgah.

# LAKE WINNIPESAUKEE

*A sailboat cruises the waters of Lake Winnipesaukee, New Hampshire's largest lake, on a perfect summer day.*

**Closest Towns:** Meredith, Wolfeboro, Moultonborough

**Directions:** For the Mount Major trailhead, from the junction of NH 11 and NH 28A in Alton Bay, follow Route 11 north for 4.2 miles to the parking area on the north side of the road. For Belknap Mountain, from the Laconia Bypass follow US 3 for 3.1 miles, then bear right on NH 11A for 2.1 miles to a right on Belknap Mountain Road. Turn left on Carriage Road and continue past a gate for 1.6 miles to trail parking area on the left. For information on S.S. Mount Washington cruises, call 603-366-5531.

At 72 square miles, Lake Winnipesaukee is the largest of the 1,300 lakes and ponds that dot New Hampshire's landscape, and the third-largest lake in all of New England. This massive lake is the product of the ice age, as there is no geologic evidence of an older lake in the vicinity. As the glaciers scoured out the giant basin, they shaped the earth into hundreds of mounds that became islands that range in size from a matter of feet to 1,200 acres. Within the lake's 236,000-acre watershed are 60 source streams, and in turn the lake's outflow serves as the headwaters for the Winnipesaukee and Merrimack Rivers.

In pre-colonial times, the Weirs Beach area at the lake's southwest corner was home to a large Native village called Aquedoctan. It was the ideal spot for an encampment, as the lake's shallow outlet offered abundant stores of fish, and was sheltered from prevailing winds by the surrounding hills. The village was ultimately abandoned in 1696 due to fears of an imminent attack by colonial settlers. More than 10,000 artifacts, including pots and spearheads, have been found in the Weirs area.

In the early 19th century, proposals were drafted to connect the lake with the Atlantic Ocean, the Connecticut River Valley, Lake Champlain, and the Saint Lawrence Seaway by a series of canals, but they never came to fruition. As the century progressed and the advent of railroads facilitated travel, the region rapidly blossomed into a popular destination for tourists looking to escape the congestion and summer heat of Boston, New York, and other Northeast cities. Many visitors enjoyed tours of the lake aboard the Mount Washington, a paddle steamer that was an icon of the lake from 1872 until it was destroyed by a fire in 1939. Today, the Mount Washington II continues the tradition, with daily cruises that stop at the harbors in Meredith, Center Harbor, Weirs Beach, and Wolfeboro.

Though the lake's shores are largely privately owned and developed, its waters remain clear and pure. They support a diverse community of fish, including rainbow, brook, and lake trout, smallmouth bass, pickerel, salmon, yellow and white perch, hornpout, and whitefish. During the spring and fall, large flocks of waterfowl, including blue-winged teal,

buffleheads, and mergansers, use the lake as a rest stop while migrating to and from their northern breeding grounds. An exciting development of recent is the increasing number of bald eagle sightings; a dozen individuals, including 8 adults and 4 juveniles, were recorded in 2010. Common loons are a familiar sight throughout the region, though recent declines in the survival of chicks on Lake Winnipesaukee is a concern.

One of the best views of the lake from above is from the 1782-foot summit of Mount Major, which rises above the south shores near Alton Bay. Here a popular 1.5-mile trail offers an easy to moderately steep climb to ledges with a panoramic overview of the lake and surrounding mountains. A short distance to the west is 2382-foot Belknap Mountain, where there are more fine views across the region. Several trails lead to the summit, including the Red Trail, which offers a scenic 0.8-mile climb. The nearby 65-acre Ellacoya State Park includes a sand beach and RV park.

On the north shores, the Markus Sanctuary and Loon Center protect 200 acres, including 5,000 feet of shoreline. A visitor center offers exhibits dedicated to loons, and the Loon Nest Trail offers an easy walk through a variety of habitats along the shore.

## SQUAM LAKE & RATTLESNAKE MOUNTAINS

*In addition to offering dramatic views of Squam Lake, the cliffs of Rattlesnake Mountain offer habitat for uncommon plants and wildlife.*

Closest Town: Holderness, NH

Contact: Squam Lakes Association, 603-968-7336.

Directions: For Squam and Rattlesnake Mountains, from Interstate 93, take exit 24 and follow US 3 for 4.6 miles to the junction with NH 113 in Holderness. Follow NH 113 east for 5.5 miles to the parking areas for Rattlesnake Cliffs on the right (east) side of the highway, and Mount Morgan on the left (west).

Ringed by low mountains and hills, Squam Lake is regarded by many as the most picturesque lake in New Hampshire. Among those who shared this opinion were the producers of the classic movie *On Golden Pond*, who chose the lake as their setting in 1981. Though much smaller than neighboring Lake Winnipesaukee, at 6,800 acres it is still the state's second-largest lake.

Squam Lake lies nestled beneath the ridges of the southern White Mountains. Rising high above the north shores is the Squam Mountain Range, which is capped by the twin summits of Mounts Morgan and Percival (2,220 and 2,212 feet respectively). From these rocky peaks, there are spectacular panoramic views across the lakes and the surrounding mountains and hills. Below Mount Morgan's summit is a steep sheer cliff and rock cave.

Mounts Morgan and Percival can be hiked individually, or combined as an easy to moderate 4.5 mile circuit that begins on Route 113 east of Holderness. The Mount Morgan Trail ascends at an easy grade along an old road for a little more than a mile, then steepens as it narrows into a forest path. At 1.7 miles, it meets the Crawford-Ridgepole Trail, and continues for another 0.2 miles to another junction. Here the Crawford Ridgepole Trail branches to the right and offers a safe climb to Mount Morgan's summit, while the trail on the left offers a trickier ascent up a series of ladders and through the rock cave.

The nearby cliffs of Rattlesnake Mountain, which is one of the region's most interesting natural areas, rise dramatically above the lake's northwest corner. Here the twin ledges of popular West Rattlesnake (1,243 feet) and the quieter, slightly higher East Rattlesnake (1,289 feet) are connected by a high ridge. A number of rare plants and natural communities grow in or near these granite outcroppings, including an uncommon Pennsylvania sedge woodland,

false foxglove, and Douglas knotweed, a small herb that is found only at a dozen sites in New Hampshire. Red pine trees, which grow in the high elevations, frame striking views across Squam Lake. At the base of the mountain is Five Finger Point, a peninsula forested with old-growth trees and one of the northernmost stands of black gums in New Hampshire. A mile-long old bridle path begins across from the Mount Morgan trailhead and offers an easy, family-friendly climb to the top of West Rattlesnake.

A short distance to the south lies the Science Center of New Hampshire, which encompasses a portion of Mount Fayal. The center offers enclosures with native wildlife such as bears, bobcats, and foxes, boat tours of Squam Lake, interpretive programs, and several miles of hiking trails.

Above the lake's east shores is Red Hill, where the lower slopes once served as pastures that were grazed by Belgian workhorses. The steep ledges known as the Eagle Cliffs offer yet another dramatic perspective of Squam Lake and the southern White Mountains, including the unmistakable summit cone of Mount Chocorua. From a roadside parking area on Bean Road on the Sandwich-Moultonborough town line, a trail offers a moderately steep, 0.6 mile climb to the cliffs, then continues to the hill's 2029-foot summit.

# RANGELEY LAKES

Closest Town: Rangeley, ME

Contact: Maine Bureau of Parks and Lands (Rangeley Lake State Park), 207-864-3858

Directions: From the south, from the junction of US 2 and ME 17 in Rumford, follow ME 17 north for 35 miles to Rangeley. For the Bald Mountain Trail, from the junction of ME 17 and ME 4 near the village of Oquossoc, follow ME 4 west, then turn south on Bald Mountain Road; the trailhead is on the left-hand side of the road. To reach the Umbagoag National Wildlife visitor center, from the junction of NH 16 and NH 26 in Errol, New Hampshire, follow NH 16 south for 5.5 miles.

In the highlands of northwestern Maine, the Rangeley Lakes, a long chain of interconnected lakes, rivers, and ponds, lie nestled beneath the backdrop of the Appalachian Mountains, forming one of New England's most picturesque settings. Historically, these scenic waterbodies, which include a half dozen large lakes, were known as the "Androscoggin Lakes," as they are the headwaters of the 180-mile long Androscoggin River, one of New England's longest waterways.

Until the early 19th century, this land was the domain of a handful of Native tribes, the most dominant of which was the Abenaki. The first settlers arrived around 1820, and by mid-century the small farming and lumber trading community of Rangeley was established. Around this time, sports fisherman from around the Northeast discovered the region's abundant stores of large fish, and the area subsequently rapidly developed into a popular destination for outdoorsmen. By the start of the 20th century, the region abounded in sportsman's camps, lodges, and hotels. Rangeley is also known for its geographic location exactly halfway between the Equator and the North Pole.

At the northeast end of the chain is the region's namesake, 6,000-acre Rangeley Lake. Though many of the grand hotels of Rangeley are now gone, the lake remains a popular destination for visitors. The 870-acre Rangeley Lake State Park on the southwest shores includes a boat launch, nature trails, and a large campground, and the Hunter Cove Wildlife Sanctuary protects an additional 100 acres along a narrow finger that juts out of the north shores.

From the northwest corner of Rangeley Lake, the diminutive Rangeley River flows a mile north to Cupsuptic Lake. Near its mouth is the "Indian Rock," where the giant brook trout that launched the region's popularity were first discovered. Cupsuptic Lake in turn drains into Mooselookmeguntic (an Abenaki word for "Moose Feeding Place"), the largest and most central of the chain. At 16,300 acres, it is one of Maine's largest lakes, and is home to rich stores of salmon and trout. Its outflow feeds Upper and Lower Richardson Lakes, which resemble a backward "S" when viewed from above. Surrounding the lake are several large public land reserve units that offer access to hiking, fishing, and wildlife watching.

The westernmost lake of the group is Lake Umbagoag, which stretches for 8,500 acres along the Maine-New Hampshire state line. It is bordered by a wildlife-rich complex of uncommon freshwater marshes and backwaters that provide homes for a number of species that are rare in New Hampshire, including nesting bald eagles, spruce grouse, and other boreal forest birds. The Umbagoag National Wildlife Refuge protects 16,300 acres of habitats here, and offers paddlers access to the Northern Forest Canoe Trail.

*October storm crosses over Rangeley Lake.*

Other wildlife present in the lakes and the surrounding northern hardwood and spruce-fir woodlands include waterfowl, osprey, beavers, river otters, mink, black bears, bobcats, deer, fishers, and moose, which are quite common and are often observed feeding in the grassy margins and wetlands along the highways.

There are outstanding views from the Rangeley Lakes Scenic Byway (Route 17), which winds through the Appalachian highlands above the lakes. At the road's height-of-land are two overlooks with views across Rangeley and Mooselookmeguntic Lakes to the distant mountains and hills, including Bigelow Mountain. The highway also passes close by Beaver Pond, where one can see wildlife such as moose, beavers, red foxes, and great blue herons (drivers should watch carefully for moose on all of the roads here, especially in the early morning and evening).

Hikers can enjoy another fine perspective of the region from the fire tower atop 2443-foot Bald Mountain, which is ideally situated on the narrow isthmus of land that divides Rangeley and Mooselookmeguntic Lakes. A moderately steep, mile-long trail leads to the summit, where there are views across both lakes and the surrounding mountains.

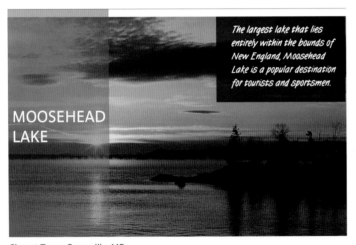

*The largest lake that lies entirely within the bounds of New England, Moosehead Lake is a popular destination for tourists and sportsmen.*

**MOOSEHEAD LAKE**

Closest Town: Greenville, ME

Contact: Maine Bureau of Public Lands (Lily Bay State Park), 207-695-2700

Directions: To reach Greenville from the south, from the center of Guilford follow combined ME 6 West/ME 15 North for 25.7 miles. To get to Guilford, from Interstate 95 take Exit 157 in Newport and follow ME 11/ME 100 north to ME 7, then ME 7 north to ME 23, then ME 23 north to Guilford.

When viewed from high above or on a map, with a bit of imagination one can make out the heavy antler and head shapes for which Moosehead Lake is named. Situated in the heart of Maine's interior wilderness between the Rangeley Lake and Katahdin regions, at 117 square miles Moosehead has the distinction of being the largest of the thousands of lakes and ponds that dot the state's landscape; it is exceeded in size in New England only by Lake Champlain. Fed by the waters of the Moose River from the north, Moosehead Lake in turn is the source of the Kennebec River, which winds for 150 miles to its mouth at Bath.

Because of the Moosehead region's remote, rugged character, it had a late European presence relative to other areas of New England. Though surveyors from Massachusetts arrived in 1764, the first settlement at Greenville wasn't established until the mid-1820s. However, as roads and transportation improved by mid-century, it rapidly became a popular destination for sportsmen and tourists, including Henry David Thoreau, who visited the area in 1853 and 1857. The mid-19th century also marked the beginning of the lake's steamboat era; for the next 100 years more than 50 boats hauled people and goods such as timber logs across the lake. One of these, the *S.S. Katahdin,* has been converted to diesel power and remains active today as a tour boat for the Moosehead Maritime Museum.

Rising above and out of the lake are the mountains and hills of the Longfellow Range, which extend across the state to Baxter State Park. Perhaps the most distinctive eminence is wedge-shaped Mount Kineo, which lies a half mile offshore from Rockwood village on the lake's west shores. This low mountain is the country's largest mass of flint, and Native Americans once traveled great distances to extract its rock for use in arrows and chisels. On its southwest face

*The distinctive profile of Mount Kineo rises above Rockwood on Moosehead Lake's northwest shores.*

are dramatic sheer cliffs that rise 700 feet above the water, while the northern slopes are more gently rounded. The 1.6-mile Indian and 2-mile Bridle Trails offer fairly easy routes to the top of the cliffs, where there are fine views across the lake. The mountain is reached by a short ferry from Rockwood ($8.00 toll) that operates hourly from 8:00 AM to 4:00 PM.

The dominant feature of the lake's southwest corner is 3196-foot Big Moose Mountain (which until recently was known as Big Squaw Mountain), where the nation's first fire tower was built in 1905. From the summit, which is more than 2,000 feet above the lake, there are outstanding panoramic views across the region, from the nearby mountains across Lily Bay to the Bigelow Mountain and Mount Sugarloaf ridges to the west. The unmarked but well-worn Fire Warden's Trail is a 6.5-mile round-trip route of easy to moderate difficulty.

As one would expect from the names of the various features, moose are quite common and visible here. One of the most reliable and easily accessible viewing areas is Lazy Tom Bog, a wetland near the village of Kokadjo near the lake's east shores, roughly 20 miles north of Greenville. Much rarer are secretive Canada lynx, whose range in New England is the northern third of Maine (a handful of tracks have been seen in New Hampshire and Vermont in recent years). Black bears, deer, fishers, coyotes, and a variety of other wildlife inhabit these woodlands.

On the lake's southeast shores near Greenville, 925-acre Lily Bay State Park is home to two campgrounds, a sand beach, a boat launch, and walking trails that explore the lake shore and the surrounding northern hardwood-spruce woodlands. Public boat launches are available at Greenville, Rockwood, and Seboomook, as well as the surrounding smaller lakes and ponds.

BOGS
chapter
eight

*Maine alone has more than a million acres worth of peat bogs, which comprise five percent of the state's landscape.*

*Bogs have historically had a rather* mixed perception among the general public; it's not uncommon to hear them characterized as wastelands inhabited by all sorts of unsavory creatures (a large bog in my hometown is named after a 19th-century counterfeiter; based on the premise that the area served as his hideout and/or final resting place). Naturalists have a different perspective on these unique wetlands, which are wonderfully rich in flora and fauna and home to many rare, threatened, and unique species.

Bogs form in glacial depressions where water accumulates without moving. This lack of motion creates an oxygen deficiency that results in acidic conditions unfavorable to all but a few highly adaptable plant species. Over time, the standing water is gradually filled by layers of dead plants called "peat." In comparison, swamps are generally better drained and home to water-tolerant trees such as red maples and cedars, while marshes have non-woody plants and slow water flows. Maine alone has more than a million acres worth of peat bogs, which comprise five percent of the state's landscape.

Perhaps the best-known bog plant is the carnivorous northern pitcher plant, which feeds on the nutrients of unwary insects that become trapped and ultimately drowned in rainwater accumulated in the plant's vase-like leaves. Also preying on insects are round-leaved sundews and colorful bladderworts, which have no roots and float freely. Other characteristic species include rhodora, which flower in pink and purple blooms in mid-spring, orchids such as yellow and showy lady's slippers, and black spruce and tamarack trees, which are tolerant of the marginal growing conditions.

A wide variety of wildlife use bogs and their edges, including moose, beavers, muskrats, river otters, turtles, frogs, waterfowl, wading birds, butterflies, dragonflies, and damselflies. Yellow-bellied flycatchers and Canada and palm warblers are among the songbirds that are often present in these habitats.

Explorers should use caution around any bog mat, as they are often fragile and the possibility of falling through and/or getting stuck

*Yellow lady's slippers are among the many rare and unique plants that grow in bogs.*

is quite real. Stay on boardwalks (some have limits for the number of people each section can support at a given time) and be sure to know the rules of each managing agency. Also be sure to bring appropriate footwear, as trails may be wet or flooded during high water periods.

A narrow boardwalk offers close-up views of Black Spruce Bog, the only natural community of its type in Connecticut.

## BLACK SPRUCE BOG

Closest Town: Cornwall, CT

Owner: Connecticut Forests and Parks (Mohawk State Forest), 860-424-3200

Directions: From the south and east, from the center of Goshen, follow CT 4 west for 4 miles to the Mohawk State Forest entrance. Turn left on the paved road and follow it for 1.2 miles to the universally accessible viewing area, then continue for another 0.2 miles to a stop sign. Turn left here on Mohawk Mountain Road (a right leads to the summit) and continue to the bog parking area at an interpretive sign on the right. If coming from the north, from the junction of US 7 and CT 63, follow CT 63 south to Goshen..

Near the base of Mohawk Mountain in northwestern Connecticut's scenic highlands is a natural community found nowhere else in the state: a tiny black spruce bog that is characteristic of northern New England, but a true rarity this far south. The story of this unusual wetland began roughly 12,000 to 15,000 years ago, when glacial ice and meltwater formed a small, two-acre pond with no inlet or outlet. Over thousands of years, a mat, which is now 40 feet thick, gradually accumulated in this basin as decaying plants slowly formed layers of peat in the acidic, nutrient-deficient environment.

Some of the first plants to emerge were sedges and grasses, then woody vegetation appeared as the mat thickened. Eventually black spruce and tamarack trees, both of which are characteristic bog species that are well-adapted to the marginal growing conditions, grew along the edges. Tamaracks are New England's only deciduous conifer tree, and are especially easy to identify in late autumn, when their needles display bright gold or yellow hues that stand out after most other trees have dropped their leaves.

One of the wildflowers that grows out of the bog mat is wild calla, which favors wetland edges. Also known as "water arum," it is easily identified by its white, oval-shaped flowers, which bloom in June and July. Other characteristic bog vegetation includes sheep laurel, northern pitcher plants, mountain holly, sundews, and sphagnum moss.

The bog is situated in the northern portion of the 3700-acre Mohawk State Forest in Cornwall. From the parking area on Mohawk Mountain Road, a short footpath offers an easy 5-minute walk to the bog's edge. Here a narrow boardwalk continues for 150 feet across the mat and around the trees before ending at a small viewing deck. In spring and summer, watch for songbirds such as Canada and chestnut-sided warblers and waterthrushes in the trees. There is also a universally-accessible viewing area on Toumey Road on the western edge of the bog.

This short outing offers visitors plenty of time to visit the nearby 1683-foot summit of Mohawk Mountain, which is easily reached by a 1.5-mile drive from the bog parking area. Here there are sweeping views across the surrounding hills and countryside of northwestern Connecticut to the Catskill Mountains and Berkshire Hills.

In addition to its value as a nature preserve, Hawley Bog is a center for research on northern pitcher plants.

## HAWLEY BOG

Closest Town: Hawley, MA

Owner: The Nature Conservancy, 617-227-7017

Directions: From the junction of MA 2 and MA 8A in Charlemont, turn south on MA 8A and cross the bridge over the Deerfield River. Turn left at the railroad tracks, then bear right on East Hawley Road and continue for 4 miles to a roadside parking area on the right, next to a small rock memorial.

Nestled in the Berkshire foothills south of the Deerfield River at an elevation of 1,800 feet, the Hawley Bog has a feel of Canada or northern New England that contrasts with the surrounding bucolic countryside of western Massachusetts. Indeed, in some years, its growing season, or time between killing frosts, is barely more than a month in length.

This bog, which is fed by rainwater, springs, and drainage from the surrounding hills, is the remnant of a past glacial lake that once filled the basin. Over thousands of years, a 30-foot thick layer of sphagnum has gradually accumulated. Many characteristic bog plants grow here, including northern pitcher plants, bladderworts, and leatherleaf. The primary prey species of the pitcher plants are ants, which represent more than half of the insects that are captured in their vases. More than 25 species of ants are found in Massachusetts bogs, including an interesting mix of both boreal and southern species near the limit of their geographic ranges.

Other colorful wetland wildflowers include blue flag iris, rose pogonia, marsh marigold, and grass pink. Trees that grow along the edges include spruces and firs, which are boreal species that thrive in harsh growing conditions, and red maples, which, thanks to their ability to colonize a variety of habitats, are one of the Northeast's most common tree species.

The Hawley Bog is well-documented, as it is part of a 65-acre preserve that is jointly managed by the Nature Conservancy and a consortium of five colleges in the nearby Connecticut Valley, who use the site for research and education. One recent study indicated a connection between the biology of pitcher plants and atmospheric air pollution. When high levels of nitrogen, a pollutant found in auto and factory emissions, are present, the plants grow larger leaves and smaller pitchers and devote less energy to feeding on insects.

From the trailhead on East Hawley Road, a short path leads through the forests bordering the bog to a 700-foot long boardwalk, which offers safe, close-up views of the vegetation. Though this trail is easy, waterproof footwear is recommended during wet periods. Visitors must stay on the boardwalk to avoid damaging the fragile plants.

ESHQUA BOG

*Uncommon showy lady's slippers, which have suffered from over picking and habitat loss, thrive at Eshqua Bog in the hills of the Connecticut Valley.*

Closest Town: Hartland, VT

Owners: The Nature Conservancy, 802-229-4425; New England Wildflower Society, 508-877-7630

Directions: From Interstate 89, take Exit 1 and follow VT 4 west to Woodstock. Just before reaching the village center, turn sharply left (south) on Hartland Hill Road and follow it uphill for 1.2 miles to a fork. Bear right here on Garvin Hill Road and continue for 1.3 miles to a pullout on the right-hand side of the road.

As if to celebrate the summer solstice and the changing of the seasons, the beautiful displays of showy lady's-slippers generally reach their peak around June 21st annually. This distinctive bog orchid is uncommon throughout much of New England and has declined in general throughout eastern North America, mainly due to habitat destruction.

One of the best places for viewing the lady's slippers and other uncommon plants is Eshqua Bog, which is nestled in the hills of the Connecticut River Valley above the town of Woodstock. This eight-acre wetland is actually a "fen," or a wetland fed by alkaline and mineral-rich groundwater (bogs are mainly fed by rainwater and are more acidic).

While it is worth a visit in any season, Eshqua Bog is especially attractive in late spring and summer, when the orchids and other wildflowers are at their peak. Yellow lady's slippers, which favor wet areas such as bogs, moist woods, and swamps, flower in late May and early June, followed in mid-late June by their showy relatives (the exact timing varies annually depending on weather). Carpets of marsh blue violets also bloom during this time. Nearly hidden amidst the vegetation are tiny round-lobed sundews, which trap unwary insects with their sticky hairs. Other flora include northern pitcher plants, cotton grass, buckbean, and Labrador tea. These northern species are holdovers from the post-glacial period, when an alpine environment existed throughout the Northeast.

The bog is protected by a 41-acre preserve jointly managed by the Nature Conservancy and the New England Wildflower Society. There are a mile's worth of easy foot trails, including a 200-foot long boardwalk that crosses the heart of the fen, allowing safe, close-up views of the vegetation. It is easily combined with another path that follows the edge of the wetland and surrounding forest; watch for birds and dragonflies along this route.

**PEACHAM BOG**

*The boardwalk at Peacham Bog is popular with both hikers and moose alike.*

Closest Town: Groton, VT

Owner: Vermont Department of Forests, Parks, and Recreation (Groton State Forest), 802-241-3655

Directions: From the junction of US 302 and VT 232 west of the center of Groton, follow VT 232 north for 5 miles. Turn right on Boulder Beach Road and follow to the nature center parking area and trailhead.

Ringed by black spruce and tamarack trees and colorful shrubs such as sheep laurel, Peacham Bog is one of Vermont's largest and most unique bogs. This 200-acre, kidney-shaped wetland lies on the edge of the state's rugged Northeast Kingdom region, which is characterized by extensive swamps and bogs.

In addition to its size, Peacham Bog is distinctive in that it is one of only two bogs in the state that has a raised, or "domed" shape, formed by the extensive peat deposits that have accumulated in its center, which is higher than the surrounding edges. These types of bogs are more common in coastal or Arctic regions, where there is more moisture and/or less evaporation. The peat is formed by decayed sphagnum moss, a well-adapted species that is the most common plant of the bog and is also known as "peat moss." After one generation of the moss dies, the next grows out of the top of the dead matter, gradually forming layers of accumulated peat.

Another common plant is leatherleaf, which grows in open water in tangled clumps that provide cover for ducks and other wildlife. Named for the texture of its leaves, it is a prolific species that can expand across a bog or pond at the rate of a foot per decade when conditions are favorable. In June, the red and pink blooms of sheep laurel add color to the margins of the bog.

Moose venture out of the surrounding forests and hills during the warm months to feed on the bog's aquatic plants, and also to escape the abundant biting flies. Much more elusive are bobcats and fishers, which make hunting rounds along the wetland-forest edges. Also present are boreal forest birds such as black-backed woodpeckers and scrub jays; these are primarily northern species that are uncommon in much of New England. The fragile bog and its surrounding environs are

*Colorful rose pogonias, which grow in peat bogs and other wetlands, bloom in late spring and early summer.*

the centerpiece of a 750-acre natural area within the 26,000 acre state forest that includes a large forest buffer. The other surrounding habitats include extensive northern hardwood forests, ponds, streams, and low mountains and hills. The 4.5-mile Peacham Bog Loop Trail offers a long but mostly easy hike to the bog. This well-marked trail branches off the Little Loop Trail near the park nature center and winds through northern hardwood forests for 2 miles to the boardwalk. One can backtrack after exploring the bog, or continue the full loop, which gains roughly 450 feet of elevation along the way. There are many other trails and features worth visiting here, including scenic vistas on Owl's Head and Big Deer Mountains; the latter offers an overview of Peacham Bog.

## Bogs

*Over thousands of years, Ponomah Bog has steadily taken over all but three acres of a large kettle pond.*

PONEMAH
BOG

**Closest Town:** Amherst, NH

**Owner:** New Hampshire Audubon, 603-224-9909

**Directions:** From Nashua, follow NH 101A west for 5 miles, then bear right on Boston Post Road and continue for 2 miles to a left on Stearns Road. Follow Stearns Road for 0.3 miles, then turn right on Rhodora Drive and continue to the entrance.

For the next 150 years or so, Ponemah Bog will offer visitors the opportunity to observe a bog as it makes its final transition from a pond. At one point in time, this wetland in southeastern New Hampshire had 100 acres of open water. Over thousands of years, the bog has slowly but relentlessly taken over, and now a mere three acres of the pond's center remain open. At its current rate, scientists estimate that it will completely fill in sometime around 2165.

Ponemah Bog is a classic example of a kettle hole bog. The pond originally formed when a large piece of ice, which was part of the glaciers during the last ice age roughly 18,000 years ago, melted in a depression in the ground. Kettle ponds have no inlets or outlets, and are largely dependent on precipitation for their source waters. The nutrient-deficient waters are an ideal environment for the formation of peat. Kettle pond bogs are spread throughout New

Hampshire's landscape, but are most common here in the southeastern region.

One of the most colorful plants that thrives here is rose pogonia, which is identified by its bright pink flowers that smell like raspberries. It thrives in moist environs such as bogs, moist woods, swamps, and wet meadows. Northern pitcher plants grow along the boardwalk, along with rhodora, cotton grass, sheep laurel, sundews, and bladderworts.

Familiar wildlife of the bog includes painted turtles, which emerge from hibernation to bask in groups atop fallen logs and rocks in early spring. It's easy to take sightings of great blue herons for granted today, but until recently they were uncommon in much of New England thanks to past hunting and habitat loss. Dragonflies and damselflies, which collectively belong to an order known as "odenates," perch on vegetation in between their hunting rounds.

Also visible on the surface of the bog mat are subtle lines marking old trenches through the peat. These are holdovers from the 1940s, when plans were drafted to drain the bog and mine it after studies indicated that it held more than 250,000 tons of commercially viable peat. Fortunately, the plan never came to fruition, and in 1954 Dr. Homer McMurray purchased the bog to maintain it as a botanical preserve. The property was subsequently donated to the Nature Conservancy in 1979.

The Bog Trail, which makes a 0.75-mile circuit along the perimeter of the bog and its surrounding forests, offers excellent views of the various habitats and plants. From the reservation entrance on Rhodora Drive, the trail winds through pine woods to a wooden observation platform. It then leaves the forest and follows a long, narrow boardwalk across the bog. At the pond, several short, one-way side trails offer views across the open water. The main path loops back to the parking area through the shrubs and trees along the edge of the bog. Though the walking is easy, visitors should be prepared for wet areas.

*Home to a variety of uncommon natural communities and wildlife, Saco Heath is one of Maine's most unusual natural areas.*

SACO HEATH

Closest Town: Saco, ME

Owner: The Nature Conservancy, 207-729-5181

Directions: From Interstate 95 in Saco, take Exit 36. After the tollbooth, take the first exit and bear left on Industrial Park Drive, then right on ME 112 (Buxton Road). Follow ME 112 for 2 miles to the parking area on the right. This lot is easy to miss; it is just east of a horse farm with large white fences on the south side of the road.

While walking the quiet boardwalks and forest trails of Saco Heath, it's hard to imagine that the development of downtown Saco and the Interstate 95 corridor lies just minutes away. This unique mosaic of habitats includes a number of uncommon natural communities and their associated flora and fauna.

The heath is a rare southern example of a raised bog, where layers of peat are higher than the surrounding water table. The bog originated from two small natural ponds that had highly acidic waters, which slowed the decay of dead plants and allowed peat to accumulate. Over time, the layers of peat in both ponds gradually merged to form the raised bog. Interspersed with the peat are areas of open water that are twenty feet deep.

Rising out of the heath are groves of Atlantic white cedar, which is at the northern limit of its range here in southern Maine. In fact, the heath is the only known place in the Northeast where cedar grows in a raised bog. Another rare community is a pitch pine bog, where individual specimens of this hardy species grow out of layers of peat and shrubs.

The cedars are the only host species for the Hessel's hairstreak butterfly, which is globally rare and found at only a handful of other sites in Maine. This small butterfly, which is active in late May and early June and is identified by its distinctive green and white underwings, has declined throughout its range due to widespread logging of cedars. It is most common in the Northeast in New Jersey and southeastern Massachusetts. Another uncommon species found here is the malleated vertigo, a tiny snail that favors boggy areas.

The plants that grow here include rhodora, northern pitcher plants, sheep laurel, round-leaved sundew, rhodora, leatherleaf, and cotton grass. The latter, which is aptly named for its cotton-like tufts, is a characteristic bog species with a wide range that includes North America, Europe, and Asia. The heath is at its most colorful in mid-spring, when many of these species are in bloom (the rhodora is especially attractive), and early autumn, when the scarlet foliage of blueberries reaches its peak.

Surrounding the heath is a buffer of forests and swampy areas. Another southern species near its northern range limit in these woodlands is black gum, which is easily distinguished by its plate-like bark. Other trees include oaks, red maple, hemlock, and white pine. These woodlands serve as an important wintering area for white-tailed deer, and also offer food and cover for moose, bobcats, and snowshoe hares.

In 1986, Saco conservationist Joseph Deering donated 475 acres of the heath to the Nature Conservancy. Following proposals to mine the heath for its peat, the state purchased additional land, and now more than 1,200 acres are protected. From the entrance on Route 112, an interpretive nature trail winds through the forest, then follows boardwalks through a swampy area. After a half mile, it reaches the edge of the heath, where a long floating boardwalk continues across the open wetlands. The out-and-back hike is 1.8 miles.

## SUNKHAZE MEADOWS NATIONAL WILDLIFE REFUGE

Closest Town: Milford, ME

Owner: U.S. Fish and Wildlife Service, Friends of Sunkhaze Meadows NWR, 207-827-6138

Directions: From Interstate 95 in Orono, take Exit 191 and follow US 2 east toward Old Town, and continue through a series of traffic lights to Milford. Turn east on County Road and continue 4.2 miles to the refuge boundary.

*Sunkhaze Meadows, which encompasses the second-largest peat bog in Maine and other wetland habitats, is one of the state's richest wildlife areas.*

by a series of lower bogs. These layers, which are comprised of accumulated peat, host a variety of plants, including rose pogonias, showy lady's slippers, pitcher plants, sundews, and bladderworts. The latter, identified by its yellow flowers, has air bladders that lure prey into submerged leaves. The bogs are divided by Sunkhaze Stream and its tributaries. The diverse forests within this watershed includes groves of silver maples and a rare 70-acre cedar swamp.

The bog has long been considered for mining and development, as it has 3,300 acres of commercially quality peat. In response to a proposal during the early 1980s, the Sunkhaze Meadows National Wildlife Refuge was established in 1988 to protect this unique watershed. Now jointly maintained by the Friends of Sunkhaze National Wildlife Refuge, the refuge offers trails for hikers and paddlers. One recommended boating route begins where Sunkhaze Stream crosses Route 2 and follows the stream to the heart of the bog (2-3 hour round trip; the launch is privately owned and boaters must park at the interpretive sign and carry their boats to the water). Another option is to begin at the Ash Landing lot where the stream crosses Stud Mill Road and paddle toward Route 2. This route passes a series of beaver dams. Walking routes include the Carter Trail, which begins on County Road and leads north for 0.3 miles to an old cabin. Here a 1.6-mile loop leads to an observation platform with views across Little Birch Stream at the edge of the bog.

A short distance east of the Penobscot River Valley lies Sunkhaze Meadows, a 5,000-acre complex of wetlands that is one of Maine's richest wildlife areas. Here waterfowl such as ringed-necked, wood, and mallard ducks cruise along open water and take cover in marshy margins, joined by 200 other species of birds in the various habitats. Throughout the warm months, a similarly diverse group of colorful dragonflies and damselflies hover on hunting rounds over the water. As many paddlers who have been obliged to portage around dams can attest, beavers are abundant as well, creating habitats that are used by river otters, mink, great blue herons, and bluebirds. Moose, bears, and other mammals are common in the surrounding woodlands.

At the heart of these wetlands is Maine's second-largest peat bog. It is unique among the state's bogs in that it has a network of raised areas, including a large domed section bordered

*Also see: Quoddy Head, ME (Coastal Northern New England chapter); Great Wass Island, ME (Botanical Areas chapter).*

# BOTANICAL AREAS
## chapter nine

*New England's varied landscape is well exemplified by its diverse botanical communities.*

*From northern bog plants* to alpine wildflowers to coastal cedar swamps, New England's varied landscape is well exemplified by its diverse botanical communities. The many habitat types include broadleaf and coniferous forests, mountains, ridges, rock cliffs, bogs, swamps, fens, and valley bottomlands.

Fed by the abundant nutrients of limestone rocks, the rich soils of western New England host an exceptional variety of plant life. At relatively compact areas such as Bartholomew's Cobble in western Massachusetts, more than 800 species have been recorded. This variety is perhaps most evident during the peak of the spring ephemeral season, when the blooms of trilliums, spring beauties, violets, columbines, and many other species add waves of color to the forest floor.

At the other end of the spectrum are places such as the sandy coast of southern New England, inland sand plains, and rocky mountains and ridges, where growing conditions are marginal. Though the overall botanical diversity of these areas is much lower, they offer the chance to observe a variety of hardy, often uncommon species that have adapted to conditions that few other plants can tolerate.

Because of New England's geographic location and historically variable climate, it is a good place to see both northern and southern species near the edge of their ranges. For example, the rhododendron groves at Pachaug State Forest in Connecticut and Little Monadnock Mountain in New Hampshire are holdovers from a brief warming period that occurred several thousand years ago, when a number of southern species migrated into the region.

As with all aspects of the natural world, timing is crucial for observing wildflowers and other flora at their peak. The woodland wildflower season generally runs from mid-April to June, during the narrow window between the start of the growing season and the full leaf out on deciduous trees, which blocks light to the forest floor. It begins earlier in the mild coastal regions and later in the northern mountains, and can vary by several weeks depending on seasonal weather conditions. Field wildflowers, such

Wildflowers such as painted trilliums thrive in the nutrient-rich soils of western New England.

as daisies, milkweed, goldenrod, and asters, bloom from late spring until the first frosts of autumn. Each species has its own phenology; some of the earliest flowers to emerge include bloodroot, round-lobed hepatica, and trailing arbutus, while others such as pink lady's slippers and blue flag iris bloom later in the spring.

Unfortunately, many of New England's native plants, including a number of rare species, are threatened by the widespread propagation of hundreds of invasive species. These plants were introduced to the region from other areas of the world, and often have prolific reproductive capabilities that enable them to crowd out native species. Some prominent examples of invasive species include garlic mustard, Japanese barberry, and purple loosestrife, which is especially visible in wetlands when it flowers during the summer. Controlling invasive plant populations is a priority for many conservation groups.

This chapter details some of the region's most unique and easily accessible botanical areas. In addition to these sites, other similar areas are detailed in the Alpine Mountains, Bogs, and Old Forest chapters.

## RHODODENDRON SANCTUARY & CEDAR SWAMP, PATCHAUG STATE FOREST

*Nearly hidden amidst the extensive woodlands of Pachaug State Forest is this globally rare swamp of rhododendrons and Atlantic white cedars.*

Closest Town: Voluntown, CT

Owner: Connecticut Department of Forests and Parks (Patchaug State Forest), 860-376-4075

Directions: From Interstate 395, take exit 85 and follow CT 138 east for 9 miles, then turn left (north) on CT 49 and continue for 0.5 miles to the main entrance. Turn left and follow the paved park road to its end, then continue straight (left) on a dirt road. After passing Mount Misery Brook, look for a parking area at a grassy field, 0.9 miles from the park entrance. The rhododendron trail begins on the right-hand side of the road, across from the parking area.

Within the bounds of the 27,000-acre Pachaug State Forest, the largest conservation area in Connecticut, lies a globally rare natural community, a swamp where Atlantic white cedar trees and rhododendrons grow together. Cedars and rhododendrons are both primarily southern species that are uncommon in New England, and to find them together is a treat. The southeastern corner of Connecticut and adjacent southern Rhode Island is unusual in that it hosts several of these unique wetlands. In northern New England, only one such community exists, near Manchester, New Hampshire.

Native rhododendrons are abundant in the forests of the southern Appalachian Mountains, but are rather scattered throughout the Northeast. They grow to the size of small trees in the south, but are more of a large shrub this far north. They are members of the overall heath family, which includes blueberries, azaleas, and mountain and sheep laurel. The rhododendrons at Pachaug grow to around 20 feet, often with their branches interlaced. The peak blooms occur around the first week of July, when the pink and white flowers add a splash of color to the swamp.

New England's cedar swamps are mostly concentrated in a belt along the south coast, with scattered sites further inland. Although there is more than 100,000 acres of swampland in Connecticut, cedars are only present at a few places, and cedar swamps are listed as one of the state's "imperiled ecosystems." Cedars, which are sensitive to flooding and only moderately tolerant of shade, have a poor reproductive rate, and are being succeeded by eastern hemlock in some areas (though hemlocks themselves are now threatened by the hemlock woolly adelgid forest pest). Cedar has declined considerably throughout its North American range because of past commercial harvesting and conversion of swamps for agricultural use.

The swamp is easily accessed and viewed by a quarter-mile (one-way) nature trail that begins near a grassy field and parking area near the base of Mount Misery in the state forest's Chapman Tract. This universally accessible path quickly leads to the heart of the swamp, then follows a short boardwalk to a wooden observation platform with a good view of Mount Misery Brook. For those with additional time, the state forest offer many miles of hiking trails and woods roads, including a short segment of the Pachaug Trail that makes an easy half-mile climb to an overlook atop 411-foot Mount Misery near the rhododendron sanctuary.

LIME
ROCK
PRESERVE

Closest Town: Lincoln, RI

Owner: The Nature Conservancy, 401-331-7110

Directions: From Providence, follow RI 146 north to the Lincoln Woods/Twin River Road exit. Bear right at the end
of the ramp and continue to the first traffic light, then turn right on RI 246. Follow RI 246 north for 2.4 miles,
then turn left on Wilbur Road and continue for 0.5 miles to the entrance at a pullout on the right (north)
side of the road.

*With its vivid displays of jack-in-the-pulpit and other wildflowers, the Lime Rock Preserve has a feel characteristic of western New England.*

With abundant and diverse wildflowers and rich soils, the Lime Rock Preserve is an oasis of botanical life in the heart of a heavily developed region. This compact, 135-acre preserve, which has long been a favored destination for botanists, lies just outside of the greater Providence area, not far from shopping malls, an airport, and busy highways.

Like the similarly rich areas of western New England, Lime Rock Preserve is home to marble ledges that provide abundant nutrients for calcareous soils, which sustain a wide variety of plant life. Thirty species that are rare in Rhode Island grow here, a total higher than anywhere else in the state. Among the many flora visible here during the peak of the woodland wildflower season are nodding trilliums, Jack-in-the-pulpit, false Solomon's seal, wild geranium, violets, trout lilies, horse balm, and red and white baneberry. One of the most colorful species is wild columbine, which grows on rocky slopes; its bright red, bell-shaped flowers offer nourishment for hummingbirds. A variety of ferns, including Christmas and sensitive ferns, also flourish here.

The preserve surrounds and provides a buffer for the Manton Reservoir, which is the water supply for Lincoln. These wetlands are part of the headwaters of the Moshassuck River, which flows through Providence to its mouth at Narragansett Bay. The river suffered substantial pollution during the industrial era, and though conditions have improved in recent decades, it has not yet fully recovered. Maintaining clean source waters amidst the development is essential for the continued health and ecological integrity of both the river and bay. Other habitats include oak-hickory forests, streams, and swampy areas.

The Lime Rock Preserve, which was established by the Nature Conservancy in 1986, is a highlight of the Blackstone Valley National Heritage Corridor, which also includes a number of historic sites such as mills, blacksmith shops, and old farms. From the entrance on Wilbur Road, the main trail follows an old railroad bed northwest through wetlands for roughly a half mile. It then forks into a loop that circles the reservoir. The path on the right branches off the main trail and quickly leads to the dam, then winds through the woods above the shore. After crossing a brook at the pond's inlet, it rejoins the railroad bed, which continues between rocky outcroppings above the pond back to the start of the loop. The walking on this 2-mile route is easy, though some areas may be wet in spring.

## BARTHOLOMEW'S COBBLE

*The limestone knolls of Bartholomew's Cobble host a great variety of plant life, including this colony of red columbines.*

Closest Town: Sheffield, MA

Owner: The Trustees of Reservations, 413-229-8600

Directions: From the junction of US 7 and MA 7A in Sheffield, follow MA 7A for 0.5 miles to Rannapo Road. Turn right on Rannapo Road and continue 1.5 miles, then turn right on Wheatogue Road and continue to the parking area and visitor center. There is a $5.00 admission fee.

As spring gradually unfolds across the southern Berkshire Hills, two limestone knolls along the banks of the Housatonic River come alive with the blooms of many colorful woodland wildflowers. Clusters of bell-shaped red columbines grow atop rocky boulders and outcroppings, while painted and purple trilliums, spring beauties, bloodroot, and violets carpet the forest floor. Among the most unusual and best-named species are Dutchman's breeches, which are easily identified by their string of white, pantaloon-shaped flowers, and jack-in-the pulpits, which have a hood-like "pulpit" that curves over the "jack," or center spathe of the flower.

After the spring ephemeral season draws to a close, the splendor continues through the end of the growing season. More than 50 species of ferns grow in and around the cobbles, representing one of the greatest varieties found anywhere in North America. An uncommon late-season wildflower that is present here are is great blue lobelia, a member of the bluebell family that blooms along field edges, swamps, and lowland woods during late August and September. The river's floodplain forest includes groves of silver maples, which are uncommon in New England, and giant cottonwood trees, which thrive in the moist valley soils.

The knolls, or "cobbles," are the centerpiece of the Bartholomew's Cobble Reservation, which encompasses 278 acres along the west banks of the Housatonic River near the village of Ashley Falls. Fed by nutrients from the limestone and marble rocks, the rich soils host a remarkably diverse community of more than 800 plant species. Because of its exceptional biodiversity and number of rare and regionally uncommon species, Bartholomew's Cobble has been a designated as a National Natural Landmark by the National Park Service.

Offering additional diversity, and a notable contrast from the floodplain, are the sunlit upland meadows and forests of Hurlburt's Hill, which rises high above the valley. Bluebirds, tree swallows, deer, foxes, and coyotes are among the wildlife that frequent the 20-acre field near the 1050-foot summit, where there are long northerly views across the southern Berkshires. All told, roughly 250 species of birds have been recorded throughout the reservation's riverine, forest, and grassland communities.

The cobbles are easily explored and viewed from a series of short footpaths that begin at the visitor center on Wheatogue Road and wind along the rocks. Those wishing to explore the riverbanks and floodplain can continue along the Bailey and Spero Trails, which offer a 1.75-mile outing that visits rocky outcroppings, views of large cottonwoods, and a clearing along the floodplain. Hurlburt's Hill and its meadows are reached by a easy to moderate climb along Woods Road or the Tulip Tree Trail; the latter branches off the floodplain near the big cottonwood. A loop hike combining all of these routes is 3.3 miles.

One of the uncommon species at Bartholomew's Cobble is great blue lobelia, which flowers in late summer.

# BEAR SWAMP RESERVATION

At Bear Swamp Reservation, rocky outcroppings come alive with the blooms of flowers and ferns each spring.

Closest Town: Ashfield, MA

Owner: The Trustees of Reservations, 413-532-1631

Directions: Take either MA 116 or MA 112 to Ashfield. From the 4-way junction of MA 116, MA 112, and Hawley Road just west of the town center, drive west on Hawley Road for 1.7 miles to the reservation's roadside parking areas.

Once cleared for farms, pastures, and orchards during colonial times, the rocky ridges and forests of Bear Swamp Reservation today host lush blooms of woodland and wetland wildflowers, ferns, and shrubs. Situated amidst the hills and valleys of the Berkshire foothills of northwestern Massachusetts, this mosaic of habitats is another example of the nutrient-rich limestone rocks and soils characteristic of western New England.

In late April and May, the rocky slopes here are carpeted with colorful spring ephemerals. Among the most prominent species are purple trilliums, which are also known as "stinking Benjamins." Named for their trio of dark red or purple petals, they are indicators of rich soils. Other familiar ephemerals include spring beauties, Dutchman's breeches, sessile bellworts, violets, and pink lady's slippers. Wetland flowers such as yellow lady's slippers bloom in marshy and swampy areas.

The revitalized forests include mixed groves of beech, birch, maple, oak, and hemlock. Other evidence of human presence includes an old mill dam and pond; today a colony of beavers acts as "managers" of this wetland. The Apple Valley Lookout, a hilltop vista with sweeping pastoral views across orchards and woodlands to the Deerfield River Valley and distant southern Green Mountains of Vermont, offers a glimpse of the region's agricultural past.

The 285-acre reservation, which is managed by the Trustees of Reservations, offers three miles of hiking trails. The quickest route to the ledges is from the main entrance on the west side of Hawley Road, where a trail leads into the woods for about 500 feet to a fork near the pond. Here the Lookout Trail branches to the right and winds along the outcroppings, offering close-up views of the floral blooms. Hikers can combine the Lookout and Beaver Brook Trails as a 1.1-mile loop. Another route worth checking is the 0.6-mile (one way) Fern Glade Trail, which branches off the Beaver Brook Trail and leads south through more ferns and wildflowers to the reservation boundary at Bear Swamp Road. The Apple Valley Overlook is easily reached by a quick 0.2-mile climb along a trail that begins on the east side of Hawley Road.

In mid-spring, purple trilliums, which are indicators of rich soils, bloom in abundance at Bear Swamp.

*Rhododendron State Park, a designated National Natural Landmark, encompasses the largest colony of rhododendrons in northern New England.*

# RHODODENDRON STATE PARK & LITTLE MONADNOCK MOUNTAIN

**Closest Town:** Fitzwilliam, NH

**Owner:** New Hampshire Forests and Parks, 603-924-5976

**Directions:** From the junction of NH 12 and NH 119 near Fitzwilliam, follow NH 119 west to the Fitzwilliam town common. From the common, continue on NH 119 west for 0.5 miles, then turn right (north) onto Rhododendron Road and follow signs to the park entrance.

In the shadow of Little Monadnock Mountain grows a 16-acre colony of rosebay rhododendrons that has the air of an exotic garden in the woods, especially when the pink and white flower blooms peak in July. This grove, which was designated as a National Natural Landmark in 1982, is the largest natural colony of rhododendrons in northern New England, and one of the largest north of the Allegheny Mountains of Pennsylvania.

The rhododendrons that grow here and at other places in New England are holdovers from a period of climate warming that occurred around 5,000 years ago, when milder temperatures allowed a number of southern trees and shrubs to migrate north into the region. When the climate cooled to its present level, these species retreated back to the south, leaving scattered colonies in favorable sites. Another nearby example of this process is the black gum swamp at Vernon, Vermont *(see Old Forests chapter)*. There are roughly 20 similar colonies of native rhododendrons scattered across central New England.

*The open ledges of Little Monadnock Mountain offer fine views of Mount Monadnock and southern New Hampshire.*

Rising above the grove is Little Monadnock Mountain, one of the many low mountains and hills of southern New Hampshire. Though its 1883-foot summit is wooded, a rock ledge known as the "North Meadows" offers a striking view of Mount Monadnock, which lies just seven miles to the north, and the surrounding countryside. A characteristic central New England mixed forest of oak maple, birch, pine, hemlock, and other species grows along the mountain's slopes, buffering the rhododendron grove.

This unique area was nearly lost to logging in the early 20th century, before Mary Lee Ware purchased the land and donated it to the Appalachian Mountain Club to protect the rhododendrons and surrounding woodlands. The property was subsequently transferred to the state of New Hampshire in 1946, and today protects 2,723 acres.

The trail network includes the universally accessible Loop and Laurel Trails, which offer an easy, half-mile long circuit through the rhododendron grove. These paths connect to the adjacent Wildflower Trail, where labeled plantings of 40 native wildflower species are maintained by the Fitzwilliam Garden Club. The Little Monadnock Mountain Trail branches off the Loop Trail at the north end of the grove and offers a moderately steep, 1-mile climb up the mountain's south slopes to the open ledges near the junction with the Metacomet-Monadnock Trail.

# KENNEBUNK PLAINS

*A young pitch pine tree rises out of the Kennebunk Plains, which offer habitat for rare plants and wildlife.*

Closest Town: Kennebunk, ME

Owner: Maine Department of Inland Fisheries and Wildlife, 207-287-8000

Directions: From Interstate 95 in Kennebunk, take exit 25 and follow Alfred Road west to West Kennebunk. Following signs for ME 99, turn left at the stop sign, then cross the Mousam River. Turn right (west) on ME 99 and continue to the plains and the Fish and Wildlife parking area on the right (north) side of the highway. If coming via US 1, from the junction of US 1 and ME 9A in Kennebunk, follow ME 9A west for 0.3 miles, then turn right on ME 99 and continue for 4.5 miles to the parking area.

While the southern Maine coast is known for its ocean beaches, it is also home to a rare inland expanse of sand known as the Kennebunk Plains. It is the largest of the handful of sand plains that are scattered across the landscape of interior New England. These unique areas, which were formed by sand and gravel deposits in glacial meltwater, are notable for their uncommon natural communities and rare flora and fauna.

The Kennebunk Plains sit atop a 70-foot layer of deposits within the watershed of the Mousam River at the boundary of the towns of Kennebunk, Wells, and Sanford. The soils hold little nutrients and water, and are therefore highly susceptible to fire. The trees and plants that grow here are hardy species that are well adapted to these marginal growing conditions. Within its bounds are 3,200 acres of open grassland, a highly uncommon natural community.

In late July and August, the plains come alive with the bright purple blooms of northern blazing star, which thrives in dry, open habitats. The Kennebunk Plains is home to the world's largest population of this uncommon wildflower, which in New England is endangered in New Hampshire (where only a half dozen populations have been recently verified) and Rhode Island, and is a species of special concern in Massachusetts and Connecticut. Its range in Maine is limited to only a handful of other sites in York County. Other rare plants include white-topped asters, which grows at only one other site in Maine, upright bindweed, which grows at four other sites, and pale green orchids.

The plains also provide habitat for a number of uncommon wildlife species, including black racer snakes, which are present at only a few other sites in the region. Ribbon snakes, which are also at the northern limit of their range in southwestern Maine, also live here. Many rare grassland birds benefit from this expanse of open land, including one of the region's largest populations of grasshopper sparrows. The warbling calls of bobolinks is a familiar sound during the spring and summer months, and eastern meadowlarks, upland sandpipers, vesper sparrows, and horned larks also call the area home.

Once the site of Native American campsites, the barrens were subsequently cultivated for large blueberry farms and other agricultural uses, which helped keep them in an open, undeveloped state. Today, several landowners combine to protect this unique area. The largest individual tract is the Kennebunk Plains Wildlife Management Area, which encompasses 1,040 acres of land south of the Mousam River and on both sides of Route 99, including 600 acres of open plains. The Nature Conservancy and other private non-profit groups own a handful of smaller parcels. A network of old dirt and sand roads offer access to the plains. Visitors should check posted signs for information about seasonal vehicle access, blueberry picking, hunting, and off-trail hiking, which is prohibited from late April to September during the grassland bird breeding season. A recommended starting point is the wildlife management area parking lot on Route 99, which includes interpretive signs.

GREAT
WASS
ISLAND

*Among the most colorful of Great Wass Island's many uncommon plants are beach head iris, which flower along the rocky shores in summer.*

Closest Town: Eastport, ME

Owner: The Nature Conservancy, 207-729-5181

Directions: From the junction of ME 187 and US 1 in Jonesport, follow ME 187 south for 10.8 miles. Cross the bridge to Beals Island, then bear left and continue through Beals village. Continue to follow the main road to Great Wass Island. After crossing a short causeway, bear right and follow signs for the Nature Conservancy to the entrance, which is 15.3 miles from US 1.

In addition to its unspoiled coastal scenery, Great Wass Island, which is the largest of an archipelago of more than forty islands off of the downeast Maine coast, is one of New England's most unique and diverse botanical areas. Throughout its extensive rocky shores and interior forests grow a notable variety of plant and forest life, including many species that are regionally uncommon. The 1700-acre island is the easternmost land mass along the Maine coast, and as such is often fogbound; the abundant moisture and humidity promote ideal growing conditions in spite of the predominantly thin, harsh soils. Many of the plants here are arctic or sub-arctic species that are at their southern range limit.

Out of the island's interior granite ledges grows the largest community of jack pines in coastal Maine. These distinctive trees, which often grow in unusual, bonsai-like forms, are the northernmost American pine species; only a half dozen other groves are known to exist in all of Maine. While jack pines are a primarily a "pioneer" species that thrive following fires and other natural and human disturbances, those at Great Wass are likely a permanent community that has adapted to the sparse soils of the ledges.

An exceptionally uncommon jack pine bog, which is the only known natural community of its type in the United States, is part of the 180 acres of coastal peatlands that are spread across the island. In addition to familiar bog species such as sundews and northern pitcher plants, a number of rare plants grow in these wetlands, including baked apple-berry, a member of the rose family with colorful summer fruits, dragon's mouth orchid, which has distinctive pink or purple crested flowers, and deer hair sedge.

More rare plants grow along the edge where the interior habitats meet the rocky shores, including beach head irises, which flower in abundance during the late spring and summer. The range of these colorful wildflowers, which are similar visually to the familiar blue flag iris, is limited in New England to the northern Maine coast and a few sites in New Hampshire. Other species include bird's-eye primrose, marsh felwort, and blinks, a tiny herb that grows in clumps. The numerous tide pools are home to a variety of unique marine creatures, including crabs, sea stars, and sea urchins.

The bulk of the island is protected by a 1578-acre preserve managed by the Nature Conservancy. The Little Cape Point Trail offers some of the best views of the island's diversity, as it winds along the interior granite ledges, passing stands of jack pine, an overlook with views across the plateau bog, and a wood bridge across one of the bogs. After 2 miles, it reaches the rocky shores. Hikers can backtrack for a 4-mile outing, or continue on a recommended 5.5 mile circuit by following the trail along the shores for 2 miles, then returning via the 1.5-mile Mud Hole Trail. Visitors should be prepared for damp conditions and mildly rugged terrain along the narrow interior paths.

*Jack pine trees, which are near their southern range limit, grow out of Great Wass Island's granite ledges and peatlands.*

# EASTERN MAINE BLUEBERRY BARRENS

*Formed by glaciers, the barrens of eastern Maine produce one-quarter of North America's total blueberry crop.*

Location: Washington County, ME

From bears to birds to humans, everyone loves blueberries, and no less than one-quarter of North America's total harvest of this small and tasty fruit comes from a 60,000-acre mosaic of barrens that are spread across Washington County and other regions of eastern Maine. In addition to their agricultural value, these rolling plains offer habitat for rare plants and wildlife and long scenic views.

The barrens are yet another legacy of the ice age. Scientists believe that after glaciers retreated from the area, the eastern Maine coast sank by as much as 1,000 feet, then began to slowly uplift. During this process, sandy marine deposits were unearthed, forming the expansive plains. These soils are ideal for cultivating low-bush blueberries, which thrive in acidic conditions that few other species can tolerate. One can often find and enjoy wild blueberries in similarly marginal environments such as rocky mountain summits and ridges.

Historically, Native Americans promoted this popular fruit by maintaining the barrens through burning regimes. Large-scale commercial farms began operation as early as the mid-1800s, and the region today remains one of the world's largest blueberry exporters. Blueberry growers manage their fields on a two-year rotation, cultivating half of the crop in one season, while growing the other half for the following year. Following the harvest in August, the bushes are pruned by mowing or burning. As autumn sets in, the fields change colors from green and blue to brilliant shades of red, offering a unique foliage viewing opportunity.

In addition to the blueberries, the barrens offer habitat for a number of rare species, including grassland birds such as bobolinks, eastern meadowlarks, vesper sparrows, upland sandpipers, and short-eared owls. These species have declined throughout New England with the regrowth of forests in recent decades. Plants that favor these environs include rhodora, teaberry, sheep laurel, wintergreen, and bracken fern.

Some of the best routes for observing the barrens include Route 193 in Cherryfield, Beddington, and Deblois, Route 9 (the scenic "Air Line" highway) in the highlands of Crawford and Wesley, and the roads that branch off of Route 1 in Columbia Falls, Harrington, and Jonesboro. A large blueberry harvest festival is held in Machias annually around the third week of August. Visitors should respect private property and obey posted signs.

*Also see: Alpine Mountains chapter; Mount Philo, VT (Unique Low Mountains chapter); Squam Lake & Rattlesnake Mountain, NH (Lakes chapter); Old Forests chapter; Bogs chapter; Cape Cod National Seashore & Forests (Coastal Southern New England chapter)*

# OLD
# FORESTS
## chapter
## ten

In addition to their aesthetic qualities, these woodlands, which presently comprise fully three-quarters (30 million acres) of the landscape, serve a variety of other essential purposes.

*Each autumn,* great numbers of tourists come to New England from around the world to enjoy the spectacular foliage displays. It is at this time that the region's forest diversity is most evident, as the various colors represent a variety of species, from brilliant red maples to evergreen spruces and firs.

In addition to their aesthetic qualities, these woodlands, which presently comprise fully three-quarters (30 million acres) of the landscape, serve a variety of other essential purposes. They provide habitat for wildlife, mitigate the effects of carbon and other human-induced atmospheric chemicals, and offer timber as an economic resource.

The region's main forest communities are distributed by climate and geography, and have also been influenced by human and natural disturbances such as storms and timber cutting. Oak-hickory woodlands are characteristic of dry, mild, regions, including much of Connecticut, southern Rhode Island, coastal New Hampshire, and southern Maine. The sandy, impoverished soils of coastal southeastern Massachusetts and northern Rhode Island host hardy, well-adapted species such as pitch pines and scrub oaks, which also occur inland on mountain ridges and sand plains.

Deciduous maples, birches, and beeches and evergreen spruces, firs, and hemlocks form the northern hardwood forest of northern New England and the uplands of western Massachusetts and northwest Connecticut. Spruce-fir forests grow in harsh, moist environments that many other species can't tolerate, such as mountain summits and ridges and boggy wetlands. On the highest mountains, clumps of stunted spruce called *"Krumholtz"* (a German word for "crooked wood") subsist in the wind-swept edge of treeline. Finally, the "transition" forest, a belt where a variety of the aforementioned species, including oaks, hickories, northern hardwoods, and hemlocks overlap, stretches from the hills of western Connecticut and Massachusetts to southeastern New Hampshire and southern Maine.

*Once a keystone species of eastern forests, the majestic American chestnut was decimated by a fungus during the early 20th century.*

Though it's easy to take forests for granted today, not long ago the landscape had an entirely different character. After European settlers arrived in the 17th century, they cut much of the region's forests for agricultural fields, and by the mid-19th century, more than three-quarters of southern New England is estimated to have been cleared. Though farming wasn't as widespread in the northern regions, most of the forests were cut for markets. Timber companies continue to own and log extensive tracts of land today, though a number of areas have been transferred to conservation groups.

After farmers abandoned the rocky soils for the more fertile lands of the Midwest, the forests began a long process of recovery. While seemingly thriving today, they remain susceptible to a variety of threats, including the spread of introduced pests and diseases. The American chestnut, which was once one of the East's most important tree species, was all but eliminated during the early 20th century by a fungus introduced from Asia. Recent threats include gypsy moths, which defoliate millions of acres annually, the hemlock woolly adelgid, which has devastated many hemlock groves in southern New England, and the Asian long horned beetle, which was discovered in central Massachusetts in 2009 and poses a significant threat to many key Northeast species; thousands of potentially infested trees have been removed to control its spread.

Significant weather events can also cause widespread, long-term damage to forests. Strong hurricanes, such as the great storm of 1938 that took an unusual inland track across central New England, occur at roughly 50-100 year intervals. Ice storms, which recently devastated large areas in 1998 and 2008, also occur irregularly, while occasional tornados and microbursts cause damage on a smaller scale. Fire frequently affected forests in the past, but is less of a factor today, due to control measures. One exception was the large blaze on Mount Desert Island in 1947, which has had lasting effects on the forests of Acadia National Park – the autumn colors visible today are deciduous trees that sprouted after the fire.

As a result of all this, very little old-growth (virgin) forest remains in New England today, even in the north woods of Maine, New Hampshire, and Vermont. However, scattered across the region are a number of small pockets of old trees that have remained undisturbed by humans since the time of European settlement. The majority of these areas are places that were inaccessible to loggers, such as mountain slopes, high-elevation swamps, and steep valleys and ravines. The old trees exist in all sorts of shapes and sizes, from towering, 150-foot high pines to stunted dwarf trees on mountaintops and ridges.

This chapter details some of the region's best places to view examples of old New England forests. A number of other areas that are detailed elsewhere in the book that also have groves of old trees are referenced at the end.

CATHEDRAL PINES

Closest Town: Cornwall, CT

Owner: The Nature Conservancy, 203-568-6270

Directions: From the three-way junction of CT 4, CT 125, and Pine Street in Cornwall, turn south on Pine Street. Follow Pine Street for 0.3 miles, then turn left on Valley Street. After 0.2 miles, bear left on Essex Hill Road and continue for another 0.2 miles to a small pullout on the left, marked with a brown sign.

For centuries, the giant trees of Cathedral Pines, which grew high out of a hillside in the Litchfield Hills of northwestern Connecticut, stood as one of the finest examples of an old white pine-hemlock forest in the eastern United States. Then, in July 1989, all but eight acres of this exemplary 40-acre grove was leveled within a matter of minutes by a powerful tornado. Although many of the giant specimens were destroyed, the large stumps, downed logs, and surviving trees continue to serve as artifacts of one of the Northeast's best-known forests.

By the 19th century, such old "cathedral" pine forests were a true rarity in New England, as most had been cut for agriculture or charcoal. The Cathedral Pines tract was not entirely undisturbed, as portions were logged in colonial times, and the trees are a combination of old and second-growth. In 1883, Cornwall resident John Calhoun purchased the land to protect the pines from further logging. The hill sheltered the trees from the brunt of the great hurricane of 1938, which blew down many of New England's other remaining old forest stands. The Calhoun family donated the property to the Nature Conservancy in 1967. Today, the grove serves as a valuable research site that offers insight into old forest dynamics.

Though the grove is best-known for the giant pines, the oldest trees are hemlocks, with several specimens over 300 years old. The white pines were generally younger, dating back roughly 200-225 years to the late 18th century. Prior to the 1989 storm, the pines grew as high as 150-170 feet; today the tallest surviving specimen is nearly 140 feet.

From the small parking area on Essex Hill Road, the preserve's blue-blazed nature trail begins at an area of fallen trees and large stumps, then winds up the hillside, passing close by several giant specimens. After about a quarter of a mile, it levels off in a younger, second-growth forest; from here walkers can backtrack down the hill to the parking area. This trail was once part of the Appalachian Trail (and is still listed in some guides and maps as such), before the latter was rerouted to the western hills of the Housatonic Valley.

The unique character of the Ice Glen, a boulder-strewn ravine in the heart of the Housatonic River Valley in the southern Berkshire Hills, inspired Herman Melville to use it as an analogy for a beautiful, wild scene in his classic *Moby Dick*: "The wood was as green as the mosses of the Icy Glen; the trees stood high and haughty...." It was also once described by fellow author Nathaniel Hawthorne as "the most curious fissure in the Berkshires."

The trees noted by Melville are still present today, as one of New England's finest old forests rises high above the 25-acre ravine. The many impressive specimens include the region's tallest documented eastern hemlock (130 feet) and second tallest white pine. A number of other trees also exceed 130 feet, and some have been dated at more than 300 years in age. The lower slopes of the hill adjacent to the ravine are also home to a number of giant second-growth trees that are approximately 200 years old.

One might expect such a setting to be miles from civilization in a remote wilderness, but the glen is, in fact, just a short distance from the center of Stockbridge and heavily-traveled Route 7. It is situated on the lower west slopes of Laurel Hill, one of the many rolling hills of Housatonic River Valley. The rugged terrain and rocky boulders made access impractical for loggers, sparing the trees from the axe during a time when much of the valley was cleared. An observation tower at the hill's 600-foot summit offers fine panoramic views across the valley to Mount Greylock and the Catskill Mountains.

The Laurel Hill Association maintains a network of trails that explore the hill and ravine. From the bridge over the Housatonic River at the end of Park Street, the main trail winds to a junction where the rocky, one-way side trail to the ravine branches to the right and winds through the mossy boulders, which can be slippery when wet or icy. After 0.7 miles, this path ends at the north end of the ravine, where there are fine views of the big trees. After backtracking to the junction, hikers have the option of a quick, 0.7-mile climb through a much younger hardwood forest to the summit viewing tower. For a different perspective of the valley, a universally-accessible, one-way recreational trail also begins at the bridge and follows the Housatonic River and its floodplain forest for 0.6 miles.

*During an era when much of the Housatonic Valley was cleared for agriculture, the rocky Ice Glen sheltered a 25-acre grove of trees from logging.*

Closest Town: Stockbridge, MA

Owner: Laurel Hill Association, 413-298-4714

Directions: From the Massachusetts Turnpike (I-90) in Lee, take Exit 2 and follow MA 102 west for 4.7 miles to the center of Stockbridge. Turn left on US 7, then quickly left again on Park Street and continue to the parking area at the road's end. The trails begin on the opposite side of the bridge across the Housatonic River.

*The forest surrounding the Ice Glen includes pines and hemlocks that are more than 300 years old and 130 feet high.*

## DUNBAR BROOK

**Closest Town:** Monroe, MA

**Owner:** Massachusetts Department of Conservation and Recreation (Monroe State Forest c/o Mohawk Trail State Forest headquarters), 413-339-5504

**Directions:** From MA 2 in Charlemont, drive 1.7 miles west and turn north on the Zoar-Rowe Road. Continue 2.4 miles to a T-intersection, and turn right on River Road. Follow River Road to the railroad crossing at Hoosac Tunnel, then continue for 4 miles to the Dunbar Brook parking area.

The upper Deerfield River Valley of northwestern Massachusetts is a landscape of steep valleys, ravines, and low mountains and hills. Not surprisingly, this rugged topography has sheltered one of the highest concentrations of old-growth forests in New England, with nearly 20 individual groves. While none of these areas is especially large, all are significant in that they represent undisturbed areas in the heart of a region that was historically heavily logged.

A half dozen of these sites alone are scattered across the Monroe State Forest, which protects 4,300 acres along the west banks of the Deerfield River. Though much of this land was cleared for farms in colonial times, these sheltered pockets were never cut and are now home to some of New England's oldest and largest trees. Among the notable specimens are the region's largest white ash (nearly 125 feet tall), the Thoreau White Pine (147 feet), an uncommon grove of big-toothed aspens (112 feet), and other giant hemlocks, birches, maples, and white pines. These trees, along with a wealth of wildflowers and ferns, benefit from the nutrient-rich soils characteristic of western New England.

While many of the old trees are hidden off the beaten path, 20 acres of large old and second-growth trees are easily viewed along the banks of Dunbar Brook, a rocky tributary of the Deerfield River that drops 700 feet over two miles as it flows through the heart of the state forest. In addition to the size of the trees, some of the clues that these groves have never been cut include the lack of stone walls and stumps, and the forest's more open character than the surrounding woodlands, where the younger, smaller trees grow closer together.

*This giant white ash at Monroe State Forest is one of many old trees sheltered by the rugged uplands of northwestern Massachusetts.*

From the trailhead on River Road, the Dunbar Brook Trail parallels the south bank of the cascading brook for 0.7 miles, where it reaches a junction at a bridge. Here one can detour on the trail to the left, which winds up a ridge with many old trees, including the giant ash. The Dunbar Brook Trail continues across the bridge, then continues along the north bank beneath giant pines to Haley Brook at 1.5 miles. At 1.8 miles, the trail reaches Parsonage Brook. More old trees, including hemlocks and red spruces, grow out of the north bank here.

The nearby Mohawk Trail State Forest protects an additional 6,500 acres along the steep slopes of the Cold River Valley. More old trees grow here, including groves of tall pines along the trails and roads near the campground. The Todd Mountain Trail offers a steep climb to a ridge with an overlook atop the valley.

*Rocky Dunbar Brook cascades between groves of giant old trees as it flows towards the Deerfield River Valley.*

# GIFFORD WOODS

Close-up of an old sugar maple at Gifford Woods, which is one of the only remaining areas of old-growth forest in the Green Mountains.

maples, including specimens that are more than 100 feet high and four feet wide. Other old trees include hemlocks (one of which is more than 420 years old), white ashes, beeches, and yellow birches. Apart from periodic sugar maple tapping, this small pocket has somehow remained undisturbed by humans and natural events such as fires and hurricanes.

Gifford Woods State Park, which protects the trees, began as a 13-acre purchase by the state of Vermont in 1931. It was subsequently expanded by additional purchases and donations, including a gift from a local resident named Walter Barrows, who noted the popularity of the old trees with tourists driving Route 100. The old forest grove was designated as a National Natural Landmark by the National Park Service in 1980. In 2003, the park acquired an additional 170 acres of the Long Trail corridor, enlarging it to its present 285 acres.

A easy interpretive trail at the ranger station offers close-up views of the big trees and exhibits and signs that detail old-growth forests. This path, which briefly follows a portion of the Kent Brook Trail, begins on the north side of the parking lot. After passing an old stump display, the trails split, and the interpretive trail curves to the left behind the ranger station. It then makes a quick loop near the campground road and returns to the parking area. The park is a popular destination for hikers, as the Appalachian Trail and other paths lead to features such as Kent Pond and the Deer Leap Overlook, where there are fine views of Sherburne Pass and nearby Killington and Pico Peaks.

Closest Town: Killington, VT

Owner: Vermont Department of Forests and Parks, 802-775-5354

Directions: From the junction of US 4 and VT 100 east of Sherburne Pass in Killington, turn north on VT 100, then left at the main entrance, which is just north of a seasonal parking area. A $3.00 day-use fee is charged at the ranger station.

It's hard to imagine that just a tiny fraction of Vermont's Green Mountains is virgin forest. After all, the region is known for its striking fall foliage, deep woods trails, and sugar maple farms that draw millions of visitors to the region annually. Yet, as recently as the mid-19th century, more than three-quarters of this landscape was barren, having been clear-cut by early settlers.

One of the few remaining old forests in the mountains is an eight-acre grove at Gifford Woods that is perhaps the most accessible example of an old northern hardwood forest in the East. Here, along the margins of well-traveled Route 100 near Killington Peak, grow giant 300-400 year old sugar

# VERNON BLACK GUM SWAMP & MILLER TOWN FOREST

*Holdovers from a period of climate warming, black gums are among New England's longest-lived trees.*

**Closest Town:** Vernon, VT

**Owner:** Vernon Recreation Department (Miller Town Forest), 802-254-9241

**Directions:** From the junction of US 5 and VT 142 in Brattleboro, follow VT 142 south for 7 miles to a right on Pond Street in Vernon, opposite the post office. Follow Pond Street for 1.2 miles, then turn right on Huckle Hill Road. After 1.4 miles, turn right on Basin Road, and continue 0.7 miles to the parking area at the road's end.

Like alpine wildflowers, cedar swamps, and rhododendron groves, black gum swamps are another legacy of New England's many historical climate fluctuations. Also known as "tupelo" or "nyssa," black gums migrated into the region from the South, where they are common, during a warming period that occurred three to five thousand years ago. After the Northeast's climate cooled to its present level, scattered communities remained in favorable sites as holdovers.

Black gums are identified by their plate-like "alligator" bark and smooth leaves, which turn bright red at the onset of foliage season. Another significant characteristic is their longevity: some individual trees in New England range in age from 400 to nearly 700 years. These specimens were never cut because of their relatively low commercial value and/or location in wetlands that were impractical for logging.

An excellent example of a black gum wetland, and one of the largest areas of old growth in Vermont, is an eight-acre grove in a high elevation swamp at the Miller Town Forest in Vernon. This wetland fills a small, 1125-foot high glacial depression on the upper slopes of a hill that rises above the farm fields of the Connecticut River Valley.

The oldest tree here is 440 years old – for a historical perspective, it began growing around 1570, or 50 years before the Pilgrims landed at Cape Cod; other individual trees are more than 400 years old. The relatively mild climate of the lower Connecticut Valley helps the black gums survive in this northerly setting. Other trees that grow in and along the margins of the swamp are eastern hemlock, red spruce, and yellow birch.

The 460-acre town forest was named for J. Maynard Miller, who was instrumental in getting the swamp and a surrounding forest buffer protected. Its 3.6-mile trail network includes the High Swamp (Red) Trail, which offers a fairly easy, 15-minute walk to the black gums. From the parking area on Basin Road, this trail leaves to the left past a private residence, makes a quick climb to the edge of the swamp, then continues along the perimeter of the wetland, with close-up views of the old trees. Other trails include the Overlook Trail, which passes a picnic area in a small clearing with a partial view toward Mount Monadnock, and the Mountain Laurel and Lower Swamp Trails, which explore the hill's forests and wetlands. A loop incorporating all of these routes can be completed in three hours or less.

NANCY
BROOK

Closest Towns: Harts Location and Bartlett, NH

Owner: White Mountain National Forest, 603-536-6100

Directions: From the eastern boundary of Crawford Notch
State Park, follow US 302 east for 3.1 miles to the
roadside parking area for the Nancy Pond Trail.

*A large old-growth red spruce forest grows on the upper slopes of Mount Nancy in Crawford Notch.*

On the mountain's upper slopes is a large area of old-growth forest dominated by red spruce and balsam fir, with a few scattered white pines. Some of the world's oldest and largest red spruce trees grow here, including individual specimens that are more than 420 years old. Though the trees generally decrease in height at these elevations, some grow as high as 85 feet. The average age of the trees is more than 250 years. This area was never logged because of the steep terrain, though the grove was damaged by the 1938 Hurricane. The forest provides habitat for rare northern three-toed woodpeckers, a boreal species at the southern limit of its range in New Hampshire, and mountain avens, a globally rare wildflower. The 460-acre Nancy Brook Scenic Area was designated in 1964 to protect the old trees.

This forest surrounds the upper watershed of Nancy Brook, which originates at Nancy Pond on the mountains upper slopes and flows through the heart of the old-growth. A half mile downstream from its source, the brook drops 300 feet at the dramatic Nancy Cascades, a tall waterfall that marks the lower boundary of the old forest. Downstream from the falls, which are 1500 vertical feet above the valley of Crawford Notch, are the remains of a old mill that once harnessed the considerable power of the flowing brook. The "Nancy" for whom the mountain, brook, and falls are named was an unfortunate woman who reputedly died of hypothermia while trying to find her fiancée at a winter camp in Crawford Notch.

The old forest and waterfalls are reached by the Nancy Pond Trail, which begins at a roadside pullout on Route 302. The lower portion of the trail is fairly easy, as it follows an old logging road for 1.6 miles to a brook crossing near the old mill site. The trail then becomes steeper and rockier as it rises to the base of the falls and the start of the old-growth at 2.4 miles. After a rocky scramble along the cascades, the trail continues through the groves to wetlands associated with Nancy Pond, which it reaches via a series of log bridges at 3.5 miles.

Home to a large area of old-growth forest, one of the region's tallest and most striking waterfalls, and a high-elevation pond, Mount Nancy is one of the most interesting and ecologically significant areas of the White Mountains. It is the namesake and highest summit of the Nancy Range, a chain of mountains in the southern portion of Crawford Notch, just south of Crawford Notch State Park.

The dramatic Nancy Cascades, one of the largest waterfalls in New Hampshire, mark the lower boundary of the old spruce grove.

## OLD BLUE & ELEPHANT MOUNTAINS

Closest Towns: Andover and "Township C," ME
Contact: Appalachian Trail Committee
Directions: From the junction of ME 5 and US 2 at Rumford Point, follow ME 5 north to the center of Andover. Continue north toward South Arm for 8.5 miles to the parking area where the Appalachian Trail crosses the highway.

*The Appalachian uplands of western Maine include a rare old-growth spruce forest between Old Blue and Elephant Mountains.*

Considering its vast interior forests, rugged and remote terrain, and low population density, it seems inconceivable that very little old-growth exists throughout Maine, apart from communities of stunted trees on the high mountains and in bogs and swamps. However, these woodlands have long been working industrial timberlands that have been owned and harvested by timber companies, which own more than 90 percent of the state's forests.

One of the state's best examples of old growth grows out of a high valley between Old Blue and Elephant Mountains, which rise above the east shores of Mooselookmeguntic Lake in the Rangeley Lakes region. Here a stand of at least 50-100 acres (some estimates indicate that this may be larger) of old red spruce and balsam fir rises high above both sides of the Appalachian Trail for more than a mile. Red spruce, which thrives in such rocky, mountainous environments, is New England's most common spruce species. The oldest specimen here has been dated at more than 310 years, and the largest diameter recorded is 28 inches. There are also giant northern hardwoods including sugar maples and yellow birches. Because the Appalachian Trail is a federally designated National Scenic Trail, the trees along the corridor are protected by the Park Service.

Access to this pristine grove requires a moderately challenging but rewarding 10-mile (round-trip) hike that begins at Black Brook Notch north of Andover. The Appalachian Trail makes a steep 0.6-mile climb to the top of the notch, where an open ledge offers fine views, then reaches the base of Old Blue at 2.3 miles. A half-mile climb leads to the mountain's 3600-foot summit, where low trees allow for excellent views. From the summit, the trail descends to the old trees in the saddle between Old Blue and Elephant Mountains, which is 800 feet below Old Blue's summit.

*Also see: Presidential Range, NH (Alpine Mountains chapter); Mount Greylock, MA (Monadnocks chapter); Wachusett Mountain, MA (Monadnocks chapter); Bear Mountain, CT (Unique Low Mountains chapter); Mount Everett, MA (Unique Low Mountains chapter); Quechee Gorge, VT (Gorges chapter); Bingham Falls Gorge, VT (Gorges chapter); Chesterfield Gorge, NH (Gorges chapter); Gulf Hagas, ME (Gorges chapter); Button Point, VT (Artifacts of History chapter).*

# COASTAL SOUTHERN NEW ENGLAND
## chapter eleven

*Within this lengthy interface, when land meets the ocean, are a remarkable array of habitats, including beaches and dunes, salt marshes, tidal flats and creeks, kettle ponds, islands, coves, bays, rocky headlands, eelgrass beds, maritime forests, and the granite mountains.*

*The erosion-prone sandy beaches and dunes of Cape Cod, seen here at Truro, were formed by glacial debris.*

*All told,* New England's coast encompasses nearly 6,000 miles of irregular shoreline stretching from Stamford, Connecticut to Lubec, Maine. Within this lengthy interface when land meets the ocean are a remarkable array of habitats, including beaches and dunes, salt marshes, tidal flats and creeks, kettle ponds, islands, coves, bays, rocky headlands, eelgrass beds, maritime forests, and the granite mountains of Acadia National Park. The portion of the coast from Connecticut to southern Maine is generally gentler and less rocky than that of northeastern Maine.

Some of the most familiar features of the south coast, including Cape Cod, Martha's Vineyard, Nantucket Island, and Block Island, were formed by deposits of rock, silt, and pebbles called "moraines" that mark the southern extent of glaciation in New England. When the ice sheets reached the south coast, the warm maritime air halted their advance and caused them to leave behind this debris, which had accumulated as they advanced across the interior. Another area similarly shaped by glaciers is Stellwagen Bank, a large underwater plateau off the Massachusetts coast known for its rich feeding grounds that support a variety of marine life.

The glaciers also were responsible for the hundreds of kettle ponds that dot the landscape of the coastal plain. These ponds, which formed when large pieces of ice melted in depressions, have no inlet or outlet streams, but are instead fed by groundwater and precipitation.

Another characteristic habitat of the south coast are its salt marshes, which are among the planet's richest and most productive ecosystems. Replenished daily by ocean tides, these support a diverse, rich food web. The marsh grasses sustain algae, fungi, and bacteria, which are consumed by bottom-feeding fishes, crabs, oysters,

*Like many other New England wildlife species, gray seals have recovered from population declines and are thriving today.*

snails, and worms. In turn, these species are prey for creatures higher up the food web, such as wading and marsh birds. These wetlands also act as buffers that mitigate the effects of strong storms and high tides. Many salt marshes have been historically abused by development, dredging, and pesticides, and as a result some wildlife species such as diamondback terrapin turtles and black-crowned night herons have suffered population declines. Significant salt marshes include the estuary at the mouth of the Connecticut River, and the Great Marsh of Massachusetts' north shore.

Further buffering the coast are some 300 miles worth of barrier beaches, which are also most common from Connecticut to Portland, Maine. These narrow strips of sand provide habitat for a variety of wildlife, including threatened piping plovers and least terns. Examples include Plum Island in northeast Massachusetts, Nauset Beach at Cape Cod National Seashore, and a 20-mile long beach that separates Trustom Pond and other waterbodies from the ocean in southwestern Rhode Island. Connecticut's coast is largely buffered by Long Island, which is also a glacial moraine.

Familiar coastal wildlife includes whales and dolphins, which migrate north from the equator during the warm months to take advantage of the rich feeding grounds. Humpbacks, which are the star attraction of boat tours, are often the most visible whales; other species include smaller finback, minke, and globally endangered right whales. Harbor seals are common along the entire New England coast in winter, and from New Hampshire northward in warm months. The much larger gray seal has made a strong recovery from substantial declines caused by hunting. Less-known and visible are the handful of sea turtles that also migrate along the coast.

Thanks to its location along the Atlantic flyway migratory corridor, the coast is also home to a wide variety of birdlife. Areas such as Hamonnasett Beach in Connecticut, Plum Island in Massachusetts, and Maine's Monhegan Island record hundreds of species yearly, including vagrants blown in by strong ocean storms. In winter and early spring, shorebirds and waterfowl such as northern gannets, razorbills, harlequin ducks, king eiders, and purple sandpipers migrate to the area from the north.

CONNECTICUT
RIVER
ESTUARY

*An exemplary river-tidal marsh ecosystem
encompasses the mouth of the Connecticut River.*

**Closest Towns:** Lyme and Old Saybrook, CT

**Contact:** Connecticut Department of Environmental Protection, 860-424-3000

**Directions:** For the boat launches and viewing areas along the lower marshes, from Interstate 95, take Exit 70 and follow CT 156 south. For the Ferry Landing Park boardwalk, from Exit 70 continue south for 0.3 miles, then turn right on Ferry Road and continue to the parking area adjacent to the Department of Environmental Protection Marine Headquarters.

At the mouth of the Connecticut River is not a large metropolis, as one might expect along the developed southern New England coast, but instead an estuary and marshlands of international significance. Bald eagles and osprey nest along the riverbanks, while large flocks of black ducks and other waterfowl use the marshy wetlands for food and cover. Beneath the water are many rare and unique creatures, such as sea turtles and shortnose sturgeons.

In effect, the river has protected its estuary by depositing large amounts of silt at the mouth, forming sandbars that are impassable for large ships. As a result, the area was unsuitable for a large port city, and thus never heavily developed . Much of these deposits, which are washed downstream from areas as far away as the river's headwaters on the Canadian border 400 miles to the north, occur during the spring freshet, when the river is recharged by snowmelt throughout its extensive watershed.

During these spring months, the Connecticut is largely a fresh water river, but as the flow decreases throughout the summer, the tides gradually move north as far as the Essex-Deep River area. The 35-mile

long estuary is one of the finest examples of an undisturbed marsh-river ecosystem in the United States.

Along the east bank of the estuary is a large area of marshes known as Great Island. More than 40 species listed in "greatest conservation need" of these habitats live here, including peregrine falcons, least terns, and such marsh and wading birds as American bitterns, king rails, and glossy ibises. A less welcome species is phragmites, a reed that invades salt marsh habitats, crowding out native vegetation; 150 acres of phragmites was removed by a combination of mowing and herbicides in 2009. The Roger Tory Peterson Wildlife Area, named for the preeminent ornithologist and author who lived in nearby Lyme, protects more than 3,000 acres here. There are good views of the marshes from boat launches on Route 156, which offer access to the estuary for boaters. A short boardwalk at Ferry Landing Park follows the edge of the marsh and river to a observation platform with a fine overview of the area. There are many options for paddlers here; a recommended guide is *The Connecticut River Boating Guide: Source to Sea* by Sinton, Farnsworth, and Sinton *(see bibliography for full citation).*

A unique area worth exploring in the upper portion of the estuary is Selden Neck State Park near Lyme, which encompasses a 600-acre roadless island that was separated from the mainland by high water in 1854. The park, which is only accessible by boat, includes four campsites and trails that lead to scenic overlooks and a historic quarry.

## TRUSTOM POND

The last wholly undeveloped pond on Rhode Island's south coast, Trustom Pond is home to a great variety of birds and other wildlife.

Closest Town: Charlestown, RI

Owner: U.S. Fish and Wildlife Service (Trustom Pond National Wildlife Refuge), 401-364-9124

Directions: From US 1 in Charlestown, take the exit for Moonstone Beach Road, following signs to the refuge. Follow Moonstone Beach Road south for 1 mile, then turn right on Matunick Schoolhouse Road and continue for 0.7 miles to the entrance on the left.

On the southwest coast of Rhode Island, a 20-mile long barrier beach stretches along the shores, broken only by a series of inlets that connect the ocean to nearby ponds.

Once constantly rearranged by the ocean tides, these inlets have been reinforced into permanent openings called "breachways." The last remaining wholly undeveloped pond here is 160-acre Trustom Pond, which is the centerpiece of one of the richest wildlife areas of the south coast.

Trustom Pond is largely a freshwater pond, with levels of salt that vary with precipitation and tides through the breachway. Bordering and buffering the pond are a variety of habitats, including maritime forests, shrubby thickets, swamps, and meadows. Thanks to this diversity, nearly 300 species of birds have been recorded on the grounds. Osprey nest high above the shores of the pond, which serves as a rest area for large flocks of waterfowl and shorebirds during spring and fall migrations. Endangered piping plovers and least terns nest on the sands of Moonstone Beach, which separates the pond from the ocean. The surrounding forests and meadows on the site of an old farm are home to bluebirds and other grassland birds, butterflies,

white-tailed deer, and eastern coyotes, which make hunting rounds in the early morning and evening.

The pond is the centerpiece of the 787-acre Trustom Pond National Wildlife Refuge, which is part of a large network of conservation areas in this region that includes the nearby Ninigret National Wildlife Refuge, which encompasses most of Ninigret Pond, the region's largest coastal pond. The refuge's easy walking paths include the Osprey Point Trail, which makes a 0.8-mile beeline from the fields at the entrance to a viewing deck on the north shores of Trustom Pond, where there are fine views across the water to Block Island Sound. The slightly shorter Otter Point Trail leads for 0.6 miles to another viewpoint on the pond's shores. Visitors can walk either route individually, or combine them as a 3-mile loop by using the Red Maple Swamp Trail as a connecting path.

## MOHEGAN BLUFFS, BLOCK ISLAND

Continually reshaped by the ocean, wind, and coastal storms, the Mohegan Bluffs rise high above Block Island's southeast shores.

Closest Town: New Shoreham, RI

Directions: From the New Shoreham waterfront, head south on Spring Street, which becomes the Mohegan Trail, for roughly 1.5 miles to the bluffs and lighthouse. The island is served year-round by ferry from Point Judith and seasonally from Providence, Newport, and New London, CT.

Of southern New England's many ocean beaches, few are as unusual and dramatic as Bluffs Beach on Block Island, so named for its location at the base of the towering Mohegan Bluffs. Here the views are not of gentle, wide sands and rolling dunes, but instead large, multi-hued granite boulders strewn at the base of towering cliffs that rise as high as 185 feet out of the ocean.

The bluffs, which stretch for nearly three miles along the island's southeast shores, draw their name from a Native American conflict that took place in 1590, short before the arrival of European settlers. A raiding party of 50 Mohegans paddled from Long Island to Block Island, where they were joined in battle by the native Manises tribe. According to lore, the battle culminated when the Mohegans were driven over the bluffs to their deaths. Earlier in the century, Italian explorer Giovanni de Verrazano noted many fires burning along the shores during his voyage in 1524, indicating a large Native population.

Ever since Block Island was formed by glacial deposits that also created Cape Cod and Long Island, the unrelenting, unbuffered forces of ocean surf, wind, and rain have continually reshaped and eroded the bluffs and shore. Large pieces of the bluffs often fall to the beach, then are broken apart and washed away by the tides. In 1993, the stately brick Southeast Lighthouse, which was originally erected in 1875 and is one of the most powerful electric lighthouses on the Atlantic coast, was moved 250 feet inland to keep it from falling into the ocean.

The bluffs and lighthouse are easily accessed and viewed from the Mohegan Trail town road, which is south of the ferry dock in New Shoreham. A wooden staircase with 140 steps offers a long but safe passage to Bluffs Beach and its sea-level perspective of the cliffs. The island's greenway network includes more than 30 miles of walking trails that explore its many natural habitats; other places worth visiting are Rodman's Hollow, a glacial depression west of the bluffs, and the Block Island National Wildlife Refuge and Northeast Lighthouse at the island's northern tip. The island is crowded with visitors during the summer but is much quieter in other months; early autumn is a prime time for viewing migrating birds and monarch butterflies.

**NARRAGANSETT BAY**

*At the southern tip of Conanicut Island, the historic Beavertail Lighthouse marks a safe passage into Narragansett Bay.*

Closest Major Towns: Wickford, Jamestown, Newport, Middletown, RI

Directions: To reach Beavertail State Park, from the junction of US 1 and RI 138 in Kingstown, follow RI 138 east across the Jamestown Bridge. Take the Jamestown exit and continue to a stop sign at the waterfront. Turn right on Narragansett Avenue, then left on Southwest Avenue and continue to the road's end at the state park entrance. For Rome Point, from the junction of US 1, RI 138, and RI 4 in Kingston, follow RI 138 for 1.8 miles, then take the RI 1A exit and follow RI 1A north for 0.6 mile to the entrance on the right.

In spite of Rhode Island's diminutive size, it boasts more than 400 miles of shoreline. Much of this land encompasses the tidal rivers, coves, beaches, and islands of Narragansett Bay, which is the largest estuary in New England. Amidst the development of the state's south coast, the bay and its surrounding environments offer habitat for a variety of wildlife, including whales, seals, and half of the state's bird species.

The bay and its adjacent shores were shaped by a complex series of processes when sea levels fluctuated after glaciers moved across Rhode Island's south coast, then stalled when they reached the maritime air. After the ice sheets retreated from the area roughly 15,000 years ago, a large fresh water lake named Lake Narragansett temporarily formed behind debris deposits. It was relatively short-lived, lasting 500 years before it drained and was replaced by salt water from the rising ocean.

In pre-colonial times, the bay and its many natural resources sustained a large Native population. The western shores were the domain of the Narragansetts, while Wampanoags occupied the eastern region. The first known European explorer was Giovanni de Verrazano, who visited Rhode Island's coast in 1524. Colonial settlers arrived during the 1630s, and established the trade post that became Providence, one of New England's largest cities, in 1636.

Within the bay are more than 30 islands of various sizes, the largest of which is Aquidneck. At its southern end are the scenic and geologically significant ridges of the Norman Bird Sanctuary (fully detailed in next entry). The nearby Sachuest Point National Wildlife Refuge encompasses 250 acres of a peninsula and rocky beaches at the mouth of the Sakonet River. It offers many scenic viewpoints and is an excellent bird watching area in all seasons; in winter it hosts a large flock of colorful harlequin ducks and other seabirds. A pair of easy walking paths loop along the perimeter of the point, offering access to the vistas and beaches.

Nearby Conanicut Island is capped on its southern shores by the rocky bluffs of Beavertail State Park, where the Jamestown Lighthouse marks an entrance to the bay. In 1749, one of the country's first lighthouses was erected on this site; it was destroyed shortly afterward during a British raid during the American Revolution. More than 30 shipwrecks have occurred off the point, including the *H.F.Payton*, which sank in 1859 with a load of granite; today some of the blocks are visible near the lighthouse. Early European settlers established sheep pastures in the island's interior during the 1630s.

On the west shores of the bay, just a few miles south of the heavily developed greater Providence area, lies Rome Point, a finger-like promontory that juts out of Bissel Cove. During the winter months, large groups of harbor seals bask on the rocks offshore from the point, offering one of the region's finest wildlife viewing opportunities. The interior woodlands are frequented by migratory songbirds, coyotes, and deer. A gravel road offers an easy, half-mile walk to the rocky shores; the tip of the point is a short distance to the north.

# HANGING ROCK RIDGE

Closest Town: Middletown, RI

Owner: Norman Bird Sanctuary, 401-846-2577

Directions: From RI 24, take Exit 1 and follow RI 138 South through Portsmouth. Turn left on RI 138A (Aquidneck Avenue) and continue to the first traffic light. Turn left on Green End Avenue, and continue to a four-way intersection. Turn right on Third Beach Road and continue ¾ mile to the sanctuary entrance on the right. A $5.00 admission fee is charged for non-members.

In addition to offering hikers outstanding scenic coastal views, the unique Hanging Rock Ridge offers a glimpse of more than 250 million years worth of geologic processes. It is one of several long, finger-like ridges that extend out of the forests and marshes at the southern tip of Aquidneck Island in Narragansett Bay, a short distance from the centers of Newport and Middletown.

Hanging Rock Ridge is comprised of "purgatory conglomerate" rock, which is also commonly known as "puddinstone." It was formed by layers of sand, boulders, and pebbles that eroded from giant mountains that once rose high above the present eastern seaboard, long before there was an Atlantic Ocean. The 70-foot high ridge was exposed during the last ice age, when glaciers stripped away layers of soil. Visible evidence of their passage includes lines scoured into the exposed ledges, and the rather abrupt, steep cliff at the ridge's south end, which, like many other eminences in New England, was "plucked" by the moving ice. Since then, gradual erosion at the base of the cliff over thousands of years has created a small overhang – hence the name "Hanging Rock."

Across the valley to the west of Hanging Rock are a pair of slightly smaller ridges, including the Red Fox Ridge. These differ from Hanging Rock in that they are comprised of igneous rock, which was formed by fire. The ridges likely never broke through the Earth's crust as lava, but instead were, like Hanging Rock, exposed by glaciers. The narrow valley between the two ridges includes marshy areas and a small pond, which offer habitat for a variety of wildlife.

The ridges are among the many diverse natural habitats of the Norman Bird Sanctuary, which encompasses 450 acres of coastal forests, salt marshes, ponds, and open meadows and offers a seven-mile network of walking trails. The Hanging Rock Trail begins near the pond in the center of the sanctuary, near the end of the Normal Universal Trail. This one-way route follows the exposed ridge to a panoramic vista at its end, 1.2 miles from the sanctuary entrance. The Red Fox Trail winds along nearby Red Fox Ridge, and offers a good perspective of Hanging Rock from the west.

*The many colors of the Aquinnah Cliffs
mark millions of years of geologic time.*

AQUINNAH
CLIFFS

Closest Town: Aquinnah, MA

Contact: Martha's Vineyard Land Bank Commission, 508-627-7141

Directions: Follow State Road west across the island to its end at the lighthouse parking area. The parking area for Moshup Beach, where a $5.00 per hour ($15.00 maximum daily) parking fee is collected in summer and on some off-season weekends, is located at the junction of State and Moshup Trail Roads. Free parking, with a 1-hour limit, is available near the lighthouse. Ferry service to the island is available from Hyannis, Falmouth, and New Bedford, Massachusetts.

Late afternoon or evening on a clear day is an ideal time for viewing the Gay Head cliffs, which rise high out of the west shores of Martha's Vineyard in a variety of shapes and formations that are more characteristic of the western badlands than anywhere in New England. At this time, the setting sun highlights the various red, pink, green, gold, and yellow tones that are present in the clay.

These colors represent 100 million years worth of geologic history, with each individual hue representing a different era. At the base of the bluffs, areas of grey and black indicate a prehistoric forest that once dominated the coast before changing sea levels altered the landscape. In later times, the ocean left behind deposits of greens and (they actually are red-colored when exposed to air) that have yielded some astounding fossil discoveries, such as teeth from early rhinoceros and crocodiles, a seal that had a stone in its stomach comprised of flint found at Hudson Bay, and a number of marine wildlife including giant sharks.

The recently discovered partial skeleton of a camel, which was found in the conglomerate gravel layers above the clay, indicates a dry period when the ocean receded from the area, while the remains of a wild horse are holdovers from a cool, grassy time.

In more recent centuries, Wampanoag Indians created pottery from clay extracted from the cliffs, while early European settlers utilized the clay for brick making, roads, and paint. This caused considerable erosion to the cliffs, which were once even more prominent than they are now;

*The brick Gay Head Lighthouse presides over the Aquinnah Cliffs at the west end of Martha's Vineyard.*

today they are protected from all activities, including digging and fossil hunting. A lighthouse was first established atop the bluffs in 1799 to mark a safe passage between the treacherous waters between Martha's Vineyard and the Elizabeth Islands, and was subsequently rebuilt as the brick Gay Head Lighthouse in 1856. The overlooks adjacent to the lighthouse offer striking views of the bluffs and the ocean.

The bluffs are easily viewed along Moshup Beach, which is widely regarded as one of New England's most scenic beaches. From the parking area, a short trail offers a quick 10-minute walk to the beach, which extends north along the base of the bluffs. The various perspectives include an especially photogenic view across a small cove and a glimpse of the lighthouse peeking over the top of the cliffs. The out-and-back walk is roughly three miles.

*The Red Maple Swamp Trail boardwalk offers close-up views of many large and unusually shaped red maple trees.*

# CAPE COD NATIONAL SEASHORE & FORESTS

*The diverse habitats of Cape Cod National Seashore include this rare Atlantic white cedar swamp.*

Closest Towns: Eastham, Wellfleet, and Provincetown, MA

Owner: National Park Service (Cape Cod National Seashore), 508-349-9052

Directions: For the Red Maple Swamp, from the rotary in Orleans follow US 6 north for 1.3 miles, then turn right on Governor Prence Road and follow signs for Fort Hill. For the Atlantic White Cedar Swamp Trail, from the National Seashore Salt Pond Visitor Center in Eastham, follow US 6 north for 5 miles to Wellfleet, then turn right at a traffic light at a sign for the Marconi Area. For Beech Forest, take US 6 to Provincetown, then bear right on Race Point Road and continue 0.6 miles to the parking area on the left.

When one thinks of the Cape Cod National Seashore, images of long sandy beaches and tall dunes invariably come to mind. Yet, within the bounds of the 45,000-acre seashore are many other habitats, including marshes, swamps, heathlands, rivers and creeks, and maritime forests. All told, the woodlands of Cape Cod have much less variety than other regions of New England, thanks to the sandy, acidic soils that only a few hardy species such as pitch pine and scrub oak can tolerate. However, scattered about this landscape are pockets of unique and uncommon natural communities that add diversity to the coastal landscape.

Nestled at the base of Fort Hill in Eastham is a red maple swamp where giant trees grow in a variety of shapes and sizes. Although many of these trees have the look and feel of old-growth, the swamp, along with virtually all of the surrounding landscape, was once cleared by early settlers for firewood. The maples weren't the only resource that was extracted from the swamp, as loads of peat were also carted away; an

Irish minister once instructed locals in the burning and drying processes. Thanks to their adaptability and ability to colonize environments such as the swamp and a variety of other lowland and upland communities, red maples are among the most common trees of the East and have the widest north-south distribution. The swamp is especially colorful in mid- to late October, when the brilliant foliage of the red maples reaches its peak, capping layers of yellows, oranges, and greens.

The boardwalk trail through the swamp is easily reached from the lower parking area at Fort Hill or from the entrance on Hemenway Road. Many walkers make a 2-mile circuit that combines the boardwalk with the Fort Hill Trail, which offers fine views of the coast and a series of large open meadows on the grounds of an old farm site.

Another unique wetland is the Atlantic white cedar swamp at the Marconi Area in Wellfleet. Atlantic white cedar is another southern species that migrated into New England during a warming period, and these swamps are regionally uncommon. Red maple trees, which also thrive in wetlands, also grow in the relatively moist, rich soils in and along the perimeter of the swamp. This small community makes for a notable contrast with the surrounding forest of pitch pine and scrub oak, which are among the few species that can grow in the acidic sandy soils and are also exposed to salt spray from the nearby ocean.

The swamp is located near a well-known historic site where Gugliermo Marconi transmitted the first transatlantic wireless communication in 1903. A 1.2-mile interpretive trail includes a long boardwalk that winds through the heart of the swamp and offers close views of the cedars and other vegetation.

At the tip of the Cape, in Provincetown, is another uncommon coastal forest community, a grove of old beech trees that grows out of a knoll above a kettle pond. In pre-colonial times, beech was likely more widespread throughout Cape Cod's landscape. When the settlers cleared the forests, many of the rich soils that support trees such as beech and maple and woodland wildflowers were also stripped away, greatly reducing the ability of these species to reestablish themselves. Beech is also a "climax" tree, meaning that it is one of the last species to cycle through areas that are disturbed, and it takes many years to reestablish itself. In contrast, "pioneers" such as pines and birches thrive when areas are cut or damaged by storms.

An easy 1.1-mile loop trail near the Province Lands visitor center begins at Beech Forest Pond and parallels the shores to the beech grove. This trail winds over the knoll, offering unique views of the forest, then returns along the edge of the pond.

# GREAT MARSH

Closest Towns: Ipswich, Newburyport, Salisbury, MA

Owners: Various. Contact: U.S. Fish and Wildlife Service, Parker River National Wildlife Refuge, 978-465-5753; Trustees of Reservations, Crane Beach, 978-356-4354

Directions: For the Parker River National Wildlife Refuge, from Interstate 95 take Exit 57 and follow MA 113 for 3.5 miles to a traffic light near the Newbury common. Turn left on Rolph's Lane and follow it for 0.5 miles, then turn right on the Plum Island Turnpike and follow it for 2 miles to the bridge to Plum Island. After crossing the bridge, turn right on Sunset Drive and continue 0.5 miles to the refuge entrance ($5.00 fee). For Crane Beach, from the junction of MA 1A and MA 133 in Ipswich, follow MA 133 east for 1.5 miles, then turn left on Northgate Road. Continue for 0.5 miles to a right on Argilla Road, which leads to the entrance. Fees are variable depending on the season and time of day; contact the reservation for more information.

*The boardwalk at Parker River National Wildlife Refuge offers views of rare marsh birds such as Virginia rails and soras.*

New England's largest salt marsh is the "Great Marsh," which encompasses more than 25,000 acres along the North Shore of Massachusetts. Five major rivers – the Merrimack, Parker, Ipswich, Essex, and Powow Rivers – and a number of smaller waterways are part of this ecologically significant watershed, which stretches from Cape Ann into southern New Hampshire. In addition to the expansive marshes, other associated habitats include tidal creeks, barrier beaches, islands, mudflats, and maritime forests. This variety is reflected by the remarkably diverse wildlife that live here, including marine invertebrates, fish, seals, turtles, more than 300 species of birds, and even deep-woods mammals such as moose, fishers, and bobcats.

The rich natural resources of this estuary have been prized by humans for centuries. In pre-colonial times, Native Americans established camps along fertile fishing areas. European settlers arrived in the mid-1630s, and harvested the marsh grasses for livestock feed and building insulation. Today, the area's highly productive soft-shell clam fisheries remain an important part of the region's economy.

Well exemplifying the Great Marsh area are the diverse habitats of the Parker River National Wildlife Refuge, which encompasses the bulk of Plum Island, a barrier beach island that separates the ocean from the mouth and estuary of the Parker River. Within its 4,660 acres are beaches, dunes, marshes, tide pools, and even a beaver wetland. Because of its variety, it is renown as one of the finest bird watching destinations along the Atlantic coast. The refuge is easily explored via an auto road that leads through the heart of the refuge, providing access to viewing areas and the beaches. The Hellcat Observation Area offers two easy interpretive trails with close-up views of marsh, forest, thicket, swamp, and dune habitats, and an observation tower that offers a fine overview of the island.

Across Ipswich Bay to the south is Castle Neck and Crane Beach, where a chain of rolling dunes rises above a popular and scenic white sand beach. Groves of pitch pine and scrub oak trees, which are common on Cape Cod and southeast Massachusetts, but much less so along the North Shore, thrive in these sandy, acidic soils. The Crane Beach Reservation, which is managed by the Trustees of Reservations, encompasses the beach and dunes. A network of color-blazed trails wind along and over the dunes, offering loop hikes ranging from easy to challenging. One recommended option is the Green and Red Trails, which form a 3-mile circuit of moderate difficulty with many fine views.

HALIBUT
POINT

*Comprised of 450 million year old granite, the rocky shores of Halibut Point are similar to the coast of northern Maine*

**Closest Town:** Rockport, MA

**Owners:** Massachusetts Department of Conservation and Recreation, 978-546-2297, Trustees of Reservations

**Directions:** From the junction of MA 128 and MA 127 in Gloucester (MA 128 Exit 9), follow MA 127 north for 6.1 miles, then turn left on Gott Avenue at the state park entrance.

With rugged 450 million year-old granite ledges and tide pools, the rockbound shores of Halibut Point at the tip of Cape Ann have a feel more similar to northern Maine coast than the gentle sandy beaches and dunes characteristic of southern New England. This wind-swept promontory was once known as "Haul About Point" by mariners, who braved the treacherous ocean waters as they navigated toward the nearby ports and harbors of Cape Ann and the North Shore.

From 1840 through to 1929, the point was the site of the Babson Farm Quarry, which excavated stone blocks out of the ledges for area construction companies. Discarded pilings from the quarry now serve as an overlook known as the "Grout Pile" that offers a panoramic three-state view of the North Shore and southern New Hampshire coastlines, the Isles of Shoals, and the sloping profile of Mount Agamenticus, which rises on the horizon above York, Maine. The base of the steep-walled quarry is filled with water today, giving it the appearance of a giant pool. During World War II, a fire tower was built near the edge of the quarry as part of a coastal defense network that guarded Boston and Portsmouth Harbors. The 60-foot structure now serves as a visitor center and headquarters.

*The historic quarry at Halibut Point once provided blocks for construction companies.*

The point is an excellent birding area, especially in the winter, when a variety of seabirds and waterfowl such as razorbills, northern gannetts, purple sandpipers, common loons, and harlequin and king eider ducks are present. In spring, flocks of migratory songbirds rest in the woods and thickets bordering the rocks, which also provide cover for cottontail rabbits and other small mammals. Harbor seals bask on the rocky ledges at low tide, then make fishing rounds as the water rises. The rocky shores are excellent tide pool habitat; among the many unusual creatures that use these basins are starfish, barnacles, and snails.

The Trustees of Reservations and the Department of Conservation and Recreation combine to protect 60 acres here; an adjacent small parcel known as "Sea Rocks" is owned by the town of Rockport. The reservation's main trail begins at the entrance on Gott Avenue and offers a short, easy walk to the quarry site, the vistas at the "Grout Pile," and short footpaths to the rocky shore.

Short footpaths lead to the rocky shores. Visitors should use caution when exploring the rocks and the high walls of the quarry.

## STELLWAGEN BANK

Closest Towns: Offshore from Provincetown, Boston, and Gloucester, MA
Owner: National Oceanic and Atmospheric Administration, 508-747-1691.
Image: "Three humpback whales surrounded by birds" © NOAA. Image from noaanews.noaa.gov

Think of Stellwagen Bank as a sort of marine Serengeti: an oasis that supports a great variety of marine life, ranging from plants and invertebrates to giant whales and sea turtles. This 117-mile underwater plateau, which stretches along the Massachusetts coast from the Race Point Channel at the tip of Cape Cod to the offshore waters of Cape Ann, rises high out of the ocean floor, with an average depth of just 100 feet below sea level. Over thousands of years, the unrelenting ocean has shaped and formed this landscape of sandy deposits, ledges, and basins.

The topography and ocean currents offer ideal growing conditions for plankton, a keystone marine food web species that sustains many species at the bottom of the food chain, including small fish, invertebrates, and shellfish. Ocean storms and currents regularly circulate these nutrients, drawing great numbers of marine wildlife to exploit this rich food resource. Among the many species that frequent these waters are humpback, fin, minke, pilot, and globally endangered north Atlantic right whales, dolphins and harbor porpoises, harbor and grey seals, basking sharks, and 100 series of fish. Sea turtles include leatherbacks, which can grow as large as 800 pounds or more, loggerheads, and uncommon Kemp's Ridleys. The bank is also visited throughout the year by a variety of seabirds from both northern and southern regions, including razorbills, Atlantic puffins, common, least, and roseate terns, sooty, greater, and manx shearwaters, and northern gannets.

For a period of time, an entirely different group of wildlife, such as giant mastodons and deer, likely once roamed this area. Like nearby Cape Cod, Martha's Vineyard, and Nantucket, the plateau is comprised of glacial deposits. After the glaciers retreated from coastal New England roughly 18,000 years ago, the bank was above sea level, with a landscape of beaches, forests, wetlands, and prehistoric wildlife. Ultimately, glacial meltwater and sea level rises fully inundated the bank approximately 10,000 to 12,000 years ago. Today, the southwest corner of the bank is a mere 65 feet below sea level.

The Stellwagen Bank National Marine Sanctuary, which is managed by the National Oceanic and Atmospheric Administration (NOAA), protects 850 acres of this vital area. The area is easily reached and viewed by tour boats, which operate from harbors along the Massachusetts coast, including Provincetown and Barnstable on Cape Cod, Gloucester and Newburyport on the North Shore, and Boston and Plymouth. Visitor centers with related exhibits include the Cape Cod National Seashore's Province Lands Visitor Center in Provincetown, the Woods Hole Aquarium in Woods Hole, the New England Aquarium in Boston, and the Gloucester Maritime Heritage Center in Gloucester. Contact the sanctuary (http://stellwagen.noaa.gov) or the Massachusetts Office of Travel and Tourism for more information.

COASTAL
NORTHERN
NEW
ENGLAND
chapter
twelve

Many finger-like rocky peninsulas, divided by
rivers and bays, extend into the ocean.

*The exposed bedrock of Pemaquid Point well exemplifies the rugged coastline of central and northern Maine.*

*The northern New England coast* holds several distinctions of the Atlantic seaboard: it is home to the highest point of land (Cadillac Mountain), the highest coastal mountain range (the Camden Hills), the easternmost point of land in the continental United States (Quoddy Head), the only fjord-like passage (Somes Sound), and the largest saltwater bay (Great Bay in New Hampshire).

Apart from a 18-mile sliver of southeastern New Hampshire, the northern New England coast is essentially Maine's domain. The Pine Tree State alone has roughly 3,500 acres of irregular shoreline spread along its many peninsulas, coves, islands, and bays. The New Hampshire and southern Maine coasts have sand beaches, dunes, marshes, and bays that are similar to southern New England. The topography is relatively level, broken only by 691-foot Mount Agamenticus, where the views extend from Cape Cod to the White Mountains. The largest salt marsh is Scarborough Marsh near Portland, where a 3000-acre watershed serves as an oasis for wildlife.

North of the Portland-Freeport area, the character of the coast becomes rockier, wilder, and less developed. Many finger-like rocky peninsulas, divided by rivers and bays, extend into the ocean. At Pemaquid Point in the mid-coast region, a popular lighthouse presides over dramatic bedrock cliffs that have been exposed and shaped by the unrelenting tides. These rocky shores are excellent habitat for tide pools, basins of ocean water that offer habitat for many wonderfully unique marine creatures, including starfish, sea urchins, crabs and sea cucumbers, and periwinkles, which are tiny snails that feed on coats of algae.

Spread throughout Maine's coast are some 4300 islands of all shapes and sizes. The best-known of these is, of course, Mount Desert Island, home of Acadia National Park, one of America's most popular natural areas. Here low granite mountains and hills rise high out of the ocean, capped by Cadillac Mountain, the highest point on the Eastern seaboard. Some assert that the tall ocean cliffs, unbroken evergreen forests, and unspoiled roadless lands of Monhegan Island represent the Maine coast at its finest. An hour or so offshore from Jonesport on the northern "sunrise coast" lies treeless Machias Seal Island, which is renown worldwide for its colonies of Atlantic puffins and other seabirds.

At the northeastern tip of the country are the spectacular ocean bluffs at Quoddy Head, which rise high above rocky beaches and the Grand Manan Channel. Here marine creatures such as endangered right whales cruise beneath spruce woodlands and a pair of rare coastal peat bogs.

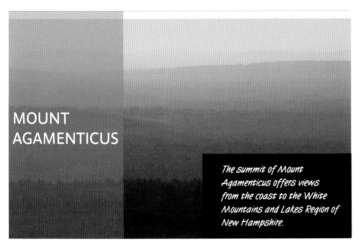

# MOUNT AGAMENTICUS

*The summit of Mount Agamenticus offers views from the coast to the White Mountains and Lakes Region of New Hampshire.*

Closest Town: Ogunquit, ME

Contact: Mount Agamenticus Conservation Region, 207-361-1102

Directions: From Interstate 95, take Exit 7 (York/Ogunquit). Bear right on Chase Pond Road and follow it for 3,5 miles, then turn left on Mountain Road and continue 2.7 miles to the auto road entrance and trails parking area.

The isolated, sloping profile of Mount Agamenticus has long been a familiar landmark of southern Maine's coastal plain. Following his 1614 voyage along New England's coast, explorer John Smith dubbed it as "Snadoun Hill" on his famous "Map of New England" (it was subsequently renamed "Agamenticus," an Abenaki term for the York River). More than 300 years later, the potential for more European visitors motivated the Army to establish the country's first radar tower at the 691-foot summit to track German submarines and warships during World War II. A ski area was established on the mountain in 1964, but it suffered from a lack of consistent heavy snow along the coast and ended operations in 1973.

Today, a observation deck at the site of the old radar tower offers some of the finest views in southern Maine, including the nearby seaside community of York and the southern Maine and New Hampshire coasts, Cape Ann, the Boston skyline, and Cape Cod in the distance to the southeast. To the west, the eastern summits of the White Mountains, including the Mount Washington and the Presidential Range and the distinctive "horn" of Mount Chocorua, are visible as a jagged ridge some 70 miles distant. Sunrises and sunsets here are often spectacular, especially following the passage of a storm.

The summit is also a prime location for viewing hawks as they travel the Atlantic flyway during spring and fall migrations. Many songbirds also use the mountain's extensive forests as a rest area during this time, while white-tailed deer, moose, wild turkeys, and other wildlife are present year-round. These woodlands were cut and cleared during colonial times, when the mountain's slopes were used as sheep pastures, but have recovered over the past century after the farms were abandoned. One 100-acre block of old second-growth forest includes white pine, eastern hemlock, black birch, red oak, and beech trees that range in age from 150 to 300 years.

Mount Agamenticus is the centerpiece of a 10,000-acre network of conservation lands. The easiest route to the summit is via the 0.7-mile auto road, which was originally built by the Army to provide access to the radar tower. The mountain's network of short, easy trails offers several options for hikers. One of the most straightforward routes is to begin on the Ring Trail at the junction of Mountain and Summit Roads and follow it to a fork. Bear left here and continue for a half mile to a right on the Blueberry Bluff Trail, which continues for an additional 0.75 miles to the summit.

# SCARBOROUGH MARSH

Closest Town: Scarborough, ME

Owners: Maine Inland Fisheries and Wildlife, Maine Audubon Society, 207-781-2330

Directions: For the Maine Audubon visitor center, from the junction of ME 9 and US 1 in Scarborough, turn east on Pine Point Road, and continue 0.8 miles to the center on the left. For the Eastern Road trailhead, from the Audubon center continue to follow Pine Point Road for an additional quarter-mile to the parking area on the left.

Given the length of Maine's coast, salt marshes are relatively uncommon, as a mere 19,000 acres worth of these rich wetlands are spread along the state's shores primarily in the southern region. The largest of these communities is the Scarborough Marsh, which encompasses roughly 2,700 acres in portions of the towns of Scarborough, Cape Elizabeth, and Old Orchard Beach. It serves as an oasis of crucial wildlife habitat in the heart of Maine's most developed region.

The marsh's watershed is comprised of several narrow, winding tidal rivers and creeks, including the Dunstan River, Mill Brook, and the Nonesuch and Libby Rivers. These waterways meet in the heart of the estuary to form the Scarborough River, which flows a short distance to meet the Atlantic Ocean at Saco Bay. The predominant vegetation of the marsh includes cord grass and salt hay, both of which are well-adapted to the salt water that few other species can tolerate. Fifteen other distinct habitats have been identified within the watershed. These include rare communities such as dune grasslands, a pitch pine bog, and Stratton Island in Saco Bay, which hosts the most diverse colony of seabirds along the Maine coast.

The marsh and its surrounding habitats support a diverse community of wildlife, including 250 bird species. Wading birds such

*Scarborough Marsh provides habitat for a great variety of birdlife, including great egrets and glossy ibises.*

as egrets, herons, bitterns, and glossy ibises hunt the marsh, while large flocks of shorebirds, songbirds, waterfall, and raptors are present during spring and fall migrations. A portion of the land bordering the marsh is managed for endangered New England cottontail rabbits, which have declined substantial across their range in recent decades. Other mammals such as deer, foxes, and star-nosed moles are present in the uplands.

Like many of New England's other marshes, the Scarborough Marsh has a long history of human use and development. In the past, colonists harvested the grasses to use as hay and dug ditches and channels to drain the water, significantly compromising the ecological integrity of the marsh. As recently as the late 1950s, the town of Scarborough drafted a proposal to fill the marsh and build an industrial park. Fortunately,

the plan never came to fruit, and it triggered concentrated efforts to preserve this fragile area. However, while the marsh itself remains free of development, much of the surrounding area has been heavily built up over the past half-century.

Today 3,100 acres of the marsh and surrounding uplands are protected by the Maine Division of Fisheries and Wildlife. The Maine Audubon Society operates a seasonal nature center on Pine Point Road in Scarborough with a viewing deck that offers close-up views of the Dunstan River and its birdlife, boat tours and access for paddlers, and a short nature trail that visits a series of salt water pools. A strongly recommended walking route is the nearby Eastern Road recreational trail, which crosses the heart of the marsh and offers excellent views of the Dunstan River and its associated habitats.

## MONHEGAN ISLAND OCEAN CLIFFS

*Visitors who spend a night on Monhegan Island are often treated to spectacular sunrises from the ocean cliffs.*

**Closest Town:** Monhegan Village, ME

**Owner:** Monhegan Associates

**Directions:** Ferry service to the island is available from New Harbor (Hardy Boat Cruises, 207-677-2026), Boothbay Harbor (Balmy Days Cruises, 800-298-2284), and Port Clyde (Monhegan-Thomaston Boat Line). Automobiles are not allowed on the island.

For those fortunate enough to enjoy a sunrise from atop the ocean bluffs of Monhegan Island, it's an experience to remember. As the rising sun slowly peeks above the open ocean, it illuminates the tall cliffs, which are among the highest along the Eastern seaboard, while groups of gulls, seabirds, and shorebirds call from the base of the rocky coves below.

The bluffs rise out of the island's east shores, or "back side," in local parlance. The southernmost of the three main cliffs is 140-foot Burnt Head, which rises high above Gull Rock and the Norton Ledges. A short distance north of Gull Cove is 160-foot Whitehead Cliff, while 160-foot Blackhead Cliff presides over the northeastern shores. From the various viewpoints, on clear days one can see east and north across the ocean to Matinicus Island, Matinicus Rock, Criehaven Island, and the Isle of Haut.

Historically, Monhegan and neighboring Manana Island, which lie roughly 11 miles offshore from New Harbor and Pemaquid Point, were inhabited by Native Americans, who enjoyed easy access to the fruitful fishing grounds of the Gulf of Maine. Early European explorers included Martin Pring in 1603, Samuel de Champlain in 1604, and John Smith in 1614. The first settlers established fishing camps and a trade post, where they conducted business with Native tribes. It was briefly captured by the French during King William's War in 1689, when the buildings and fishing boats were destroyed. A lighthouse was erected atop the island's height-of-land in 1820, then replaced in 1850 by the present structure. For the past century, the village, which has a small year-round population, has hosted a popular seasonal artist colony.

Thanks to the efforts of the Monhegan Associates, which have protected roughly two-thirds of its total area, Monhegan Island retains a refreshingly wild, pristine character The island has 17 miles worth of walking trails that wind along the rocky shores and through the unbroken interior spruce-fir woodlands. The most direct routes to the bluffs are Trail 7, which leads from the lighthouse to the Whitehead Cliffs, and Trail 4, which connects the village to Burnthead Cliff. For those with time for a longer outing, Trail 1 follows the perimeter of the shores. It is a mildly rugged route with some rocky areas and elevation change, especially around the high bluffs. A full circuit along the shoreline is 3.7 miles; hikers can also make shorter loops by using the other trails as connecting paths. When planning a route, day visitors should factor in the time between ferry rides; overnight accommodations are available in the village.

At Pemaquid Point, one of Maine's
most familiar lighthouses rests
atop high bluffs that have been
shaped by the relentless ocean.

PEMAQUID
POINT

The spectacular ocean cliffs of Monhegan Island rise as high as 160 feet out of the ocean.

The point lies at the tip of Pemaquid Peninsula, which is bordered on the east by Muscongus Bay, and on the west by Johns Bay. It was one of the first places in New England to be settled by Europeans, who arrived during the mid-1620s and subsequently established a fur-trading center. The lighthouse was commissioned in 1826, and upgraded to Maine's first fully automated light in 1934.

Over thousands of years, the relentless surf has carved and scoured a variety of shapes and features into the exposed bedrock. The cliffs, many of which are metaphoric gneiss, are a geologist's delight; the various colors represent minerals such as quartz, mica, and feldspar. The lighter, whitish rocks are igneous, with granite and pegmatite grains. The long vertical ridges and grooves were created as the crashing waves forced stones and boulders against the cliffs. The small depressions and basins offer tide pool habitat for sea urchins, starfish, blue mussels, and other marine organisms.

The seven-acre property was transferred from the Coast Guard to the town of Bristol in 1940. There are fine views of the cliffs and ocean from the lighthouse, and visitors can explore the rocks and tide pools below (use caution when walking along the cliffs and watch carefully for high surf, which can be dangerous). The fishermen's museum, which once served as the lighthouse keeper's residence in the days before automation, is home to a series of maritime artifacts, including the original Fresnel lens from the Baker Point Light.

Closest Town: Bristol, ME

Owner: Bristol Parks Department, 207-677-2494

Directions: From Interstate 295 in Brunswick, take Exit 28 and follow US 1 north to its junction with ME 130 in Damariscotta, then follow ME 130 south for 14.5 miles to the park entrance ($2.00 fee).

Of all of the attractions and features in Maine, the ocean cliffs and lighthouse at Pemaquid Point were chosen as the subject for the official state quarter. This especially scenic area, where the Pemaquid Lighthouse sits atop high bedrock ledges, has long been a favored destination for artists, photographers, and tourists.

# CAMDEN HILLS

*The many trails at Camden Hills State Park lead to vistas with striking views of the central Maine coast.*

Closest Town: Camden, ME

Owner: Maine Bureau of Parks and Lands (Camden Hills State Park), 207-236-3109

Directions: From the center of Camden, follow US 1 north for 2 miles to the state park entrance on the west side of the road. For the Maiden Cliffs trails, from the junction of US 1 and ME 52 near the center of Camden, follow ME 52 north for 3.2 miles to the parking area on the right. A $3.00 fee is charged at the state park entrance.

In the heart of Maine's mid-coast region, the Camden Hills rise high above one of the state's most picturesque harbors, forming one of the most distinctive backdrops along the Eastern seaboard. The scenery here has long attracted tourists and affluent permanent and seasonal residents to the Camden area.

These rolling hills, which range from 450 to 1,385 feet in elevation, are capped by 1,385-foot Mount Megunticook, which is the highest mainland point of land on the Eastern seaboard and second-highest overall, surpassed only by Cadillac Mountain on Mount Desert Island. Although its summit is wooded, there are fine views from the nearby 1300-foot high "Ocean Lookout" ledges.

Thanks to easy access from an auto road and stone observation tower, Mount Battie is the most-visited summit of the range. Though it is barely half the size of Mount Megunticook at 780 feet, the mountain's location at the southern end of the chain affords sweeping panoramic views from the Camden waterfront to the mountains of Mount Desert Island and Acadia National Park across Penobscot Bay to the east. During the war of 1812, a gun battery was built atop the summit to deter British raiders.

At the western edge of the range are the dramatic Maiden Cliffs, which rise 800 feet above Megunticook Lake. Here there are more excellent views that offer a different perspective of the mid-coast region, including the lake and the surrounding hills and countryside. All of the park's overlooks are excellent areas for bird watching, especially during the spring and fall when hawks and songbirds are migrating along the Atlantic flyway.

The hills are the centerpiece of the 5700-acre Camden Hills State Park, which was established as a Maine state park in 1947 after the National Park Service originally acquired most of the land to save the mountains from development. 30 miles of trails traverse the reservation and provide access to the various features. The park auto road offers an easy route to the top of Mount Battie, which can also be reached on foot via the Mount Battie Trail, which begins outside of the state park on Harden Avenue.

Mount Megunticook hikers have several options, including the mile-long Megunticook Trail, which begins at the park auto road and ascends the southeast slopes. It can also be reached from the west via the Maiden Cliff and Ridge Trails, which begin on Route 52 near Megunticook Lake. The former offers a easy to moderate climb to the top of the Maiden Cliff ledges. For those seeking a more involved outing, a one-way traverse of the hills from Maiden Cliff to Mount Battie involves six miles of hiking spread among five of the state park trails.

SOMES SOUND

*Flying Mountain rises out of the southwest corner of Somes Sound and offers sweeping coastal views.*

**Closest Town:** Somesville, ME

**Contact:** U.S. National Park Service (Acadia National Park), 207-288-3338

**Directions:** Follow ME 3 across the causeway to Mount Desert Island, then bear right on ME 198/ME 102 and continue south to Somesville. For Flying Mountain, from Somesville, follow ME 102 south for 4.5 miles, then turn left (east) on Fernald Point Road and continue 1 mile to the parking area and trailhead.

was the first area of Mount Desert Island to be settled, lies at its northern tip. Portions of Acadia National Park encompass the uplands on both side of the sound above its mouth. On the east rises 852-foot Norumbega Mountain, while across the valley are Acadia (681 feet), St. Sauver (679 feet), and Flying (284 feet) Mountains. From Flying Mountain's summit, which is easily reached by a short, moderately steep 0.3-mile trail, there are views across the mouth of the sound to Fernald Point, Northeast Harbor, and the nearby islands. One can backtrack for a 0.6-mile round-trip, or continue north on a longer outing that explores the adjacent mountains and valleys.

Another excellent option for exploring the sound is a boat tour. Several operators offer cruises from the nearby harbors that offer fine views of the dramatic cliffs and their associated wildlife, including colonies of basking harbor seals, a 100-year old osprey nest, and a variety of shorebirds and seabirds.

The narrow valley of Somes Sound, which stretches for seven miles across the heart of Mount Desert Island and gives the island its distinctive kidney shape, is a landscape unique to the Eastern seaboard. While New England's coast has many long bays and some high rocky headlands, the sound is its only area with high, steep, fjord-like walls.

True fjords are characteristic of coastal and mountain regions with cool climates, such as western Europe, northwestern North America, New Zealand, and Tasmania. In these areas, glaciers scoured deep U-shaped valleys into the bedrock, forming passages as long as the 217-mile Scoresby Sund in Greenland. Because Somes Sound lacks the overall vertical relief and glacial sediments present in other fjords, it is classified by modern geologists as a *fjard*, or a smaller, glacially submerged valley.

The mouth of the sound is flanked by Northwest and Southwest Harbors, while the village of Somesville, which

*Boat tours offer an excellent opportunity to view harbor seals and other wildlife of Somes Sound.*

**CADILLAC MOUNTAIN**

Closest Town: Bar Harbor, ME

Owner: U.S. National Park Service (Acadia National Park), 207-288-3338

Directions: From the junction of US 1 and ME 3 in Ellsworth, follow ME 3 south for 18 miles. After crossing the Mount Desert Island causeway, bear left and continue to follow ME 3 toward Bar Harbor. The park visitor center is off of ME 3, 3 miles north of Bar Harbor. Ellsworth is reached via ME 1A from Bangor, ME 3 and US 1 from Augusta, or US 1 from the south coastal region.

*The highest point of the Eastern seaboard, Cadillac Mountain's summit has been shaped by glaciers and fires.*

As the signature attraction of one of America's most popular national parks, Cadillac Mountain is one of the iconic natural features of the Northeast. This granite eminence is the highest point of the Eastern seaboard, rivaled only by the Camden Hills across the bay. Tens of thousands venture to the 1530-foot summit annually, drawn by the sweeping 360-degree views that include Frenchman Bay, Bar Harbor, the Porcupine Islands, and the Atlantic Ocean. During the fall and winter months, the sunrise is visible from Cadillac's summit before any other place in the continental United States.

The barren summits and ridges of Cadillac Mountain and many other of Acadia's eminences have been shaped by the forces of fire and ice over thousands of years. Because granite absorbs very little water and promotes a dry environment, it offers ideal conditions for fires, which have denuded much of the vegetation. Although the elevations of these eminences are modest and the frequency of fires isn't terribly high, the continuous effects of storms, fog, and wind keeps forests from developing in the intervals between fires.

The island's most recent significant inferno occurred in October 1947, when a period of especially dry and windy weather set the stage for fires that burned more than 17,000 acres, including nearly 9,000 acres of the national park. More than 250 buildings, including many estates and several hotels, were destroyed, and panicked residents evacuated the island by car and boat. More than 60 years later, the effects remain evident, appropriately enough, in the flame-like autumn colors of the maples, birches, and aspens that sprouted following the fire. These deciduous trees, which thrive following disturbances, now are mixed with the evergreen spruces, firs, and pitch pines that were predominant before the fire.

Also visible at the summit are grooves that were scoured into the granite by glacial debris roughly 20,000 years ago. The legacy of the moving ice is indeed evident throughout Acadia National Park in the form of the rounded mountain summits, steep valleys, lake and pond basins, and erratics such as Bubble Rock *(see Artifacts of History chapter)*. The glaciers and associated sea level rises along the Maine coast also combined to separate Mount Desert Island from the mainland.

Cadillac Mountain is located in the eastern portion of Acadia National Park, a short drive from Bar Harbor. The summit is easily reached in season via the park auto road, which winds up the northwest slopes. Hikers can take their choice of several moderate to challenging trails, including the spectacular South Ridge trail (7 mile round trip), which features excellent extended views across the island from along an open ridge, and the shorter (2.8 mile), rugged West Face trail, which begins at Bubble Pond and makes a beeline up the west slopes.

*Autumn wildflowers grow out of fractures in the exposed rocks atop Cadillac Mountain.*

*Rocky, treeless Machias Seal Island is famous for its
nesting colonies of Atlantic seabirds.*

MACHIAS
SEAL
ISLAND

Closest Towns: offshore from Jonesport and Cutler, ME
Owner: Canadian Wildlife Service.

The Maine coast is undeniably a popular destination in summer not only for human tourists, but also for tens of thousands of Atlantic puffins, razorbills, terns, and other seabirds that journey to Machias Seal Island to breed and raise their chicks. Here the birds enjoy an ideal combination of abundant rocky crevices and burrows for nest sites, the fertile fishing grounds where the Gulf of Maine meets the Bay of Fundy, and a minimal human presence that is restricted to lighthouse keepers, wildlife researchers, and carefully controlled tour groups.

This treeless 20-acre island, which lies 10 miles east of Jonesport, is actually a disputed territory of the United States and Canada, thanks to an ambiguous clause in a treaty following the American Revolution. Though a lighthouse has been maintained since the 1830s by the United Kingdom and then Canada, the United States has not recognized that as signifying ownership.

The island's best-known inhabitants are 3,000 pairs of Atlantic puffins, which are easily distinguished by their huge, bright orange beaks. For much of the year, puffins live ocean-bound lives far out at sea, but during the summer breeding season, they come ashore to lay eggs and raise their chicks in the island's

innumerable rocky crevices. Though puffins have historically thrived at Machias Seal Island, they suffered significant declines along the rest of the Maine coast due to habitat loss and hunting, to the point that only a single pair was recorded at Matinicus Rock at the onset of the 20th century. Fortunately, conservation efforts have allowed them to recover strongly in recent decades.

Also present during the breeding season are razorbills, which are the size of a small duck and bear some resemblance to penguins with their black and white bodies. They are named for their sharp bills, which enable them to efficiently catch fish. They are present along the New England coast during spring and fall migrations and in winter, when flocks may be seen off of places such as Cape Ann and Cape Cod.

Of all the seabirds that venture to the island, none undertake a longer journey than arctic terns. These hardy fliers travel an average of 15,000 to 22,000 miles annually, the greatest distance of any migratory bird. In spite of this, they are also long-lived, as individuals as old as 34 years have been documented. They are at the southern limit of their range along the Maine coast and are listed as threatened statewide, as they presently are known to nest on only 10 islands.

Other birds that inhabit the island and surrounding waters include common terns, common murres, eider ducks, Leach's storm petrels, northern gannets, and sooty shearwaters. Roger Tory Peterson and Marlin Perkins are among the many naturalists who have visited the island and observe the seabird colonies.

Access to the island is by tour boats based out of Jonesport, Cutler Harbor, and Grand Manan, New Brunswick. Reservations in advance are strongly recommended; contact the individual operators for specific information about their tours. Those that land on the island have the opportunity to view the birds at close range from wooden observation blinds.

*Inimitable Atlantic puffins, which are easily distinguished by their outsized
orange beaks, nest in rocky burrows at Machias Seal Island.*

# QUODDY HEAD BLUFFS

*The rising sun illuminates the high ocean bluffs at Quoddy Head, the easternmost point of land in the United States.*

Closest Town: Lubec, ME

Owner: Maine Bureau of Parks and Lands (Quoddy Head State Park), 207-733-0911

Directions: From the junction of US 1 and ME 189 in Whiting, turn east on ME 189, following signs for Quoddy Head State Park and Lubec. Before reaching the center of Lubec, turn right (south) on South Lubec Road and continue to the road's end at the state park entrance.

Millions of years ago, layers of hot magma rose out of the Atlantic Ocean floor in the area of present-day Lubec, Maine, the easternmost point of the United States. When this hot liquid rock cooled off, it formed a dark, solid rock known as "gabbro." Long after other layers of rock eroded away, the gabbro remains in the form of ocean bluffs that rise as high as 90 feet above the Grand Manan Channel.

The striking views from the bluffs include Canada's Grand Manan and Campobello Islands across the channel to the east and northeast respectively; the latter is home to a 2800-acre international park and is connected to Lubec by a bridge. Wildlife is abundant here: whales, seals, and dolphins migrate to these fertile feeding grounds during the warm months, and fortunate observers may see a right whale, which are endangered worldwide. The diverse birdlife includes seabirds, shorebirds, waterfowl, boreal species, and birds of prey such as bald eagles and osprey.

Atop the bluffs sits one of Maine's most recognizable lighthouses, the candy-striped, red and white West Quoddy Head Light. It was erected in 1858 as a replacement for the original lighthouse, which was built in 1808 with the dual motivations of marking a safe passage around the treacherous rocks and also establishing a territorial claim against Great Britain.

These shores are also home to two coastal boreal peat bogs, a natural community that is uncommon in Maine. In the heart of the forests west of the lighthouse lies the 7-acre West Quoddy Head Bog, which is ringed by evergreen spruce and fir trees. At the west end of the bluffs is 40-acre Carrying Place Cove Bog, which is a designated National Natural Landmark. It is a rare example of a raised coastal bog, with cliffs of peat moss that are 10 feet high. Over the past half-century alone, the ocean has eroded away 150 feet of the bog. In addition to the characteristic New England bog species such as pitcher plants, sundews, sheep laurel, and Labrador tea, northern subarctic plants such as black crowberry and baked appleberry are also present.

The 532-acre Quoddy Head State Park has 4.5 miles worth of trails that explore all of these habitats. Near the park entrance, there are fine views of the bluffs and ocean from the lighthouse and the Inland Trail, a quarter-mile long path that connects to the Coastal and Bog Trails. The latter offers a 650-foot long interpretive boardwalk that loops along the

*Flowering northern pitcher plants at West Quoddy Bog, one of two rare coastal bogs at Quoddy Head State Park.*

perimeter of the bog. For those seeking a longer outing, the Coastal Trail follows the bluffs and shore for two miles, while the Thompson Trail winds through the interior woodlands for 1.25 miles. Both routes meet near Carrying Place Cove, making a loop hike possible.

*Also see: Great Wass Island (Botanical Areas chapter).*

# ARTIFACTS
# OF
# HISTORY
## chapter
## thirteen

*A few unique artifacts, such as dinosaur tracks, ancient fossils, and glacial boulders, offer especially valuable insight deep into the planet's past.*

*Vermont's Button Point is one of New England's most unique historic sites.*

*While every natural feature reflects* history to some degree, a few unique artifacts, such as dinosaur tracks, ancient fossils, and glacial boulders, offer especially valuable insight deep into the planet's past, often in scales of time that are nearly impossible to comprehend.

For perspective, consider the age of a 500-year old old-growth tree, such as one of the long-lived black gums that have survived, sheltered in the region's remote swamps. Its life began in the 16th century, well before European settlers arrived in North America. However, if we compare its age to that of the 190 million year-old dinosaur tracks in the Connecticut River Valley, the percentage

barely registers. And consider that the tracks in turn are less than half the age of the 500 million year-old coral reef off of Button Point in Vermont, which is a holdover from a period when a tropical ocean covered the site of the present Lake Champlain Valley (something for New Englanders to ponder during the heart of a hard winter).

By comparison, the glaciers are a relatively recent phenomenon; our old black gum represents a full five percent of the time since the close of the last ice age. In addition to shaping or creating many of the region's natural features, the ice sheets moved millions of boulders across the

landscape. Two of the most unusual were the giant Madison Boulder, which is one of the world's largest glacial erratics, and Bubble Rock, which was deposited on the slopes of a mountain in Acadia National Park. In some areas, clearly defined fields of boulders called "trains" indicate the exact course that the glaciers followed. These rocks ultimately had a significant effect on the region's natural human history, as the soils proved inhospitable for early farmers, who largely abandoned the region by the mid-19th century. This enabled the forests that are now synonymous with New England to gradually recover over the past 150 years.

The dome at Dinosaur State Park protects a large cluster of dinosaur tracks and includes a museum and gift shop.

# DINOSAUR STATE PARK

# DINOSAUR FOOTPRINTS RESERVATION

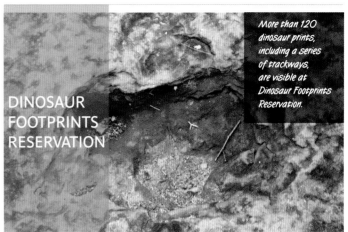

More than 120 dinosaur prints, including a series of trackways, are visible at Dinosaur Footprints Reservation.

Closest Town: Rocky Hill, CT

Owner: Connecticut Forests and Parks (Dinosaur State Park), 860-529-5816

Directions: From Interstate 91 south of Hartford, take Exit 23 and travel east on West Street for 0.8 miles to the park entrance. The exhibit center is open Tuesday to Sunday from 9 AM to 4:30 PM year round ($6.00 admission adults, $2.00 children). The nature trails are open 9 AM to 4 PM year-round.

Closest Town: Holyoke, MA

Owner: The Trustees of Reservations, 413-532-1631

Directions: From Interstate 91 northbound, take Exit 17A and follow MA 141 east to US 5, then follow US 5 north for 2.2 miles to the roadside pullout on the right. From Interstate 91 south, take Exit 18 and follow US 5 south for 5.2 miles to the pullout on the left.

Ever since a teenage boy named Pliny Moody uncovered a set of prints while plowing his family farm in South Hadley, Massachusetts in 1802, the Connecticut River Valley has been a hotbed for dinosaur discoveries. More tracks and fossils have been found in the valley than at any other place in the world, and many preeminent scientists have conducted research in the area.

Because Moody's find predated the overall concept of dinosaurs by a half century, the prints were originally believed to have been made by a giant bird. They turned out to be the first of many discoveries that have been made in the valley over the past 200 years. In 1818, a well-preserved skeleton was uncovered in sandstone rocks during the blasting of a well in East Windsor, Connecticut. Noted geologist Edward Hitchcock cataloged more than 20,000 fossils in the valley before his death in 1865. In 1885, paleontologist Othneil Charles Marsh uncovered two more skeletons and a portion of a third (the other half remained encased in the abutment of a stone bridge for nearly a century) in a quarry near Manchester, Connecticut.

One of the more recent and significant finds occurred in August 1966, when a bulldozer operator named Edward McCarthy uncovered a large group of tracks while clearing the site of a planned state office building in Rocky Hill, Connecticut, near the west banks of the Connecticut River. More than 2000 other prints were subsequently uncovered in the vicinity, one of the largest concentrations in North America. The tracks, which are 10 to 16 inches long, are called *Eubrontes*, a reptile from the Triassic era (detailed more in Dinosaur Footprints Reservation entry). The prints were originally made in soft mud, and then covered by sediments that protected and preserved the prints. In August 2006, another series of prints was found at a nearby construction site on West Street, ironically during the park's 40th anniversary week.

Shortly after its discovery, the Rocky Hill site was designated as a National Natural Landmark and Dinosaur State Park was established. 500 of the exposed tracks remain visible beneath a 55,000 square-foot geodesic dome, while the others remain buried in order to ensure their preservation. In addition to the tracks, the dome includes a visitor center with dioramas, displays of other Connecticut Valley fossils, and a gift shop. The park also includes an arboretum and a nature preserve with two miles of walking trails.

Based on studies of fossils and geology, scientists generally surmise that roughly 200 million years ago, the Connecticut River Valley was a sub-tropical land of giant evergreen trees, ferns, swamps, and lakes. As the dinosaurs roamed the sandstone shores of what is now the west bank of the Connecticut River near Holyoke, they left evidence of their presence in the form of a tracks that remained well-preserved for years in sedimentary rock.

These tracks were discovered in 1845 by Edward Hitchcock, a pioneer in dinosaur research who was also the Massachusetts state geologist and a president of Amherst College. According to recent research by Yale University, the prints belong to three distinct, but related species from the late Triassic and early Jurassic eras. Because it's impossible to conclusively prove relationships between dinosaur tracks and skeletal remains, scientists name and categorize them separately.

The largest prints, which are known as Eubrontes, were made by a relatively large dinosaur that is believed to have been 20 feet tall. Eubrontes tracks are generally 10-20 inches long and feature three toes with claws. It was likely similar to Dilophosaurus, the well-known dinosaur that has been featured in books and the movie Jurassic Park. The tracks at Holyoke and Rocky Hill, Connecticut are the world's best-known Eubrontes prints, which have also been found in Australia, France, Italy, Poland, Spain, and Slovakia.

Also present are the three to five inch-long tracks of Grallator, a small dinosaur that is

*The Dinosaur Footprints Reservation is one of many sites in the Connecticut River Valley where dinosaur tracks and fossils have been uncovered.*

also known as the "Stilt Walker." Analysis of Grallator strides indicates they were likely among the fastest dinosaurs of the Valley, perhaps capable of reaching 20 miles per hour. Another species evident here is Anchisauripus, a medium-sized creature that was likely 7-10 feet tall. Clusters of prints called "trackways" indicate that some of the dinosaurs may have traveled in groups. In addition to the tracks, there are also fossils of prehistoric fish, plants, invertebrates, and the markings of an ancient pool along the riverbanks.

The eight-acre Dinosaur Footprints Reservation, which is managed by the Trustees of Reservations, is located adjacent to Route 5 on the banks of the Connecticut River. From the roadside pullout, a short footpath leads to the track viewing area, which is marked with an interpretive sign. In addition to the tracks, there are views of the river here and access to the water for paddlers.

Out of the southeast shores of Lake Champlain juts Button Point, a little peninsula with a long and rich natural and cultural history. It is one of the most significant areas of the Champlain Valley, as it is home to many unique artifacts of the area's geologic and natural history.

A short distance offshore from the tip of the point is the site of an ancient, 500 million year-old coral reef that dates back to a time when the site of the present valley was a tropical ocean near the equator. Preserved in its limestone rock of the point are the fossils of marine creatures from this era, including gastropods (large sea snails), and trilobites (crabs).

Visible in the point's exposed rock are long, distinct grooves called "striations," which were scoured by debris in glaciers as they advanced across the Champlain Valley during the last ice age. The glaciers also deposited a variety of clays along the point, which subsequently, through a variety of processes, became shaped like buttons – this is how the point was named.

Much younger by comparison, but no less significant, is the small block of ancient forest that rises out of the point. The venerable specimens here include old-growth white cedars, which range in age from 300 to 500 years, along the shoreline and old hemlocks,

*Button Point is home to fossils, an ancient reef, an old-growth forest, and scenic Lake Champlain views.*

**BUTTON POINT**

Closest Town: Vergennes, VT

Owner: Vermont Forests and Parks (Button Bay State Park), 802-475-2377

Directions: From the center of Vergennes, drive south on VT 22A for 0.5 miles, then turn right on Panton Road and follow it for 1.4 miles, then turn right on Basin Harbor Road. Follow Basin Harbor Road for 4.4 miles to a left on Button Bay Road and continue to the park entrance, where a $3.00 admission fee is charged.

oaks, and white and red pines in the interior.

Among the early European visitors to these shores was Samuel de Champlain, who explored the point during his voyage in 1609. During the American Revolution, Benjamin Franklin, Benedict Arnold, and Ethan Allen also passed through the area.

The point is part of a 14-acre natural area within 253-acre Button Bay State Park, which includes a large campground, boat launch, and nature center. From the parking area, an easy walking trail leads west toward

the nature center, then forks into a figure-8 shaped circuit that explores the point. The shore views offer a good perspective of just how narrow Lake Champlain is for much of its length – it's hard to imagine that it's the largest lake in New England and one of the largest in the country. Across the water to the east rise the peaks of the eastern Adirondack Mountains, while the ridge of the central Green Mountains is visible in the distance to the east. The round-trip is a 1.4 miles with minimal elevation change.

# MADISON BOULDER

Of the innumerable glacial erratics that are scattered across New England, none match the size of the giant Madison Boulder.

Closest Town: Madison, NH

Owner: New Hampshire State Parks, 603-485-2034

Directions: From the junction of NH 113 and NH 16 west of Conway, drive south on NH 113 for 2.5 miles, then turn right on Boulder Road. Follow Boulder Road for 0.9 miles, then bear right at the park entrance and follow the dirt road to its end at the boulder parking area. From the south, from Madison center travel north on NH 113 for 2 miles, then turn left on Boulder Road.

Of the innumerable glacial boulders that are spread across the hillsides of North America, none match the sheer size and weight of the Madison Boulder, which is the largest known glacier boulder in New England and one of the largest in the world. This massive, rectangle-shaped granite slab, which lies at the southeastern corner of the White Mountains between the towns of Madison and Albany is 83 feet long, 37 feet wide, and nearly 25 feet high. It is estimated to weigh around 6,000 to 8,000 tons, roughly as much as an ocean freighter.

The Madison Boulder is an "erratic," or rock that differs geologically from its surrounding environment. Though early 19th century scientists believed that these boulders were washed to their present locations by ancient floods, they are now believed to have been moved by the glaciers. The largest rocks such as the Madison Boulder were relocated just a few miles by the ice, but smaller boulders and pebbles were carried much longer distances, more than 100 miles in some instances.

Because the big rocks didn't travel very far from their original location, it is often relatively easy to trace where they came from. Many geologists believe that the Madison Boulder was likely plucked off of the Whitten Ledge in Albany, which is roughly two miles northwest of its present site. This distance is consistent with that traveled by other giant boulders, and there is a gap in the high ridge that generally matches the boulder's size and shape. However, others, citing the similarities between the boulder and rocks found at Mount Willard in Crawford Notch, have speculated that it may have come all the way from the notch, a distance of 25 miles.

The boulder, which was designated as a National Natural Landmark in 1970, is the centerpiece of a 17-acre natural area that was donated to the state of New Hampshire in 1946. It is easily reached and viewed from a short loop trail that begins at the end of the park's dirt road and offers an easy five-minute walk around the boulder. Those looking for a longer outing can park at the welcome sign and walk the dirt road for a half-mile round-trip. The park is unstaffed and open year-round. In late spring and summer, watch for groups of white admiral butterflies along the road and in the parking area.

# BUBBLE ROCK

Though it looks in imminent danger of falling, Bubble Rock has graced the slopes of South Bubble Mountain since the last ice age.

Closest Town: Bar Harbor, ME

Owner: U.S. National Park Service (Acadia National Park), 207-288-3338

Directions: From the junction of US 1 and ME 3 in Ellsworth, follow US 3 across the causeway to Mount Desert Island. Enter Acadia National Park at the Hulls Cove Visitor Center, and follow the park loop road for 6 miles to the Bubble Pond parking area on the right (west) side of the road.

When viewed from below, Bubble Rock looks rather precariously perched along the slopes of Bubble Mountain in Acadia National Park. Indeed, it's something of a tradition for hikers to pose for pictures while pretending to push it off the ledge. However, in spite of its appearance, this elephant-sized eminence sits solidly lodged in a subtle depression that was carved out of the mountain's granite slopes. Viewed against the backdrop of the park's surrounding lakes and mountains, it makes for a striking and photogenic scene.

Bubble Rock, which is also known as Balance Rock, weighs approximately 14 tons. During the last Ice Age, it was enveloped by glaciers, which carried it to its present location and deposited it along the upper east slopes of South Bubble Mountain, a short distance below its 766-foot summit. South Bubble is one of the twin peaks of Bubble Mountain, which is one of Acadia's most familiar landmarks. These distinctive, rounded humps rise high above the north shores of the Jordan Pond, which is famous for its historic restaurant, scenic views, and carriage roads and nature trails. At 872 feet, neighboring North Bubble is the slightly higher of the two. Both offer fine views of Jordan Pond, Eagle Lake, Pemetic Mountain, and other Acadia landmarks.

The trail to the Bubbles begins at a parking area off of the park loop road just north of Jordan Pond. This path climbs gently for a half-mile to a well-marked junction where the trails to each summit diverge. From here, the South Bubble Mountain Trail offers a short, steeper climb to the summit and the boulder, which is reached by a short side trail. Hikers have the option of backtracking for a 1.5-mile round-trip, or making a longer expedition that includes the trails to North Bubble and Jordan Pond.

*Also see: Hanging Rock Ridge, RI (Coastal Southern New England chapter), Aquinnah Cliffs, MA (Coastal Southern New England chapter).*

# Bibliography

Alden, Peter, Cassie, Brian, et al. *National Audubon Society Field Guide to New England*. New York: Alfred A. Knopf, 1998.

Appalachian Mountain Club. *Maine Mountain Guide: Eighth Edition*. Boston, Massachusetts: Appalachian Mountain Club, 1999.

Burk, John S. (editor). *AMC Massachusetts Trail Guide, 9th Edition*. Boston, Massachusetts: Appalachian Mountain Club, 2009.

Burk, John S. *The Wildlife of New England: A Viewers Guide.* Hanover, New Hampshire: University Press of New England, 2011.

Bushee, Joseph. *Waterfalls of Massachusetts: An Explorer's Guide to 55 Scenic Wonders.* Amherst, Massachusetts: New England Cartographics, 2003.

Casanave, Suki. *Natural Wonders of New Hampshire: A Guide to Parks, Preserves, and Wild Places.* Castine, Maine: Countryroads Press, 1994.

Connecticut Forests and Parks Association. Connecticut *Walk Book: The Complete Guide to Connecticut's Blue-blazed Hiking Trails.* Middlefield, Connecticut: CT Forests and Parks Association, 1997.

Davis, William. *Massachusetts Wildlife Viewing Guide.* Helena, Montana: Falcon, 1996.

Dodge, Harry W. *The Geology of Button Bay State Park.* Vermont Department of Forests and Parks, Development Department, and Geological Survey, 1962.

Emblidge, David. *Exploring the Appalachian Trail: Hikes in Southern New England.* Mechanicsburg, Pennsylvania: Stackpole Books, 1998.

Farnsworth, Elizabeth. *Metacomet-Mattabesset Trail Natural Resource Assessment.* Royalston, Massachusetts, 1984.

Feintuch, Burt and David Watters editors. *The Encyclopedia of New England: The Culture and History of an American Region.* New Haven, Connecticut: Yale University Press, 2005.

Ferguson, Gary. *National Geographic Guide to America's Outdoors: New England.* Washington, D.C.: National Geographic Society, 2000.

Fergus, Charles. *Trees of New England.* Guilford, Connecticut: Falcon, 2005.

Foster, D.R., and J.D. Aber. *Forests in Time: The Environmental Consequences of 1000 Years of Change in New England.* New Haven, CT: Yale University Press, 2004.

Friary, Ned, and Glenda Bendure. *Walks and Rambles on Cape Cod and the Islands: A Naturalist's Hiking Guide, 2nd edition.* Woodstock, Vermont: Backcountry Press, 1999.

Howe, Nicholas. *Not Without Peril: 150 Years of Misadventure on the Presidential Range of New Hampshire.* Boston, Massachusetts: Appalachian Mountain Club, 2009.

Johnson, Charles. *The Nature of Vermont: Introduction and Guide to a New England Environment.* Hanover, New Hampshire: University Press of New England, 1998.

Jorgenson, Neil. *A Guide to New England's Landscape.* Barre, Massachusetts: Barre Publishing, 1971.

Kershner, Bruce, and Robert Leverett. *The Sierra Club Guide to the Ancient Forests of The Northeast.* San Francisco, California: Sierra Club Books, 2004.

Kulik, Stephen, Pete Salmansohn, Matthew Schmidt, and Heidi Welch. *The Audubon Society Field Guide to Natural Places of the Northeast: Inland.* New York: Hilltown Books, 1984.

Lanza, Michael. *New England Hiking: The Complete Guide to more than 380 Hikes: 3rd Edition.* Emerysville, California: Avalon, 2002.

Little, Richard. *Dinosaurs, Dunes, and Drifting Continents: The Geology of the Connecticut River Valley.* Earth View LLC, 2003

Laubach, Rene. *Audubon Guide to the National Wildlife Refuges: New England.* New York: St. Martin's Griffin, 2000.

Massachusetts Department of Conservation and Recreation. *Mount Everett State Reservation Summit Resource Management Plan.* Boston, Massachusetts: Massachusetts Executive Office of Environmental Affairs, 2006.

Middleton, David. *A Photographer's Guide to Vermont.* Woodstock, Vermont: Countryman Press, 2003.

Motzkin, G., Orwig, D., and D. Foste. *History and Dynamics of a Ridgetop Pitch Pine Community, Mount Everett, Massachusetts.* Petersham, Massachusetts: Harvard Forest Paper No. 25, 2002.

National Geographic Society. *National Geographic's Guide to the State Parks of the United States.* Washington, D.C.: National Geographic Society, 1997.

Neff, John W. *Katahdin: An Historic Journey.* Boston, Massachusetts: Appalachian Mountain Club, 2006.

Parsons, Gregory and Kate Watson. *New England Waterfalls.* Woodstock, Vermont: Countryman Press, 2003.

Putnam, William L. *The Worst Weather on Earth: A History of the Mount Washington Observatory.* Gorham, New Hampshire: Mount Washington Observatory and New York: American Alpine Club, 1991.

Riccuti, Edward. *The Natural History of North America.* New York: Quadrillon Publishing, 1999.

Rutland Regional Planning Commission. *Phase 1 Stream Geomorphic Assessment, Mill River, Rutland County Vermont.* Rutland, Vermont: Rutland Regional Planning Commission, 2007.

Scofield, Bruce. *Hiking the Pioneer Valley.* Amherst, Massachusetts: New England Cartographics, 1995.

Sinton, John, Elizabeth Farnsworth, and Wendy Sinton. *The Connecticut River Boating Guide: Source to Sea.* Helena, MT: Falcon Press, 2007.

Sterling, Dorothy. *The Outer Lands: A Natural History Guide to Cape Cod, Martha's Vineyard, Nantucket, Block Island, and Long Island.* New York: W.W. Norton, 1978.

Thieret, John W. (revising author), William A. Niering, and Nancy C. Olmstead. *National Audubon Society Field Guide to North American Wildflowers: Eastern Region.* New York: Alfred A. Knopf, 2001.

Tougias, Michael J. *New England Wild Places: Journeys through the Back Country.* North Attleboro, MA: Covered Bridge Press, 1997.

Wessels, Tom. *The Granite Landscape: A History of America's Mountain Domes, From Acadia to Yellowstone.* Woodstock, Vermont: Countryman Press, 2001.

Wetherell, W.D. *The Smithsonian Guides to Natural America: Northern New England.* Washington, D.C.: Smithsonian Books, 1995

Van Diver, Bradford B. *Roadside Geology of Vermont and New Hampshire.* Missoula, Montana: Mountain Press Publishing Company, 1987.

Vermont Forests, Parks and Recreation and David Laing. "Quechee Gorge Geology: Legacy of the Last Ice Age." Unpublished brochure.

Vose, Arthur. *The White Mountains: Heroes and Hamlets.* Barre, MA: Barre Publishing Company, 1968.

Zielinski, Gregory and Barry Keim. *New England Weather, New England Climate.* Lebanon, NH: University Press of New England, 2003.